D1757398

This is the first systematic attempt to establish Sheridan as a major figure in the history of English comedy and as the outstanding playwright between Congreve and Wilde. Leading scholars address Sheridan's roles as playwright, as manager of Drury Lane theatre for more than thirty years, and, for almost as long, as a Member of Parliament, where he proved himself a master of rhetoric in another theatre of great personal confrontations.

The essays examine the theatrical world in which Sheridan worked, discuss his major plays, and include a modern director's observations on the production of his work today. The volume also contains important new assessments of Sheridan's political career and the image he projected through his speeches. It offers a much-needed contemporary evaluation of this multi-faceted man and his work.

Sheridan studies

Sheridan studies

Edited by

James Morwood

and

David Crane

Published by the Press Syndicate of the University of Cambridge
The Pitt Building, Trumpington Street, Cambridge CB2 1RP
40 West 20th Street, New York, NY 10011–4211, USA
10 Stamford Road, Oakleigh, Melbourne 3166, Australia

First published 1995

Printed in Great Britain at Redwood Books, Trowbridge, Wiltshire

A catalogue record for this book is available from the British Library

Library of Congress cataloguing in publication data

Sheridan studies/edited by James Morwood and David Crane.
p. cm.
Includes bibliographical references and index.
ISBN 0 521 46466 8 (hardback)
1. Sheridan, Richard Brinsley, 1751–1816. 2. British drama (Comedy) – History and criticism. 3. Dramatists, British – 18th century – Biography. 4. Theatre managers – Great Britain – Biography. 5. Legislators – Great Britain – Biography. 6. Political History, English – 18th and early 19th century I. Morwood, James. II. Crane, D. Lisle
PR3683.S55 1995 822'.6–dc20 95–49681 CIP

ISBN 0 521 46466 8 hardback

Contents

Illustrations

Notes on contributors

MARK S. AUBURN is Senior Vice President and Provost of the University of Akron. He has written *Sheridan's Comedies, their Contexts and Achievements* (1977).

MARC BAER is Professor of History at Hope College, Michigan. He has written *Theatre and Disorder in Late Georgian London* (1992).

CHRISTOPHER CLAYTON teaches history and politics at City of London School. His doctoral dissertation was entitled *The Political Career of Richard Brinsley Sheridan* (Oxford University, 1992).

DAVID CRANE is a Research Fellow at the University of Wales (Lampeter). He is concerned with the theatre both in practical terms and as a writer. He has edited Buckingham's *The Rehearsal* (1976) and Sheridan's *The Critic* (1989).

JACK D. DURANT is Professor of English at North Carolina State University. He has written *Richard Brinsley Sheridan* (1975) and compiled *Sheridan: A Reference Guide* (1981).

JAMES MORWOOD is Head of Classics at Harrow School. He has written *The Life and Works of Richard Brinsley Sheridan* (1985).

CHRISTOPHER REID is Senior Lecturer in English at Queen Mary and Westfield College, University of London. He has written *Edmund Burke and the Practice of Political Writing* (1985).

ERIC RUMP is Associate Professor of English at Glendon College, York University, Toronto. He has edited *The Comedies of William Congreve* (1985) and *Richard Brinsley Sheridan: The School for Scandal and Other Plays* (1988).

RICHARD TAYLOR is Associate Professor of English at East Carolina University. He writes on late eighteenth-century literature and has written *Goldsmith as Journalist* (1993).

PETER WOOD has had a long and distinguished career as a director. At the National Theatre, as well as producing *The Rivals* and *The School for Scandal*, he has staged Farquar's *The Beaux' Stratagem* and Congreve's *Love for Love* (twice).

Some dates in Sheridan's life

1751 Richard Brinsley Sheridan born in Dublin in September or October.

1762–*c.* 1767–8 At Harrow School.

1766 His mother, Frances Chamberlaine Sheridan, dies at Blois in France.

1770–1772 At Bath.

1772 Elopes to the continent with Elizabeth Linley (March); fights two duels over her with Captain Thomas Mathews (May and July).

1773 Marries Elizabeth Linley at Marylebone Church on 13 April.

1775 First performances of *The Rivals* (17 and 28 January), of *St Patrick's Day* (2 May) and of *The Duenna* (21 November), all at Covent Garden. Son Thomas born on 17 November.

1776 Opens Drury Lane as principal manager (24 September).

1777 First performances of *A Trip to Scarborough* (24 February) and of *The School for Scandal* (8 May) at Drury Lane. Elected a member of the Literary Club in March.

1778 First performance of *The Camp* (15 October) at Drury Lane.

1779 First performances of *Verses to the Memory of Garrick* (11 March) and *The Critic* (30 October) at Drury Lane.

1780 Elected MP for Stafford on 12 September.

1782 Under-Secretary of State for the Northern Department (27 March–1 July).

1783 Secretary to the Treasury (21 February–18 December).

1787 Delivers a famous speech in Parliament in the proceedings against Warren Hastings (7 February).

1788 Speaks at the trial of Warren Hastings in Westminster Hall (June). Confidential adviser to the Prince of Wales in the Regency Crisis (November–December).

1792 Death of his first wife at Bristol Wells on 28 June.

1794 Drury Lane reopens on 21 April after being closed for reconstruction in 1791. First performance of *The Glorious First of June* (co-written with James Cobb) on 2 July.

1795 Marries Hester Jane Ogle on 27 April.

1796 Son Charles Brinsley born on 14 January.

1799 First performance of *Pizarro*, adapted from Kotzebue's *Die Spanier in Peru*, at Drury Lane (24 May).

1804 Treasurer of the Navy in the Ministry of All the Talents. Wins Parliamentary seat for Westminster after the death of Charles James Fox (November).

1807 Defeated in the Westminster election but becomes MP for Ilchester.

1809 Drury Lane Theatre destroyed by fire on 24 February.

1811 Advises the Prince Regent in the Second Regency Crisis.

1812 Defeated at the Stafford election and so loses a seat in Parliament.

1816 Dies at Savile Row on 7 July; buried in Westminster Abbey on 13 July.

Introduction

One could say that a good book of essays will have a fundamental coherence and yet will draw strength from the diversity, the contradictoriness even, of its parts. If that is so, then Sheridan makes a particularly apt subject for such a volume. At the end of his life it can only have been by the most strenuous act of the imagination that he was able to see himself whole. For over thirty years he had been a failed and scheming politician of the reforming party, and for a similar length of time the only intermittently enthusiastic but ultimately accountable manager of Drury Lane theatre, the destruction of which by fire in 1809 finally ruined him financially. Before his career in politics effectually began, he had been the author of the three most famous comedies of the age. That success, however, was long past when he died in 1816, and it appears that Sheridan took this as a comment on the failure of the latter part of his life when he moved among great men in reality and not only on the stage, to the extent that he was reluctant to recall it and wished to be buried next to Fox in Westminster Abbey and not, as happened, between Handel and Johnson and close to Garrick – and the despised Cumberland – in Poets' Corner.[1] He died in wretched poverty: the bailiffs at the door now that he was no longer protected by immunity as a Member of Parliament from arrest for debt, his desperately ill wife doing what she could for her dying husband in a house without food or warmth or anything much in the way of furniture. And yet a few days later dukes walked in his funeral procession to his literary resting place. So much greater is literature, as he might always have uneasily suspected, than the play of what seems like real power in human affairs.[2]

The evidence indicates that Sheridan did not often see himself whole in the way that this volume of essays suggests is possible. One might almost say that in the end he valued least what he did best, the writing of plays. As a playwright he is at the centre of a large world which extends back in time to Shakespeare and the Restoration theatre and forward to Wilde and the present day. As Peter Wood suggests in the last chapter, it is some index of the health of the modern theatre that it can or cannot tolerate a fully elaborated production of a Sheridan comedy. As a politician Sheridan was – and the change of tense seems appropriate – part of what appeared to be a large world, but that world is now past and its battles are over. Even at the time Sheridan was hardly centre stage, since in a political career lasting more than thirty years he held minor office for a total of barely two.

The portraits of Sheridan in this volume vary greatly from chapter to chapter, but we hope that the organic quality of a life which moved from the theatrical stage to the stage of politics and which extended from the minutiae of political intrigue to the larger shapes and movements of literary tradition, will become apparent. In the compass of a single volume we have tried to present Sheridan so that nothing important of him is lost, even though we have had to omit extended treatment of those *chefs-d'oeuvre* of dramatic opportunism, *The Duenna* and *Pizarro*. If the whole can seem to make significant sense, then we shall feel, editors and contributors alike, that the volume has been worth compiling.

The essays begin with the theatre, and with Mark Auburn's account of the theatrical scene in the age of Garrick and Sheridan. We hope that the reader will gain a vivid sense of what it was like to go to the London theatre in the 1770s, in the decade when Sheridan replaced Garrick as manager of Drury Lane and produced his three great plays. The theatre was then at the centre of popular culture in a way that television rather than theatre is now; as Peter Wood says, it was not 'Art', and the response it received was enthusiastic rather than decorous. As Auburn also suggests, Sheridan's own attitude to it was not decorous either: he became manager of Drury Lane because he saw it as a way of making money. His attitude towards Drury Lane as a speculative investment went hand in hand with, and no doubt partly fuelled, his theatrical enthusiasm: both as a playwright and later as a reforming politician, Sheridan was human in his desire for money and fame.

The dream of money failed him, but Sheridan's early sense that the theatre was a good investment in fame led him, as Eric Rump notes, to revive three of Congreve's comedies in the opening months of his first season at Drury Lane. It is as though he saw a major part of the comic tradition lying dormant in the late eighteenth century, and it was a tradition to which he was aware he could contribute greatly. Partly as an act of theatrical piety but partly also to establish an arena for himself, he took the bold step of reviving the licentious comedy of the last age, altered with rather less boldness to suit the less licentious taste of his own time. In some way then, as Rump argues, Sheridan's Congreve revivals, coming between his first major success with *The Rivals* and the fortifying and establishing of that success with *The School for Scandal*, link him explicitly with that earlier and still evidently vigorous tradition. Rump's essay joins with the pieces by Morwood and Crane in offering an alternative or supplement to Auburn's view that as a playwright Sheridan owes far more to his contemporaries and his actors than to his long-dead precursors.

Richard Taylor, in his account of the way in which contemporary reviewers struggled to make sense of *The Rivals*, stresses Sheridan's originality in the way in which he challenged the received ideas of contemporary critics, rather than stressing his debt to either the living or the dead. Great originality and a profound response both to the contemporary theatre and the theatrical tradition seem to characterize Sheridan's work as a comic playwright; for as James Morwood suggests in examining Molière's influence on *The School for Scandal*, the root system which fed Sheridan's own comic energies was broader than Congreve, drawing on a tradition which goes back to the great French master of comedy; and David Crane shows, with a detailed look at the relationship between *The Critic* and one specific Restoration play, both how Sheridan focussed upon and how he transformed a still living tradition of performance of Buckingham's *The Rehearsal*.

The Critic, with its intense involvement in contemporary political events, opens also in a different direction, and is a point of meeting between Sheridan's theatrical and political energies, a place too where the seriousness and the unseriousness of Sheridan's whole understanding of life tricksily and subtly hold hands. It is perhaps somewhere near the heart of the matter with Sheridan to understand how closely grave concerns and play went together: he was satirist and showman, reformer and politician, a serious friend or enemy and a contemptible cartoon figure. The patriotic finale of *The Critic* is both ludicrously successful bombast and love of country, and (as Peter Wood suggests) it cannot be well played except both as farce and magic.

The mixture of farce and magic reminds one of Shakespeare, and it does not seem too much to say that Sheridan is at a pivotal point in a comic tradition which links Shakespeare and Wilde. But again, as Richard Taylor reminds us, he is also his own man, not to be explained simply as a meeting point of influences. Both Taylor and Rump deal with Sheridan's attitude to the sentimental theatre of his day. The latter is eager to disassociate him from it altogether, while the former discusses his not altogether unfriendly exploitation of it.

And slippery he is indeed, giving more than one account of himself to the world, as is evident from the essays by Jack Durant and Christopher Reid. These two pieces hold together the literary and political parts of this volume, concentrating on Sheridan's fundamental ability, both as playwright and political activist, in his command of language. Differing pictures, however, emerge from the two essays.

Jack Durant concentrates on Sheridan's claim that language should honestly, accurately and simply convey the honest truth, and uses his political speeches, especially against Warren Hastings, to enforce the point that Sheridan wished fundamentally to endorse 'language as a vehicle of truth'. Looking back upon the plays from this angle, we see the various corruptions of language displayed there as intended satirically. There is a stark contrast between this and Morwood's view of the playwright's moral relativism, and also Christopher Reid's sense that the House of Commons which Sheridan entered in 1780 was 'a theatre of great personal confrontations', and that as a consequence it drew forth from him a rhetorical ability to improvise, a ready ingenuity of mind, so that, as Fox said, 'he could contrive to give an argument what turn he pleased'. This is Sheridan more as Mr Puff than the plain honest dealer; and indeed, even the honest dealer could be a rhetorical persuader by his honesty, and the more effective no doubt the more he believed in the honesty of his position. We enter upon the accounts of Sheridan's political life towards the end of this volume with a sense of the simplicity behind the art and the art behind the simplicity, which drove him as a political reformer upon such a complex and finally unsuccessful course.

In his political life, by contrast with his playwriting life, other people were of course contriving the plot, much as Sheridan would have liked himself to be the master plotter. And if the plot is written by another hand, then the sense one has of playing a leading role may in the end be subverted by events, leaving one's great gifts stranded amid small successes and trivial manoeuvres. It is with a feeling that although in *The Critic* Puff achieved a cunningly unexpected success with his play, *The Spanish Armada*, no such glittering finale awaited Mr Puff in real life, that we pass in Sheridan's political career from the early triumphs in the speeches against Warren Hastings to the sorry record of his later years.

Christopher Clayton gives an overall view of Sheridan's political career, suggesting that behind all the manoeuvres there remained a fundamental integrity and consistency of purpose. The Sheridan portrayed here resembles the image of the man as he appears in Durant's essay. Sheridan's failure as a politician is, in this estimation, not the result of any sense of unreliability or dishonesty but is rather the consequence of his unaristocratic birth. Mark Baer, by contrast with Clayton, focuses tightly upon the borough of Westminster and the Westminster Association, in order to give, both in parliamentary and extraparliamentary terms, an account of Sheridan's rise and fall as a political reformer. Baer also suggests that one of the key reasons for Sheridan's failure was his 'innate theatricality', his ability to play a role, to invent himself. Politics may have a complicated plot, but it works with simpler ideas of character, whether good or bad, than a playwright would. This is not to say, of course, that politicians are in fact simple people, only that their trade requires them to appear so; Sheridan perhaps passed too joyously and evidently from such a simple account to more complex delineations of himself, more subtle presentations of possibilities, as the circumstances of the moment engaged his energies. Baer emphasizes the frequency with which he was caricatured in political cartoons in the late Georgian era and how often and (in political terms) damagingly he was seen as a theatrical figure. Clearly his theatricality made him a public presence, and also a political failure. You couldn't easily credit the performance, but arguably his failure was no failure of basic integrity; it revealed him as a more fully accounted for human being than he would have been as the great reformer.

The volume ends with Sheridan's survival. Peter Wood gives an account of the two productions he staged at the National Theatre, *The Rivals* (1983) and *The School for Scandal* (1990). We have a sense from this of the breadth and variety of the response Sheridan asks of players, of audience, and, last and least, of critics. It is as important for the theatre of our day to keep a good hold on Sheridan as it was for him to hold fast to the living theatrical tradition that fed his own genius and was in turn revitalized by his individual contribution to it. Peter Wood suggests that the present-day theatre is in a state of crisis and that for its health it should try again to accommodate Sheridan's comedies in all their original largeness of life. The same may surely be said of present-day politics: arguably what the House of Commons needs today is what it had in abundance with Sheridan: great speakers and failed politicians, not successful politicians unable to utter a single living word. In the end the acid test is whether the words one speaks and writes confer life; and in the desert land of bureaucratic machine-speak that we inhabit, it is time to look to Sheridan again.

Notes

1 *Memoirs, Journal, and Correspondence of Thomas Moore*, ed. Lord J. Russell (London, 1853), iii, p. 233.
2 Charles Butler, *Reminiscences* (London, 1827), ii, p. 80.

References are to Sheridan, *Plays*, ed. C. Price (Oxford, 1975).

I

Theatre in the age of Garrick and Sheridan

MARK S. AUBURN

This chapter presents a broad, general overview of London theatre in the age of David Garrick and Richard Brinsley Sheridan, spanning slightly more than six decades. Some memories of the English literary critic Charles Lamb provide a context to sections on what it was like to go to the theatre; how the major theatres contrasted with other theatrical entertainment; what plays would be seen; and what characterized the acting, the careers of six representative actors who created roles for Sheridan, Sheridan's creative debts, and Sheridan's management. Two general assumptions undergird the essay. First, theatre in this era shaped and was shaped by human consciousness in roughly the way that television functions in the late twentieth century; it was an aspect of popular culture which opens a society to our understanding in the same ways that the rise of professional sports teams or municipal bands and orchestras or great museums and libraries might do for other ages and places. Second, the written plays which have come down to us two centuries later can best be understood in the contexts not just of the social mores and literary conventions of the time but also of the raw materials, human and physical, with which the playwrights had to work and which shaped their artistic choices perhaps more than the dramatic traditions to which they were heirs. Knowledge of the London theatre in the second half of the eighteenth century helps to illuminate Sheridan's achievement.

GOING TO THE THEATRE

About forty years afterwards, Charles Lamb recalls his first trip to the theatre. In an essay called 'My First Play' (*London Magazine*, December 1821), 'Elia' tells us of a rainy day on which his law-clerk father promised a chance to go to Drury Lane, if the rain abated; the family had 'orders', or free tickets, obtained by his godfather Fielde, an oil dealer who supplied the Theatre Royal in Drury Lane, and the precocious child watched 'from the window the puddles, from the stillness of which I was taught to prognosticate the desired cessation'. Lamb was five years old when his mother carried him into the pit at Drury Lane on 1 December 1780, and four decades later he writes with excited clarity about seeing that night Thomas Arne's dramatic opera *Artaxerxes* followed by David Garrick's farce *Harlequin's Invasion*. 'The orchestra lights at length arose, those "fair Auroras"! Once the bell sounded. It was to ring out yet once again – and incapable of the anticipation, I reposed my shut eyes in a sort of resignation upon the maternal lap. It rang a second time. The curtain drew up – and I was not past six years old, and the play was *Artaxerxes*!'

Drury Lane was the theatre which Richard Brinsley Sheridan owned and managed for thirty-five years from 1776, most of his adult lifetime. He had written and helped to produce two enormously popular plays, *The Rivals* (January 1775) and *The Duenna* (November 1775), at the Theatre Royal in Covent Garden, close by Drury Lane. When Sheridan bought through a complicated financial arrangement part of the royal patent for Drury Lane in 1776, he confirmed his place as the theatrical manager who would succeed David Garrick (1717–79), since 1747 the most powerful shaping force in theatre throughout the English-speaking world. Sheridan gave two great plays to Drury Lane, *The School for Scandal* (May 1777) and *The Critic* (October 1779), several entertainments, and one political spectacle, *Pizarro* in 1799; but there was no lasting theatrical literature after he became a Member of Parliament in 1780.

As one of the three-quarter-of-a-million residents of London in the 1760s and 1770s (the era of Garrick's influence and Sheridan's playwriting), you might have joined the 12,000 or so who went to the theatre or the opera in any given week, or the 2,300 or so who could have crowded into the Theatre Royal in Drury Lane on that clear-skied evening, although in fact only about a thousand were in attendance on 1 December 1780. Like most Londoners, at four p.m. you had your dinner, and earlier that day you had read in the *Public Advertiser* details concerning the performances to be available tonight at Covent Garden and Drury Lane; or perhaps you had seen stuck up somewhere in London one of the more than 150 'large' playbills distributed six mornings a week. (The advertising posters are to be distinguished from the smaller but otherwise identical handbills available at the theatres themselves.) Particulars about tonight's presentation, one of about 180 available every year between September and May at the two 'patent houses', legally chartered theatres, may have influenced your decision to go tonight; or perhaps you just wanted to be seen at the theatre. Whatever your reasons for going, you would make your way to Drury Lane an hour or forty-five minutes before the 6.15 p.m. starting time (depending upon the length of daylight, the play might begin at 5.30, 6.00, 6.15 or 6.30). There you would find yourself in a large crowd of people pushing their way past a small entry door through the narrow five- or six-foot-wide corridors which led to the auditorium.

Only a few people would possess, like the Lamb family this night, 'orders' or free admissions provided by the management of the theatre. Most would be seeking to buy places in one of four seating areas: the pit (three shillings), the boxes (five shillings), the first gallery (two shillings), or the second gallery (one shilling). This was an era when Dr Johnson related that thirty pounds a year would be sufficient for a single gentleman to survive in London and when a skilled craftsman might earn about twenty shillings a week, so attendance at the London theatres was a treat, as a percentage of income just about what it costs to go to the West End or Broadway theatre today – that is, it was expensive. Generally, social class as much as buying power determined where you sat. The nobility and the gentry occupied the boxes which were ranged in a double horseshoe just above the level of the stage proper; people of some means in trade or business sat on the nine or ten rows of backless benches in the pit. These benches rose slightly beyond the sunken orchestra pit from a few feet below the apron of the stage directly before it to nearly even with the boxes in the back of the house, where those sitting in the last row of the boxes would be about fifty-one feet from the apron of the stage. Tradesmen and others would pay two shillings for a bench seat in the first gallery, above at the rear of the horseshoe formed by the two tiers of boxes, and labourers and servants would spend a shilling to occupy the second gallery at the top of the auditorium above the first gallery. (These galleries did not project above and beyond the pit and the boxes, in the manner of most modern balconies, but were flush above the boxes at the rear of the horseshoe.) Unless you had arranged for a box seat by paying in advance half the five-shilling fee, you would pay your entire price as you entered the corridor, be given a ticket which was in fact a metal token, and surrender that token to a doorkeeper as you reached the doorway entrance to your seating area.

1 The auditorium of the Theatre Royal in Drury Lane, following the refurbishment by Robert Adam in 1775–6.

Upon giving up that token in a poorly lit, crowded corridor, you would rush through a door into your seating area and jostle for one of the unreserved seats. There you would encounter much more light than you, the average eighteenth-century Londoner, saw in the night. In this era of candlelight and oil lamps, no place would be more brightly illuminated than this auditorium, except perhaps masquerades at the great pleasure gardens. Crowded together on your backless bench, you might focus upon the green stage curtain (and it was always green by custom) at the proscenium arch, whose rising would signal the start of the evening's entertainment; or you might look around at the smartly dressed people in the boxes, who had begun to arrive to take the places on the benches which their servants had been holding for them – even in the boxes, there were no reserved seats and no backs to the benches. Certainly you would hear and see women selling oranges, apples, and playbills – 'Chase some oranges, chase some numparels, chase a bill of the play,' Lamb says he heard them cry, meaning 'Choose some oranges, choose some non-pariels [a variety of apple], choose a [playbill].'

Stagewards there was a slightly sunken area where the orchestra performed – ten or so musicians, who began to play when the prompter (whom we would now call the stage manager) rang the bell about twenty minutes before the performance. Above the orchestra area was an eleven-foot deep forestage sweeping into the horseshoe of the auditorium so far that two pairs of the boxes on either side were actually 'on stage'. On either side of the twenty-eight-foot wide, twenty-one-and-one-half-foot high proscenium arch were two doors, both practical and both used for regular entrances and exits by the performers. The green curtain rose to reveal scenery in five or six tongue-and-groove slots ranged backward toward the rear wall of the stage, spectacular visual representations of imagined or real locations. In an age before photographs or television, this scenery substantiated remembered reality or imagined circumstance more vividly than any recreated visual experience with which the audience might be acquainted; so central was this scenery to London theatre-going (I have argued elsewhere) that in January 1775 the Covent Garden manager Thomas Harris and the 24-year-old Richard Brinsley Sheridan included the second scene of the fifth act of *The Rivals* mostly because there was a new, very good representation of the South Parade at Bath among the scenery of Covent Garden.[1]

The actors worked mostly on the forestage, in front of this scenery and of the proscenium. Even though some 2,300 could have been crowded into the auditorium of Drury Lane in December 1780, the effect when the actors came forward was remarkably intimate. With audience around them and in front of them, the actors made their appeals directly to the assemblage, sometimes bowing upon first entrance or when applauded. Sight lines were relatively short even if some angles were acute, and acoustics were not bad when the audience was quiet, especially since actors seem to have assumed stentorian tones in delivery.

The stage machinery constantly amazed its audiences, though we might consider it rudimentary. Garrick managed to get the lounging beaux and noblemen off the stage and from behind the scenes in 1762 (where they had felt privileged to be since 1660), and the theatrical illusion could become more realistic. Particularly after European designer Philippe Jacques de

2 The Screen Scene from *The School for Scandal*, showing the proscenium of the Theatre Royal in Drury Lane, following the refurbishment by Robert Adam in 1775–6. Note the directional lighting from the stage left wings.

Loutherbourg began working for Garrick at Drury Lane in 1773, contemporaries remarked upon realistic effects achieved through cut-out scenes and other devices. The basic scene unit was a flat, as today. It was in fact what we call a 'shutter', held in place by a groove placed on the raked floor of the acting area behind the proscenium and supported above by grooves on a batten. Five or six pairs of these tongue-and-groove shutters would rank backward from the proscenium. Drops were less common, though the stages were equipped with fully rigged stagehouses and used movable battens to fly masking curtains and even (we believe) additional lights. Together, the flats (masked at the top) would present perspective views of particular scenes, and the actors would on occasion work within those scenes, though more usually in front of them on the forestage. The illumination could accomplish some variation; metal shutters on the oil-fed footlights, for instance, could be rotated so as to dim the effect, and de Loutherbourg introduced the notion of placing coloured fabric in front of the lights. Not much furniture would be placed within the acting area; an easy chair, like that in *She Stoops to Conquer*, might be the only piece. On the other hand, practical properties abounded, as we know from inventories and price lists.

Costumes were sumptuous even if not historically accurate. Better-paid actors acquired their own costumes at the theatre owners' expense and perhaps were allowed to use those costumes when they acted elsewhere (as did most of the leading performers during the June-through-August period when the two patent theatres were dark and only Samuel Foote's third licensed theatre in London, the Haymarket, was open). All other actors were provided with stage dress by the management, and a staff of tailors and seamstresses was maintained for this purpose. All costumes belonged to the theatre, and actors could not borrow them for use elsewhere without permission. In any given performance of, say, *Julius Caesar*, a few principal characters might be costumed according to an idea of Roman garb while others might dress as contemporary gentry. (An occasional notice on playbills about a revival is 'dressed according to the time' or 'the characters new dressed in the habits of the country'.)

Although the two major theatres were open six nights a week (never on Sunday) from mid-September to May, the height of the season was from November through to early February. When Lent began, every Wednesday and Friday evening was given over to performances of oratorio, with Handel's *Messiah* a particular favourite. Passion Week was dark; not even oratorio was permitted. Soon after Easter began the benefits for the actors and other employees of the theatres; on such nights, depending upon their status, these servants of the theatre could choose the entertainment and would personally sell tickets, keeping the portion of the profits beyond a house charge calculated to reflect the expense of opening and lighting the theatre. (Sheridan raised that charge to £105 in 1776; by the time the new huge Drury Lane opened in 1794 it was £200.) Sometimes these benefits could raise half or more of their annual salaries. Tradition gave over the performances on 4 or 5 November to Nicholas Rowe's *Tamerlane*, which was viewed as an allegory of William III's accession to the throne of England and triumph over Louis XIV; and in December one night would often feature George Lillo's *The London Merchant; or, The History of George Barnwell*, a tragic, exemplary tale which everyone believed that young apprentices in business should see, particularly close to Christmas because they might be released from duty to come to the theatre. After 1766, when a nobleman arranged for Samuel Foote to receive a special dispensation (in compensation for Foote's losing a leg in a horse-riding accident), there was also a London summer season, from late May to the end of September, at the 'little' theatre in the Haymarket; it attracted a slightly different audience, and Lamb does not record being present as a child at any of its productions. Its brief season was calculated so as not to conflict with the winter season at Drury Lane and Covent Garden.

Charles Lamb remembers a second ringing of the prompter's bell, though there may have been three before the green curtain rose and the entertainment proper began. Lamb tells us of seeing as 'mainpiece' the dramatic opera, *Artaxerxes*, and as the 'afterpiece' Garrick's pantomime-farce *Harlequin's Invasion*. By about 1714, custom dictated that the theatrical evening should consist of two major dramatic pieces, one a five-act comedy or tragedy or three-act musical and the other a two-act comedy or farce or pantomime. Interspersed earlier in the century were various entr'acte performances ranging from songs to dance to monologues to tightrope walking ('rope dancing') and even juggling, though entr'actes (other than dances) were fewer by 1780. When a new play was performed as the mainpiece or an old play was given a major revival or some other special occasion demanded, there would be a prologue and epilogue, usually performed by a single actor or sometimes (as in Sheridan's original prologue to *The Rivals*) by a pair. And on every theatrical evening, following the last act of the mainpiece, an actor, manager, or proprietor would announce the play to be performed on the next night, an announcement which would often stimulate active participation by the audience, especially if the entertainment planned did not meet with their approval.

Indeed, compared with the generally quiet behaviour of theatre audiences today, the participation of audiences in the Garrick-Sheridan era was vociferous. Numerous foreign visitors in the last half of the eighteenth century remark upon the noise in the London playhouse. Though footlights on the stage and more lights on the scenery were revealed behind the proscenium upon the rising of the green curtain, the lights of the great chandeliers in the auditorium were not dimmed, and so audience and actor were each illuminated throughout the presentation. Only the prompter's bell and the act music, not a dimming of light, signalled the performance. Thus, throughout the representation, members of the audience saw one another, saw the actors, saw the musicians; and the interaction was constant. In 'Play-House Memoranda' (*The Examiner*, 19 December 1813), Lamb remarks upon how people in the boxes modelled boredom; those in the pit sharp criticism; and those in the galleries warm adulation or angry disagreement. Many contemporary comments indicate that applause and shouts punctuated most performances, with calls for repetition of songs or speeches being commonplace and warm rounds of applause or boos and hisses occurring throughout the representation. In tragedy, both men and women could be seen shedding tears and dabbing them up with handkerchiefs; in comedy, not only laughter but comments to one's neighbour were commonplace.

And if conversation and distraction were common among the audience, the practice of half-price tickets offered later in the evening added to the general confusion. At the conclusion of the third act of the mainpiece (the second act, if it were a three-act dramatic or comic opera), all seats went on sale: for half-price, you could enter the auditorium and remain for the rest of the evening. (For many years, you could also leave about this time and claim a refund.) Suddenly, a box seat cost two shillings and six pence, a place in the upper gallery six pence. Since only on very crowded nights were the doors to the pit 'screwed' shut, one could expect new arrivals everywhere in the auditorium to be claiming spaces about a third of the way through the theatrical evening. Moreover, though most Londoners took their dinner at 4.00 p.m., many had begun to shift their dining hour later and thought it proper to delay, so that some fashionable people did not arrive before 8.00 p.m. They, too, would cause disruption as they dismissed servants from the benches in the boxes which they had reserved and were scrutinized by the other theatre-goers.

These were hardy people, able to sit on backless benches in frequently cold auditoriums for five hours or more; the presentation which began at 6.00 p.m. rarely ended before 10.30 or 11.00. Having obtained a seat in most cases through personal competition, they expected their money's worth. And though we children of electric machinery and light would probably think what they saw rudimentary, they were entranced by it: like Mr and Mrs Dangle in *The Critic*, Londoners loved their theatre with a passion, discussed it endlessly, and were as personally attached to the actors and managers as today's fans are to football players or cricketers or television stars.

MINOR THEATRES

The foregoing description applies mostly to the two major theatres of the age of Garrick and Sheridan, Covent Garden and Drury Lane, and it ignores the King's Theatre (a quite similar space) where opera was performed throughout the winter season, and the 'little' theatre in the Haymarket (similar but with fewer seats). The most telling fact about London theatre from 1660 to 1832 is that the performance of plays was officially limited to two holders of 'letters patent', which guaranteed the owners of patents at Drury Lane and Covent Garden the exclusive right to present plays with spoken dialogue. For nearly two centuries, a play with mostly spoken dialogue could not legally appear except in one of the two theatres which constituted the London monopoly during the regular season or after 1766 in the Haymarket Theatre during the summer months.

But lots of other theatrical performances occurred in and around London on any given night, either by special licence and usually for charitable purposes or because they had been defined not as plays but as 'musical' performances or puppet shows. Myriad theatrical afternoons or evenings of a single performer doing impressions or favourite monologues were offered; two-foot-tall puppet shows of the same plays seen at the patent houses were produced; many were the spectacles which employed narrative and character lines which we would recognize as plays, performed at pleasure gardens or the equestrian amphitheatres like Astley's, the Royal Circus, or Sadler's Wells; even more numerous were the performances of burlettas, allowed because all words were sung either in aria or recitative. Londoners' appetite for performance was satisfied by dancers and acrobats, mimics, mimes, jugglers and tightrope walkers, musicians and singers, performing horses and learned pigs and other trained animals of all varieties, in assembly halls, in taverns, in parks, in what were theatres in all but name, well within the twenty-mile radius of London to which the patents applied. The urge to duplicate the entertainment provided by the royal patent houses was constant, and not every violation against their monopoly of the spoken word could be prevented or punished, in the way that the actor John Palmer was punished when he was imprisoned as a rogue and vagabond (those weighty words from the Elizabethan statutes against actors) on 9 November 1789 for speaking prose at the Royal Circus.

THE REPERTORY

Two facts shaped the theatre of the Garrick-Sheridan era. First, it was an age of repertory. Second, it was an age of acting.

If you decided to go to the theatre, in any given nine-month season you would have about fifty choices of mainpieces at each theatre and slightly fewer of afterpieces. On an average, thirty of these mainpieces would be older comedies long established in the repertory; for instance, in the 1779–80 season, a spectator could have seen twenty-two five-act comedies which also had been performed in 1747–8, Garrick's first season as manager of Drury Lane. Thus, the repertory was fairly static; of the fifty-two new five-act comedies produced between the Licensing Act in 1737 and Sheridan's assumption of the management of Drury Lane in 1776, twenty-seven did not survive the season and only seven lasted ten seasons or more.

If we examine the thirty-three seasons at the two winter theatres from Garrick's assumption of the Drury Lane management in 1747 to 1780, when Sheridan entered Parliament, we find that Farquhar's *The Beaux' Stratagem* (1707) and Colley Cibber's adaptation and completion of Vanbrugh's *The Provok'd Husband* (1728) were the most popular five-act comedies, each receiving slightly more than 200 performances at the two houses. Next comes Benjamin Hoadly's *The Suspicious Husband* (1747) with more than 190 performances, Susanna Centlivre's *The Busy Body* (1709) with more than 180, and Richard Steele's *The Conscious Lovers* (1722) with more than 170. Shakespearean comedies were well represented, *The Merchant of Venice* (170 performances) the most popular, then *Much Ado About Nothing* (123), *The Tempest* (109), *As You Like It* (101), and *The Merry Wives of Windsor* (94) appearing nearly every season. Ben Jonson's *Every Man in his Humour* (165) and Vanbrugh's *The Provok'd Wife* (130) and two other Centlivre plays, *The Wonder* (130) and *A Bold Stroke for a Wife* (84), appeared frequently. Farquhar's *The Recruiting Officer* (121), Molière's *L'Avare* in Henry Fielding's adaptation as *The Miser* (111), Beaumont and Fletcher's *Rule a Wife and Have a Wife* (111) were as frequently seen as Congreve's *Way of the World* (111) and *Love for Love* (105). Other stock pieces by Cibber included *She Wou'd and She Wou'd Not* (78), *Love Makes a Man* (73), *The Careless Husband* (73), *Love's Last Shift* (44), and *The Refusal* (37). Farquhar was also represented by *The Constant Couple* (64) and *The Twin Rivals* (34), while Steele's *The Funeral* (58), Jonson's *The Alchemist* (76),

Vanbrugh's *The Relapse* (49) and *The Confederacy* (52) were perennial favourites. Of Dryden not much was seen except in revisions of *Amphytrion* (39) and *The Spanish Friar* (49). By far the most popular comedy at both houses was not a five-act spoken piece but John Gay's musical, *The Beggar's Opera*, performed some 464 times in these thirty-three seasons. The most popular of tragedies was *Romeo and Juliet*, seen some 340 times. Roughly two-thirds of the mainpiece repertory was comedy.

Thus, the staple of the London stage in the Garrick-Sheridan era was older comedy, portions of it Elizabethan but much more from early in the eighteenth century and by authors we do not often read today. The absence of Etherege and Wycherley deserves notice, although in Garrick's chastened 1766 version remnants of *The Country Wife* were occasionally seen. In his useful introduction to *The London Stage, 1660–1800*, Part 5 (1968), C. B. Hogan gives figures for the last twenty-four years of the century, without much change to report in the mainpieces. Comedies and musical comedies abounded, headed by *The School for Scandal* (261), *The Beggar's Opera* (229), Isaac Bickerstaff's *Love in a Village* (168), *The Duenna* (164), and *Hamlet* (164). In the top ten, the only other serious plays are *Macbeth* (150) and *Romeo and Juliet* (119). Newer plays other than Sheridan's did break into the repertory, notably Colman and Garrick's *The Clandestine Marriage* (1766), Colman's *The Jealous Wife* (1761), Cumberland's *The West Indian* (1771), Goldsmith's *She Stoops to Conquer* (1773), and Arthur Murphy's *The Way to Keep Him* (1761); all established themselves into the 1780s and were still occasionally performed in the 1790s.

The afterpiece repertory, on the other hand, reflects an audience demand for novelty and spectacle, particularly as the size of the theatres was expanded in the 1770s and again in the 1790s. When C. B. Hogan lists the top eighteen afterpieces from 1776 to 1800, only Garrick's reworking of Milton's *Comus* comes from before the period; the rest were written after 1776, and most of us would recognize the title only of the eleventh on the list, *The Critic* (1779), with 131 performances in the last twenty-one seasons of the century, as against 200 of John O'Keeffe's *The Agreeable Surprise* or 215 of *Comus*. The other musical pieces, topical farces, and dramatic extravaganzas have been lost to memory.

What to say about the repertory and how it characterizes audience tastes? Well, first, the drama's laws the drama's patrons give, to quote Samuel Johnson. This theatre responded to popular taste. Though that taste was fickle (particularly with regard to new plays), though it accepted serious drama which we consider bombast and comedy which we fault for failure of feeling, the popular taste bred great acting.

Second, again from Johnson (though not in his famous prologue for Garrick), 'Pleasure upon the whole consists in variety'. In every age, theatre only works if it makes money; and it only makes money if people pay for an experience which the backers can provide at less expense than the receipts. Patrons make the theatrical programme. Increasingly through the Garrick era and even more (as Sheridan recognized) in the last quarter of the eighteenth century, they wanted music and spectacle, pantomime and spectacle, procession and spectacle. The pleasure of an often-seen play with a different ensemble or a varying interpretation still brought an audience, and so did an occasional new comedy by Elizabeth Inchbald or a new burletta in the style of Kane O'Hara's *Midas*. Covent Garden held 1,400 until 1782, and in the next decade it held about 2,300; from 1792 to 1808 its capacity was 3,000. Drury Lane from 1775 could offer seats to 2,300 patrons, and after its reconstruction in 1794, on crowded nights 3,611 theatre-goers could be seated. Did changes in taste, such as a growing desire for spectacle, help to increase the size of the houses? Did a desire to raise profits lead the managers to enlarge the houses? Did spectacle become the norm because the auditoriums became larger and the intimacy between actor and audience member in that constantly lit space diminished? The answer to each of these three questions is 'Yes'.

THE ACTING

David Garrick first appeared in London theatres in October 1741, acting without a playbill credit. By 1747, his 'natural' style had so captured the attention of the London theatre-going audience and his popularity so won their approbation that he was able to become the manager of the Theatre Royal in Drury Lane. His amazing achievements would influence dramatic performance for the next three decades. His emphasis upon ensemble acting countered a tradition of formal and individualistic presentation which had marked London acting for several decades: actors portrayed the universal rather than particular truths of their characters; they represented the passions which they found in their roles; they acted exemplars rather than people. When the great Irish actor Charles Macklin portrayed Shylock in *The Merchant of Venice* (February 1741) as a realistic human being rather than a formal comic stereotype, he drew from Alexander Pope the famous response, 'This is the Jew which Shakespeare drew'. The long-lived Macklin performed both before and after Garrick assumed his great role in remaking London theatre.

Garrick stressed an idea which seems simple today: that all the actors are working together, as an ensemble, to make a play live. Each actor supports every other actor to create a dramatic presentation which imitates life. Each actor is part of an effort to give breath and vitality to a *False Delicacy* or *The West Indian* or *The Battle of Hastings*. Each actor submerges his or her ego in the production. Actors act with each other, not alone. They maintain eye contact with their fellow actors, and they do not idly watch the audience when not speaking. They have studied the manuals which outlined the proper posture and gesture to display the various passions, but instead of assuming these only individually, they share them with their fellow performers.

Garrick's idea was new for London and for the actors. But his idea brought great crowds to Drury Lane after 1747, and it affected the way Covent Garden did business as well. The concept of ensemble acting, so foreign to the London stage in 1747, would bring audiences steadily for nearly three decades.

And so would Garrick's personal acting. Any count of the most popular plays in the Garrick-Sheridan era would show such anomalies as Benjamin Hoadly's *The Suspicious Husband* (1747), which hardly anyone bothers to read today: Garrick's representation of Ranger in that play made it a great favourite. Benedick, Archer (in *The Beaux' Stratagem*), Sir John Brute (in *The Provok'd Wife*), Hamlet, Richard III, Macbeth, Romeo, and Lear were among the most popular of the ninety-six roles which Garrick performed. (*Othello* did not appear much before the rise of Kemble, because Garrick decided not to play it.) His acting, and his staging through ensemble performance at Drury Lane, kept the lesser as well as the more famous roles on stage for many years.

That the audiences in this age demanded great acting from recognized stars is clear from what happened after Garrick's retirement. A brother and sister, John Philip Kemble and Sarah Siddons, were hired at Drury Lane, Sarah in 1776, then again in 1782, John in 1783. They were to be associated with that theatre for twenty years. The brother would be acting manager for a number of years, and the sister would become the most effective tragic actress of the century. Neither was cast in Garrick's mould. Instead, they returned the theatre to the formal presentational styles which had obtained before Garrick's reign, even if they kept a good part of the ensemble technique. By the end of the century, Siddons's name alone would draw a capacity crowd; and J. P. Kemble's triumphs as Rolla in Sheridan's *Pizarro* (1799) would draw the largest receipts that Drury Lane had realized in many years. But the theatrical equation had changed; now Kemble and Siddons addressed audiences of three thousand or more, and ensemble became less important than individualistic performance. Every testimony suggests that they seized the attention of audiences with their performances. What those audiences in the 1790s wanted were stentorian representations in spectacle-filled productions, and they got them.

THE ACTORS

If the playgoers were hardy, so too were the actors. With rehearsals and other duties, it was not unusual for them to be at the theatre from ten in the morning until midnight, six days a week, perhaps with time off at three or four for dinner. When the theatres-royal were closed for the summer, stars would undertake arduous tours to the provinces, sometimes matching in eight to twelve weeks their annual London salaries; other actors might engage at the Haymarket or Sadler's Wells or even the stalls of suburban market towns: the gift of talent, looks, voice, carriage, and agility might fail at any moment, and so its present value deserved constant exploitation.

Only leading actors could negotiate for their roles. A youngster trying to earn a place at one or two pounds a week would be expected to sing and dance as well as act, and once engaged an actor who failed to take any part that the acting manager assigned would be fined. Most new members of the company would have been seasoned in the provinces, where they learned and performed many roles until they settled into a pattern of specialities. But parts learned in the provinces might not be available in the city, where an established actor or actress was already in possession of a character and loath to give it over, since the following among the audience guaranteed their benefits. Thus, most actors were exceedingly versatile in their art, possessing a great variety of skills, not least of them the ability to perform a vast number of parts. Garrick, we have seen, had ninety-six roles; many actors had a hundred or more which they could perform at a day's notice. And what must we make of Thomas Hull's 225 parts or John Bannister's 425? These were not just walk-on roles.

The line that an actor took would be well known not just to the audience but also to the playwrights. And it is undoubtedly the case, especially for Sheridan, that plays would be crafted with those skills and associations in mind. For instance, it was Jane Green (1719–91) who created Mrs Malaprop.[2] Active at Covent Garden from 1754 to the end of the 1779–80 season, she had begun by playing pert chambermaids and graduated to more substantial comic roles. As she grew stout, country hoydens and Lucys of ballad opera were succeeded by eccentric maiden ladies and silly hostesses, so that she recreated the affected Mrs Heidelburg for Covent Garden performances of Colman and Garrick's *The Clandestine Marriage* and brought first life to the confused Mrs Hardcastle in Goldsmith's *She Stoops to Conquer* (15 March 1773). Clearly, Mrs Malaprop was the kind of role in which she could excel. Although Sheridan left *The Duenna* to Covent Garden and Thomas Harris (he had probably sold the rights; Jane Green portrayed Margaret, and it was never performed throughout the century at Drury Lane, except for one benefit performance), he took *The Rivals* with him to Drury Lane and turned to Elizabeth Hopkins (1731–1801) to recreate Malaprop. Like Jane Green, Elizabeth Hopkins inherited the role of Mrs Heidelburg, in her case upon the retirement of Kitty Clive at Drury Lane. Shrill of voice, possessed of a peevish countenance, she was mistress of the stage mother, the old eccentric, the dowager and the crabbed aunt; and she was so inclined to corpulence that near the end of her life she was said to have weighed nineteen stone. Wife of the long-time Drury Lane prompter William Hopkins (d. 1780), Elizabeth also created Mrs Dangle; and it was she who played Margaret in the one pre-1800 Drury Lane performance of *The Duenna* on 18 May 1795.

One other example of an actor whose abilities shaped Sheridan's early comic characters is John Quick (1748–1831). First engaged in London by Samuel Foote at the Haymarket on 18 June 1766, he acted Mordecai in Macklin's *Love à-la-Mode* for Ned Shuter's benefit at Covent Garden on 9 June 1767 and was engaged there for the next thirty-one years. By the 1790s he was the second-highest paid performer with a salary of £14 a week and benefits bringing as much as £400. He brought a turkey-cock air to low comic parts – country boobies, servants, old men, stage Jews and other exotics – and George III is said to have come to Covent Garden only to see Quick. Quick's range was broad. Among his regular characters were Mungo in Isaac Bickerstaff's popular comic opera, *The Padlock* (23 October 1770), Foresight in *Love for Love*, Touchstone, Launcelot Gobbo, Dogberry and Trinculo, Cimberton in *The Conscious Lovers*, and Major Oakley in *The*

3 John Quick as Isaac Mendoza in *The Duenna*.

Jealous Wife. But it was as Tony Lumpkin in *She Stoops to Conquer* (15 March 1773) that his talent for whimsy and exuberance must have caught Sheridan's imagination and shaped Bob Acres, created by Quick, as well as Dr Rosy in *St Patrick's Day* and Isaac Mendoza in *The Duenna*. So much did London audiences expect of Quick the comic line that when, for his benefit on 6 April 1790, he acted Richard III, he was caricatured as 'Little Dicky'

4 The Screen Scene from *The School for Scandal*. Thomas King as Sir Peter Teazle, Frances Abington as Lady Teazle, William Smith as Charles Surface, and John Palmer as Joseph Surface. Painted by James Roberts and exhibited in 1777.

and made no further London forays into tragedy. (He had been successful as Richard III in Bristol.)

The careers of six other actors may join these in exemplifying the lives and talents of all these evanescent artists. Each created roles in Sheridan's plays after his move to Drury Lane, and each achieved remarkable distinction in his craft.

Thomas King (1730–1805) won fame as Ranger in *The Suspicious Husband* under the management of Thomas Sheridan in Smock Alley Theatre, Dublin. As a young man in 1748, King had been tried at Drury Lane by Garrick in a variety of supporting roles; then he spent most of the next decade acting abroad or in the provinces. Permanently installed in London by 1760, he could not be expected to take roles like Ranger which belonged to Garrick; yet by 1764–5, he had become Drury Lane's chief comedian after Garrick. Though he could do clowns, valets and fops, it was as the generous-minded but absurd Lord Ogleby in *The Clandestine Marriage* (20 February 1766) that he established the line of aristocratic eccentrics by which for the final thirty-five years of his career he would be best known. The actor and critic Francis Gentleman valued his amiable personality and appreciated the warm sensibility which he brought to Lord Ogleby. These qualities must have informed his conception of Sir Peter Teazle just as much as his brusque manner earned praise for his recreation of Sir Anthony Absolute in the 1776 Drury Lane revival of Sheridan's first comedy, or his creation of Puff, author of 'The Spanish Armada' in *The Critic*. King was Sir Joseph Wittol in *The Old Batchelor*, Tattle in *Love for Love*, and Witwoud in *The Way of the World* during Sheridan's revivals of Congreve in that first 1776–7 season of his management at Drury Lane. King had had these roles for some years, and his range remained as large throughout his fifty-five years on stage. But it was as the elderly nobleman or knight that he excelled. I once gave credence to the report that King's Sir Peter was an 'old fretful dotard', but I now doubt that report. King's roles as warm if eccentric old men confirm him in a line of amiable humorists for which he was much beloved.

Tom King earned David Garrick's affection and respect, and Richard Sheridan brought him in as acting manager at Drury Lane (something between producer and artistic director) from 1782 to 1788, until King finally quit the post in disgust at Sheridan's lackadaisical management. Like a number of other principal performers, King sought opportunities to invest his earnings and his expertise in the theatre, and from October 1771 to 1785 he owned and managed the theatre in Sadler's Wells. During the summer of 1779 he produced there *The Prophecy; or, Queen Elizabeth at Tilbury*, a musical piece capitalizing upon London's excitement over the declaration of war with Spain and the reports of Spanish and French squadrons in the Channel. It was also one of the proximate causes for *The Critic*, first performed a few months later with King as the putative author of the absurd 'Spanish Armada' which informs the second and third acts. King achieved remarkable popular acclaim in another area: his performance of prologues could often guarantee a respectful hearing of new plays, particularly comedies, into the ninth night of presentation, when the author would get his or her third and final benefit. On 10 June 1800, he acted Sir Peter Teazle for the 254th time, having missed only two announced performances since 8 May 1777.

Frances Abington (1737–1815) was discovered by that great actor of low comic parts, Ned Shuter (1728–76), who saw her at the Haymarket in the summer of 1755 and found her employment at the theatre in Bath. (Shuter was not 'perfect' as Sir Anthony Absolute in the 17 January 1775 première of *The Rivals* and may have been one cause for the initial failure of Sheridan's first play.) 'Fanny Barton' in her earliest years, Mrs Abington played at Drury Lane from 1756 to 1759, then spend half a decade in Ireland before returning to London, where she had been reared, motherless, in a strolling life as a flower girl. From 1765 until November 1782, she acted at Drury Lane; for the next eight years she was part of the Covent Garden company (another casualty of Sheridan's inept management) until she retired on 12 February 1790. She recreated Lydia Languish at Drury Lane, performed Hoyden in *A Trip to Scarborough*, and was the first Lady Teazle. In Sheridan's 1776–7 revivals of Congreve, she was Laetitia in *The Old Batchelor*, Prue in *Love for Love*, and Millamant in *The Way of the World*, a range of characters indicative of her versatility.

'Nosegay Fan' set standards for London style as well as acting. Her voice did not meet contemporary expectations for a graceful young lady, but she was so able to modulate her tones and to articulate her words that she won regular applause. She could converse in French and Italian and knew a surprising range of contemporary literature. What she wore and how she did her hair affected the choices of many ladies in the capital, and she was regularly (and professionally) consulted on matters of fashion: in the early sketches for *The School for Scandal* is a joke about Lady Teazle's having her coach remodelled so as to admit a towering headdress, but that joke vanishes in the final script, and Fanny Abington is cited in the press for a 'remarkably low' coiffure in her performance of Lady Teazle. Gaiety, ease, humour, elegance and grace marked her person and her acting. She often argued with Garrick, accusing him of giving Jane Pope better parts; and she began flirting with Covent Garden from the earliest months of Sheridan's management at Drury Lane, though it was six years before she jumped to the other company.

No comic acting line since Colley Cibber earned more audience approbation than the fop; but Garrick himself abandoned such roles once he had discovered James William Dodd (1740?–96). Highfill, Burnim, and Langhans in their notice on Dodd cite a scouting letter from Dr John Hoadly to Garrick about Dodd's appearance on the Bath stage – his white 'calf-like' face, his dancing-master mincing, his surprisingly good, deep singing voice (which must have set up an absurd contrast) – and Garrick brought both

Dodd and his wife Martha to Drury Lane in 1765. Although in the next thirty-one years he would occasionally descend to low comedy or attempt, usually for his benefits, to rise into tragedy, it was as coxcombs, fops, country boobies, and silly beaux in comedy of manners and sentimental comedy that Dodd excelled. Early on, some critics thought he might try to dethrone King as the leading comedian of Drury Lane, but his natural range was not so great as King's. Still, his £8 weekly salary in 1776–7 indicates his substantial value to the company. For Sheridan he recreated Acres, performed Lord Foppington, and created Sir Benjamin Backbite and Dangle. Some thought his Osric the finest of the century, and his Sir Andrew Aguecheek was equally famous. James Boaden, in his *Memoirs of Kemble*, tagged him with the epithets 'the prince of pink heels, and the soul of empty eminence', tottering rather than walking the stage.

In 'On Some of the Old Actors' (*London Magazine*, February 1822), Charles Lamb gives a loving portrait of Dodd's powers:

> In expressing slowness of apprehension, this actor surpassed all others. You could see the first dawn of an idea stealing slowly over his countenance, climbing up by little and little, with a painful process, till it cleared up at last to the fullness of a twilight conception – its highest meridian. He seemed to keep back his intellect, as some have had the power to retard their pulsation. The balloon takes less time in filling than it took to cover the expansion of his broad moony face over all its quarters with expression. A glimmer of understanding would appear in a corner of his eye, and for lack of fuel go out again. A part of his forehead would catch a little intelligence, and be a long time in communicating it to the remainder.

Thinking that he saw Dodd on the street going about his business in a sober, manly fashion, Lamb asks:

> Could this sad thoughtful countenance be the same vacant face of folly which I had hailed so often under circumstances of gaiety; which I had never seen without a smile, or recognized but as the usher of mirth; that looked out so formally flat in Foppington, so frothily pert in Tattle, so impotently busy in Backbite; so blankly divested of all meaning, or resolutely expressive of none, in Acres, in Fribble [in Garrick's *Miss In Her Teens*], and a thousand agreeable impertinences? . . . Care, that troubles all the world, was forgotten in his composition. Had he had but two grains (nay, half a grain) of it, he could never have supported himself upon those two spider's strings, which served him (in the latter part of his unmixed existence) as legs. A doubt or a scruple must have made him totter, a sigh have puffed him down; the weight of a frown had staggered him, a wrinkle made him lose his balance . . . Shakespeare foresaw him, when he framed his fools and jesters.

5 James Dodd as Lord Foppington in *A Trip to Scarborough*.

And surely Sheridan knew his pattern in creating the immortal Backbite. As Boaden wrote, 'he left you no doubt whatever of the superior happiness of a coxcomb'.

John Palmer (1744–98) recreated Jack Absolute and created Tom Fashion, Joseph Surface and Sneer for Sheridan. His reputation for intrigue and hypocrisy as well as his acting of Lord Plausible in *The Plain Dealer* earned him the sobriquet 'Plausible Jack'. After playing small parts with Samuel Foote at the Haymarket, he was first engaged at £1 a week by Garrick at Drury Lane in 1763–4; he left during the 1764–5 season and rejoined in 1766–7, rarely straying for the next thirty years. His value to the company may be judged by his £17 weekly salary in 1790. Few leading actors possessed Palmer's range; he was adept in low and high comedy, in farce, in tragedy. Though he is remembered best for Joseph Surface, he played Macduff to Kemble's Macbeth on many occasions. Outside London he performed Richard III, Shylock, Hamlet, and Othello, and within the city there was no role too small for his versatile talents. In a one-year period from 18 June 1797 to 18 June 1798, he acted 170 nights in sixty-five different characters, a dozen of which were new. His total roles probably exceeded 375; he died on stage in Liverpool, performing in the title character of *The Stranger*. Some thought his movement in tragedy too abrupt and violent, although this criticism may reflect a preference for the more formal and deliberate style that John Philip Kemble brought to London in the 1780s; but while Palmer's delivery in tragedy was both discriminating and animated by feeling, he was preferred in comedy.

In 1785, 'Plausible Jack' thought he had found a loophole in the Licensing Act of 1737. He convinced officials of the Tower of London to give him a licence to perform within the Liberty of the Tower at a theatre to be erected in Well Street, Wellclose Square, slightly to the south of the old theatre in Goodman's Fields. With a silent partner, he organized 120 renters at £50 each, the stockholders to receive a shilling a night for the first hundred nights of each of the first twenty-one seasons plus free admittance to the theatre. By December 1785, the cornerstone for the Royalty Theatre was laid, and by 20 June 1787 the 2,600-seat theatre actually opened, in spite of published threats from Thomas Linley (for Drury Lane), Thomas Harris (for Covent Garden) and George Colman (for the Haymarket). Palmer acted as Jacques in *As You Like It* and also in the farce, *Miss In Her Teens*, and spoke an opening address composed by Arthur Murphy for the occasion. Skirting the licensing issue by advertising the performance as a benefit for the London Hospital (which he subsequently paid), Palmer tried to hold his company together; the renters had not provided sufficient capital to build the theatre, he was deeply in debt, and the licensees were publicly threatening any of their actors with arrest for performing at the Royalty. Palmer managed to reopen on 3 July 1787 with musicals and pantomimes, and several of the company were briefly jailed as 'rogues, vagabonds, and sturdy beggars', though not Plausible Jack himself. Musical and burletta performances continued sporadically until April 1788 and then ceased. There is an anecdote which ought to be true but sounds too neat. Palmer, creator of Joseph Surface, seeks his old acting job back at Drury Lane and apologizes to Sheridan for his attempt to break the patent monopolies: Jack says, 'If you could but see my heart, Mr Sheridan –' 'Why, Jack!' replies Sheridan, 'you forget: I wrote it.'

Charles Lamb remembered Jack Palmer in 'On Some of the Old Actors' for his air of 'swaggering gentility':

> He was a *gentleman* with a slight infusion of *the footman* . . . When you saw Jack figuring as Captain Absolute, you thought you could trace his promotion to some lady of quality who fancied the handsome fellow in his topknot, and had bought him a commission.

Lamb detailed Palmer's special qualities in Joseph Surface:

> Jack had two voices, both plausible, hypocritical, and insinuating; but his secondary or supplemental voice still more decisively histrionic than his common one. It was reserved for the spectator; and the *dramatis personae* were supposed to know nothing at all about it. The *lies* of Young Wilding [in Samuel Foote's *The Liar*], and the *sentiments* in Joseph Surface, were thus marked out in a sort of italics to the audience. This secret correspondence with the company before the curtain . . . has an extremely happy effect in some kinds of comedy, . . . of Sheridan especially . . .

Lamb waxes rhapsodic in 'On the Artificial Comedy of the Last Century' (*London Magazine*, April 1822), and declares that the hero of *The School for Scandal*, when Palmer had the part, was Joseph Surface:

> . . . the gay boldness, the graceful solemn plausibility, the measured step, the insinuating voice – to express it in a word – the downright *acted* villainy of the part, so different from the pressure of conscious actual wickedness – the hypocritical assumption of hypocrisy . . . made Jack so deservedly a favourite in that character . . . He was playing to you all the while that he was playing upon Sir Peter and his lady. You had the first intimation of a sentiment before it was on his lips. His altered voice was meant to you, and you were to suppose that his fictitious co-flutterers on the stage perceived nothing at all of it.

It is no mean place in history to be remembered as Joseph Surface by so acute an observer as Charles Lamb; but we should not forget Palmer's Toby Belch, his Falstaff, his Henry the Eighth, his Bajazet (*Tamerlane*), Count Almaviva, Don John, even his Stukely (*The Gamester*). His versatility and range were greater than those of most of his peers.

King, Abington, Dodd, and Palmer exemplify all of the actors who trained up in the Garrick era and who became the raw material for Sheridan's Drury Lane comedies. At the end of Garrick's career came two other actors, a sister and a brother, who typify theatre not in the age of Sheridan but in the age of the Kembles.

Sarah Siddons (1755–1831) was born to Roger and Sarah Ward Kemble; Roger was a provincial manager, and actress Sarah was the daughter of John and Sarah Ward, managers of another company of itinerant actors. Sarah Siddons's siblings John Philip, Charles, Stephen, Frances, Elizabeth, and Julia Ann all performed in London, and her sister Jane acted in the provinces in the 1790s. The sons of the family were raised Catholic, the daughters Protestant. By the time she was fifteen, Sarah had won the affections of William Siddons, an actor in Roger's company who was twenty-six. But her parents did not approve and sent her into service (then companionship) to Lady Mary Greathead; Roger fired Siddons. Two years at Guy's Cliffe in Warwick did not cool the couple's ardour, and by November 1773 Sarah and William were married and acting in Roger Kemble's company.

When she was eighteen, Sarah had appeared in twenty-three characters, her favourites being Alicia in *Jane Shore*, Portia in *The Merchant of Venice*, Belvidera in *Venice Preserv'd*, widow Brady in *The Irish Widow*, Rosalind in *As You Like It* and Clarinda in *The Suspicious Husband.* Garrick sent Thomas King to scout her, and King was much impressed by her performance as Calista in *The Fair Penitent*, but it was another year before Garrick asked the Reverend Mr Henry Bate to scout her once again and then to settle upon terms for her London première. When that occurred at Drury Lane on 29 December 1775 and thereafter through Garrick's last spring on stage, it went badly. Sarah most likely felt intimidated, and Garrick's casting of her was not strong (perhaps he could not take roles from established actresses for her). In any event, she was not re-engaged for autumn 1776 and must have suffered bitter disappointment. From 1778 to 1782, however, she became an established leading actress in the theatre at Bath, and when she reappeared in London at Drury Lane on 10 October 1782, the seasoning of the provincial theatre had done its work: twenty-four times she was Isabella in *Isabella; or, The Fatal Marriage* to tremendous applause, repeated her Calista and Belvidera, graduated to the title character of *Jane Shore*, acted a total of eighty times that season, and in January 1783 performed no fewer than five times in five different roles for George III – an unprecedented run of theatre-going for the monarch. Her December benefit, as Belvidera, earned her £335 plus personal gifts to a total of £800, and as Zara in *The Mourning Bride* for a second benefit in March 1783 she was rumoured to have earned £650. The town was in love.

Among many critics, of course, the love was not perfect. As the successor to the vastly popular Susanna Maria Cibber (now dead nearly two decades but well remembered), Sarah was expected to achieve new heights in tragic acting. Meanwhile, she was frequently compared to Ann Crawford (formerly Mrs Spranger Barry), reigning tragic queen at Covent Garden; it was generally conceded that Siddons was prettier but offered more to the mind and less to the heart than Crawford. In comedy Sarah earned commendation for the perfection of her art, in tragedy for the perfection of nature. (One can never be sure in the eighteenth century just what 'nature' meant in the context of acting, let alone of philosophy or of literature.) In tragedy she brought the greatest crowds. Her first London performance as Lady Macbeth occurred when she was not yet thirty, on 2 February 1785, and Charles Lamb later remarked that when theatre-goers spoke of Lady Macbeth they were really thinking of Mrs Siddons *as* Lady Macbeth. A clue to the fact that her acting, howsoever formal and studied, still upheld something of the Garrick tradition of ensemble playing comes from an appreciation of her response to Shylock's 'On what compulsion must I?' As Portia, she launched into 'the quality of mercy' speech as a true answer to Shylock and his aggressive question and to the Duke and the magnificoes, not as the studied piece of recitation directed at the audience heard so frequently from other actresses in that famous scene.

Mrs Siddons's mature years were neither smooth personally nor calm professionally. In late 1789 she denied being ill, but her friend Hester Lynch Thrale Piozzi became concerned about her health during a prolonged visit to the Piozzi country home; yet it was not until August 1792 that Mrs Siddons's ailment was diagnosed as venereal, an unfortunate gift from her husband, from whom she was often estranged. During this discomfort in the 1790–1 season at Drury Lane, she performed only six times. She earned large amounts of money from her acting in London – for instance, £30 a night for twenty-four appearances while the Drury Lane company performed at King's in 1791–2 during the reconstruction of its theatre, and nearly £500 for her benefit – yet still she felt compelled to undertake arduous tours of Ireland and the provinces during the summer, often matching or exceeding her London earnings. Despite Sheridan's owing her fully £2,100 plus her previous season's benefit in November 1799, she had amassed by 1802 £53,000 in the funds. She never liked the enlarged Drury Lane, calling it 'a wilderness of a place', for her voice would not fill the huge auditorium; she remarked how happy she was to have earned her reputation in a smaller house. Her last new role was Hermione in *The Winter's Tale*, 25 March 1802; shortly thereafter she left Drury Lane for good, another casualty of Sheridan's management, and after a season in Ireland she joined her brother John Philip Kemble at Covent Garden, where he had gone as part owner and manager in 1803–4. She would act there every season until her retirement in 1812 except 1804–5, when the boy actor Master Henry Betty caused a craze for his female tragic roles at Drury Lane and she refused to be drawn into a competition. After 1812, she foolishly appeared a few times, evoking sad comparisons with the actress she once had been. Still, William Hazlitt could write in the *Examiner* of 16 June 1816,

> She raised the tragedy to the skies . . . It was something above nature. We can conceive of nothing grander. She embodied to our imagination the fables of mythology, of the heroic and dignified mortals of elder time. She was not less than a goddess, or than a prophetess inspired by the gods. Power was seated on her brow, passion emanated from her breast as from a shrine. She was Tragedy, personified. She was the stateliest ornament of the public mind . . . To have seen Mrs Siddons was an event in everybody's life . . .

If Sarah Siddons was the Tragic Muse for London and the British Isles through the eighties, nineties, and into the early nineteenth century, her brother John Philip Kemble (1757–1823) was not only the Tragic Hero until the rise of Edmund Kean in the teens of the next century but also the best acting manager since David Garrick. His father Roger Kemble sent him to a Roman Catholic seminary in 1767, but Kemble did not take to the priesthood. By June 1778 (his apprenticeship was with Tate Wilkinson, the 'wandering patentee') he had mastered sixty-eight roles in tragedy and fifty-eight in comedy; over one period of 345 nights with Wilkinson he performed 102 roles in ninety-nine plays.

The years of seasoning allowed Kemble at twenty-six a better introduction to London audiences than his sister had had at twenty. Arriving in London in August and taking advantage of the hospitality of his friends Joseph and Elizabeth Inchbald to help publicize his appearance, he first trod Old Drury's boards as Hamlet on 30 September 1783. Memories of Garrick's interpretations abounded, and Kemble's steady, static declamatory style did not always compare favourably. (Even Sarah found him too cold and formal for the passionate, tumultuous Jaffier in *Venice Preserv'd*, one of Garrick's occasional roles. There was something literary in many of Kemble's interpretations which put some people off.) But audiences came,

6 Sarah Siddons as Lady Macbeth and John Philip Kemble as Macbeth, painted by Thomas Beach and exhibited in 1786.

and his fame increased. His wide range of tragic parts and his performance with his sister inspired many adherents. The studied gesture and the intelligent intonations pleased those who put Garrick's memory out of their minds.

By 23 September 1788 John Philip Kemble had become the acting manager for Drury Lane. Thomas King had left that post, and Kemble felt compelled to tell the public that his management was not being assumed 'under *humiliating circumstances*' as some (knowing Sheridan) apparently thought. For the next eight seasons, including the wandering time before the construction of the new theatre, Kemble would give Old Drury not only the gift of his acting and directing but also the fruits of his pen. For instance, his studious preciseness as Coriolanus in his revision of Shakespeare's late play, with authentic-seeming properties and costumes, began to cement a popular association of his art with the Roman heroes. He added many other adaptations to the Drury Lane stock such as *Measure for Measure*, *All's Well That Ends Well*, *Alexander the Great*, *The Plain Dealer*, *Macbeth*, *The Roman Actor* (from Massinger), *Celedon and Florimel* (from Dryden and Cibber), *The Merry Wives of Windsor* and *Much Ado About Nothing*. Garrick had done much the same thing in adapting older plays, and in the late 1770s the public had expected as much from Sheridan, though they got little more than some revivals of Congreve and the revision of Vanbrugh. Still Kemble enlarged his art: he even essayed after William 'Gentleman' Smith's retirement the unaccustomed comedic role of Charles Surface, in which Lamb liked him very much indeed.

At the end of the 1795–6 season, Kemble resigned his post as acting manager for Drury Lane. Yet he remained as an actor in the company, and in 1799 he created his first original role for Sheridan – Rolla in *Pizarro*, with his sister Sarah playing Elvira. Nearly £14,000 was grossed in the thirty-one nights before the season closed, fully one-quarter of the receipts for the year. In the 1800–1 season Kemble resumed the responsibilities of acting manager for Drury Lane: he hoped to buy one-quarter of the patent for £25,000, but Sheridan's title was judged unclear by the attorneys, and at the conclusion of the 1801–2 season Kemble resigned from the theatre entirely. After a grand tour, in April 1803 he purchased one-sixth of the Covent Garden moiety for £22,000; he remained there as an actor and as the acting manager until the 1811–12 season when he retired.

Two events must have complicated Kemble's life. While he made lots of money for the new Drury Lane with its forty-three-foot wide proscenium and its 3,611 seats after its 12 March 1794 opening, he got into trouble in the autumn of 1795 for his revival of *Venice Preserv'd*: new dressed for the larger house but always judged a political piece, it was taken to be inspiring rebellion. Kemble (and Sheridan) persisted in offering it, probably because of a tremendous investment in scenery and spectacle. After its third performance on 29 October 1795 the play was banned for seven years. Fifteen years later he faced the 'old price' riots, which destroyed the interior of his new home in Covent Garden when the theatre attempted to increase the price of tickets permanently. Again, he seems to have persisted too long in a course of which the audience did not approve. But he managed the actors and the choices of plays well into the nineteenth century, and he was responsible for raising the money to recreate Covent Garden after the 1808 fire. Never possessing Garrick's range of emotion or his affecting style, Kemble's intellectual precision held audiences for three decades. He was not 'natural', and he certainly could not match Edmund Kean's passionate, fiery, romantic energy; but he was the measure of the great tragic roles for a generation or more. When he retired in the early years of Edmund Kean's ascendancy, he was remembered as Garrick's successor.

SHERIDAN'S CREATIVE DEBTS

The physical space and its potential, the actors and their capacities, the repertory and its tradition, the audience and its expectations, the literary precursors – these elements constrained the boundaries of creation for playwrights of the Garrick-Sheridan era. Sheridan articulated his awareness of one aspect in a letter to his father-in-law, Thomas Linley (some time in October 1775; *Letters*, i. 86), when he wrote about their upcoming production of *The Duenna* that 'We dare not propose a peep beyond the ancle on any account; for the critics in the pit at a new play are much greater prudes than the ladies in the boxes.' If he understood the necessity of avoiding bawdry and sexual suggestion lest the audience rebel before the requisite nine performances had earned him three benefit nights, he also must have understood much more. Certainly he had not been present when the audience insisted that Samuel Johnson's Irene be garrotted off-stage rather than on, but he cannot have misunderstood the audience's power to dismiss a new piece with only one hearing like William O'Brien's *The Duel* (Drury Lane, 8 December 1772) or the near damnation of his own first comedy. If Sheridan were to experiment, it would be within the context of the drama which the drama's patrons supported.

Hence, I think that Sheridan owed most of his playwriting debts not to his long-dead precursors but to his immediate contemporaries and to the actors who were giving life to the characters every evening as they performed plays in that broad repertory. Congreve Sheridan must have known and loved: the act of reviving Congreve's three best comedies when he assumed management and ownership of Drury Lane in 1776 represented a labour of affection and a payment of literary debt, though an uncertain investment of human capital, given the return. Wycherley and Etherege he did not try. Vanbrugh he attempted to reform, and in fact he did a very credible job of tightening the plot of *The Relapse* in his significant revision called *A Trip to Scarborough*: his biographer Thomas Moore lamented that (from his early nineteenth-century perspective) Sheridan's re-drawing mistook the fact that the characters were so licentious that they are 'luminous from putrescence – to remove their taint is to extinguish their light', and this criticism is not unfair from one who rightly saw that comedy after about 1750 was character-centred rather than plot-centred and who hence had little appreciation for the masterful job that Sheridan did in tidying Vanbrugh's bifurcated plot scheme. From Shakespeare, Sheridan took not situation but characters in situation, and from *Much Ado About Nothing* especially he learned a great deal about his craft. Farquhar, Steele, Cibber, and Centlivre, among the earlier eighteenth-century authors, also helped him to form his art.

Charles Lamb in 'On the Artificial Comedy of the Last Century' (*London Magazine*, April 1822) links *The School for Scandal* to Congreve and Wycherley, even though Sheridan's play 'gathered some allays of the sentimental comedy which followed theirs'. This judgement deserves attention. Hugh Kelly's *False Delicacy* (Drury Lane, 23 January 1768) and Richard Cumberland's *The West Indian* (Drury Lane, 19 January 1771) played throughout the 1770s and satisfied a taste very like that met by the Julia-Faulkland line of *The Rivals*. Although *She Stoops to Conquer* (15 March 1773) was often seen as Goldsmith wanted it to be as opposing 'a new species of Dramatic Composition [sentimental comedy] . . . in which the virtues of Private Life are exhibited, rather than the Vices exposed; and the Distresses rather than the Faults of Mankind, make our interest in the piece' ('An Essay on the Theatre; or, a Comparison between Laughing and Sentimental Comedy', 1772), the Neville-Hastings plot of Goldsmith's play appealed to the same tastes that made *False Delicacy* and *The West Indian* hits and kept *The Conscious Lovers* in the repertory. Sentimental comedy was a great force in the 1770s, and Sheridan used that particular audience expectation as much as any other of his contemporaries.

The actors, their specialities, and the theatre's other capabilities influenced what Sheridan tried to do as a playwright. Covent Garden was the home of 'low comedy', that is comedy which uses the jape, the leer and the pratfall. Drury Lane was the home of 'high comedy', refined, sensitive, measured, more verbally dependent. A reading of *The Rivals*, *St Patrick's Day* and *The Duenna* – the plays which Sheridan did for Covent Garden – will show their dependence upon low comic skills; a reading of *A Trip to Scarborough*, *The School for Scandal* and *The Critic* will show their dependence upon witty language and graceful acting, the 'high comic' style for which the Drury Lane company was famous, and *The Camp* and *The Critic* show a dependence upon spectacle, which with Philippe de Loutherbourg Drury Lane could produce much better than Covent Garden. (The final scenes of *The Critic* were visually stunning in the minds of early spectators.) Sheridan wrote his plays with a contemporary tradition at hand, and though his final conceptions reflect a small debt to the great plays of Congreve and Wycherley and Shakespeare, much more debt must be ascribed to the actors in the two different companies with which he worked, to the playwrights who gave the two houses many comedies in the 1760s and 1770s, and to the companies of actors whose particular skills he exploited.[3]

SHERIDAN'S MANAGEMENT

Sheridan owned Drury Lane and managed it from 1776 to 1811, a period exceeding in length David Garrick's management and ownership from 1747 to 1776. Sheridan had in his hands the entertainment of 12,000 or so Londoners a week and the livelihoods of several hundred theatre workers and their families – actors, dancers, singers; ticket collectors and property men; billstickers and accountants; guards, scenemen, scene painters, and machinists; charwomen and janitors; chief operating officers like his deputy acting managers, his prompters, and his treasurers – all the myriad workers who make a theatre into a business that represents the strongest human passions and relieves them all. And yet, with this awesome responsibility for the personal circumstances of his subordinates and with the executive authority to assure that investors would recoup what they had wagered, he rarely showed a profit like that of the Garrick years; he was often in arrears in paying wages (particularly to the leading actors); and he balanced his debts to investors so precariously that by 1815 Samuel Whitbread, a successful and hard-headed businessman who at Sheridan's request in 1809 had taken over management, committed suicide in despair of ever being able to pay Drury Lane's bills.

Sheridan's management began auspiciously. He had impressed two of the three owners, David Garrick and Dr John Ford, and he brought his father-in-law Thomas Linley as an ally in the purchase of the Drury Lane patent and as music director for the theatre. In his financial manoeuvrings in the summer of 1776 and the spring of 1778 (when he bought Willoughby Lacy's moiety), it appears that Sheridan laid out no more for his nine-fourteenths share than £1,300 cash for a property valued at between £60,000 and £70,000. Much was hoped of him. A man who in one ten-month period had produced two great money-making comedies, tossed off a farce and a season-opening prelude, and graced several plays with prologues and epilogues could be trusted to earn with his pen and talents the money to pay off renters and shareholders and theatre servants, and to make good on annuities. Instead of an actor like Garrick who developed himself into a superb businessman or a businessman like Thomas Harris at Covent Garden, who became an extraordinarily knowledgeable producer, Drury Lane would have an author and acting manager whose sense of theatrical taste and dramatic talent would enlarge its repertoire and bring crowds such as those which had thronged to Garrick's farewell performances.

Despite the rage for seventy-five nights of *The Duenna* at Covent Garden, Garrick's forty-seven performances in 1775–6 brought in an average of £266 a night. In 1776–7, by contrast and excluding benefit nights for which figures are unreliable, 151 nights brought Drury Lane an average of only £191; Covent Garden that season averaged £212 on the 133 non-benefit nights. As acting manager as well as part owner, Sheridan exerted himself tremendously. He cut Garrick's popular *A Christmas Tale* to after-piece length and presented it thirty-two times; he refurbished the pantomime *Harlequin's Invasion* and offered it twenty-eight times; he made cuts and changes to *The Old Batchelor* (last acted in 1758) and *Love for Love* (last acted in 1771) and with a repeat of the previous season's *The Way of the World* made November and December a Congreve revival; he added now-lost changes to *The Tempest* principally to display de Loutherbourg's art, and a scene to *The Beggar's Opera* to point the moral; he put important finishing touches on Sir George Collier's *Selima and Azor*, for which the author thanked him effusively in the preface to the published edition; he wrote an epilogue for G. S. Ayscough's *Semiramis* and a prologue for William Woodfall's alteration of Richard Savage's *Sir Thomas Overbury* at the rival house. By late February his extensive revision of *The Relapse* as *A Trip to Scarborough* came forward, and on 8 May 1777 *The School for Scandal* appeared. Since as acting manager (with the prompter William Hopkins) he oversaw rehearsals and distributed roles, his Drury Lane version this season of *The Rivals* (16 January 1777) must have sparked considerable interest in comparison with its opening two years before; it averaged £217 a night. The real money-maker, of course, was *The School for Scandal* at an average £233, still not up to the £275 average for the twelve nights announced in the previous year as Garrick's last in a particular role, but fairly remarkable so late in the season. (It brought in a stunning £255 a night in the 1777–8 season in its forty-five appearances.) If we count Sheridan's efforts as a director, a play-doctor and an author, fully 179 of the 181 nights of that first season at Drury Lane featured something from his talents. It was a hopeful start.

But before Sheridan went to Parliament on 12 September 1780, there would be only three more pieces indisputably his own: *The Camp* (15 October 1778), the *Verses to the Memory of Garrick, Spoken as a Monody* (11 March 1779), and *The Critic* (30 October 1779). There was some play-doctoring for Henry Fielding's long-lost comedy, *The Fathers* (30 November 1778), some impromptu for de Loutherbourg's art in *The Wonders of Derbyshire* (8 January 1779), various prologues and epilogues, and probably some cutting and pasting for a revision of Henry Woodward's old personal vehicle, *Fortunatus* (first produced 26 December 1753; revived by Sheridan 3 January 1780). After his election we have less evidence until the 1790s. He may have helped Thomas Lewis O'Beirne with *The Generous Imposter* (22 November 1780) and been part of *Robinson Crusoe* (30 January 1781), in which a song from *The Duenna* was featured. A two-act farce by John Dent called *The Statesman* was announced to be in rehearsal on 21 December 1781, but it never appeared. Perhaps he took a hand in *Richard Coeur de Lion* (24 October 1786), which is credited to Elizabeth Linley Sheridan and John Burgoyne. In the 1790s we can be reasonably sure that Sheridan was one artistic force behind *The Glorious First of June* (2 July 1794), a spectacle at the newly opened Drury Lane to celebrate Admiral 'Black Dick' Howe's cutting up of the French fleet off the Bay of Biscay, and then in the revival of James Cobb's *The Haunted Tower* (first performed 24 November 1789) sometime in 1794 to use the scenery and machinery from *The Glorious First of June* once again. (It was in rehearsal on 18 October 1794 and was performed on 20 October; however, there was no advertisement of new scenery.) The initial appearances of Benjamin Thompson's translation of Kotzebue's *The Stranger* (24 March 1798) show marks of Sheridan's style of revising plays in light of audience response, just as he did for his own version of another Kotzebue piece, *Pizarro* (24 May 1799), that vastly popular vehicle for Kemble and Siddons. The Patmore manuscripts show numerous corrections to several unpublished plays in what Professor Cecil Price identifies as Sheridan's hand (watermarks from 1797 and 1802 on two of the MSS); there is an outline of incidents for *The Forty Thieves* (8 April 1806), otherwise attributed to C. W. Ward and George Colman the Younger; and both Richard and his son Tom, by then part of the Drury Lane management, made corrections to Theodore Hook's adaptation of Pixérécourt's *Les Mines de Pologue*, acted as *The Siege of St Quintin, or, Spanish Heroism* (10 November 1808). But the playwriting and the play-doctoring after 1780 was less management than hobby.[4]

Garrick saw owning the patent as an opportunity to shape taste and produce great theatre, to educate the public through events (ill-starred though they were) like Noverre's *Chinese Festival* or his own *Shakespeare Jubilee*. Sheridan saw owning the patent as a speculative investment designed to make money. If he had left it at that, if he had truly given over the day-to-day management to others, he might have earned regular profits. But especially after he went to Parliament, he meddled, he became a micro-managing executive. He delighted in the planning and the intrigue of large-scale investment, but he paid only sporadic attention to the day-to-day details by which real fortunes are gradually secured. And when he did attend to those details it was often at the expense of the authority of his hired deputies, who would find their hard-won discipline undermined by their owner's acquiescence to whim and fancy. He knew it of himself: in a letter from about October 1788, Sheridan writes to his friend Joseph Richardson (1755–1803): 'The Theatre tho I am now more than ever interested in it, must continue a Secondary Object to me . . .'[5] But it was a secondary object in which, countless times, he felt his judgement superior to that of his hired executives. Sheridan had at least eight deputy or acting managers, three prompters, and at least three treasurers; by contrast, from his assumption of the management of Covent Garden in 1767 to the end of the century Thomas Harris had two managers, one prompter, and two or three treasurers. Among Sheridan's letters and notes are numerous agreements which assigned his authority to one or another of his subordinates, all, alas, regularly broken. The executive who fails to trust his subordinates and countermands their authority creates dissension and demoralization in any organization of people, leaving it not an organic concatenation whose boundaries are known but a confused conglomeration of different talents and specialities working at cross-purposes with one another, suspicious of current favouritism, uncertain of rewards and punishments. Though he was, if not an excellent financier, at least an effective con-man, as an executive Sheridan's powers of persuasion in person – which were more considerable than those of almost any contemporary – betrayed him into slipshod, officious, damaging management, truly 'humiliating circumstances' for his subordinates.[6]

Sheridan's first prime deputy was his father as acting manager (at £600 a year – which Richard paid promptly), beginning for the 1778–9 season, after Richard had tried it for two seasons by himself. The *Morning Chronicle* (25 September 1778) was overjoyed: 'the father, is not less polite, or less a man of ability, than his son, but he is at the same time one of the most punctual persons in existence. In every sense of the words, he is a man of business, and God knows such a man is much wanted at Old Drury.' Thomas Sheridan had been a remarkable manager at Smock Alley in Dublin, and his knowledge of the theatre and its ways was encyclopaedic, his judgement fine except when faced by what he took to be an affront, then clouded, peevish, and self-destructive. He insulted authors and actors and contrived to quarrel yet again with Garrick, who had been so very good to his son since the sale and had become a genuine friend; Thomas did not attend Garrick's funeral, though he must have had some responsibility for mounting Richard's *Monody* two months later. He lasted as acting manager only to the end of the 1779–80 season.

Subsequent managers and prompters included Joseph Younger (1780–4), Thomas King (1782–8), Thomas Linley, Sr, the co-patentee and director of music (1784–8), John Philip Kemble (1788–96; 1800–2), John Grubb, Richard Wroughton (1796–8; 1800–9), and James Aikin, and several others organized into a kind of committee of senior performers. Of these managers, the finest was J. P. Kemble (with James Wrighten, W. Powell, Stokes, and Westley), and three of the seasons under Kemble's direction are the only ones in Sheridan's entire career in which Drury Lane earned anything like Garrick's profits. Kemble brought many alterations and additions to the repertoire, was instrumental in the opening of the enlarged house in 1794, and of course kept his sister Sarah Siddons mostly at Drury Lane, where she never failed to draw large houses. Sheridan could articulate his appreciation: in the 1788 letter to Joseph Richardson cited in note 5, Sheridan writes, 'I like Kemble *very* much in his new Department, and I have no Doubt of going on prosperously'. At the outset of Kemble's man-

7 The enlarged auditorium and proscenium of the Theatre Royal in Drury Lane, following the 1794 reconstruction by Henry Holland. Note the increased number of side boxes. The play is *Coriolanus*.

agement, then, Sheridan could behave generously and perhaps without interference. But it did not last, and Kemble, disgusted with Sheridan's meddling and failure to pay his salary, quit at the end of 1796, though he kept acting. His return as acting manager in 1800 was prompted by a desire to have an ownership position, and he was prepared to pay £25,000 for a one-quarter share; but the attorneys could not assure him of Sheridan's clear ownership of what he wished to buy, and on 11 November 1801 he informed Richard Wilson, an attorney and a member of the Drury Lane Board of Management, that he considered himself and Sheridan 'entirely free from our mutual Engagements relative to the Sale and Purchase' (May, May and Merriman gift cited in note 5). After a year's tour of the continent he bought into Covent Garden instead, took his sister with him, and managed there until 1812; he was instrumental in gathering the funding to rebuild Covent Garden after its burning in 1808.

It is remarkable that Sheridan was able to keep Drury Lane open all those years, until the fire of 24 February 1809. His manipulations of finances were secretive, cunning, sometimes generous, but effective when combined with his immunity from arrest for debt which was granted by his being a Member of Parliament. But he mortgaged too deep. Professor Judith Milhous calculates that during Garrick's last season between 6 and 10 per cent of the theatre's expenses were payments due to renters' shares; but for Drury Lane under Sheridan, the similar figures were 13 to 17 per cent, and that does not include monies due to non-renting shareholders.[7] Henry Holland's construction of the new Drury Lane of 1794 had cost £160,000 rather than the £80,000 predicted; when it could not be completed for want of capital, with more pride than prudence, more generosity than judgement, Sheridan took the whole debt upon himself, borrowing, selling boxes, neglecting his backers and creditors. In the vast new structure, expenses for mounting productions were far higher than before; Colman's *Blue Beard* on 16 January 1798, for instance, cost £2,000 to mount at Drury Lane, and at a time when companies enlarged only slightly, the percentage of expenses paid as salaries fell from 64 per cent in 1775–6 to 27 per cent in 1799–1800. Annual income at Drury Lane increased from £34,000 in 1775–6 to between £50,000 and £60,000 by the end of the century, but profits decreased.

By 1801–2, the financial fate of Drury Lane became the province of the Court of Chancery. Sheridan successfully managed his case so as to retain control (several of the unpublished May, May and Merriman letters concern this action), but he was bound by the Court's findings to pay his creditors in a priority and to accept a new management committee. When the 'fireproof' Drury Lane burned to the ground on 24 February 1809 (with Sheridan's own personal furniture and many of his papers), Sheridan might have been able to retain real control; but he was dilatory in seeking public donations as Kemble had done for Covent Garden, probably because he continued to put his faith in his abilities as a speculative investor. He dithered for three months, then sought the help and advice of an old friend, Samuel Whitbread, a prosperous brewer. Whitbread agreed to head a committee, and he exerted himself energetically on behalf of the houseless Drury Lane company, but he asked that Sheridan withdraw from the management. Thinking probably that he could accept that condition *de jure* but continue to act *de facto*, Sheridan agreed. But what Whitbread knew, and what was continually reaffirmed as he sought to gather investors to rebuild the theatre, was that people would not invest if Sheridan were to have any further part in the management. By 1811, Sheridan was definitely out of management. The next year Sheridan had the further blow of losing his seat in Parliament, for which he blamed Whitbread's failure to provide £2,000 at the last minute to help secure his election; Sheridan thought the money due to him for his investment in Drury Lane ownership, but Whitbread was severely undercapitalized in the on-going reconstruction project and could not afford it.[8] When final settlements were made, Sheridan was not paid in cold cash but, as he had done for so many years to so many of his backers and creditors, in shares. So, by 1811, Sheridan's thirty-five years as owner and manager of Drury Lane were at an end.

LEAVING THE THEATRE

The great green curtain has fallen. Young Charles Lamb would begin to doze in the maternal lap were it not for the activity of leaving. The crowding into the narrow corridors is less excited than it was before the play, and the fresh air of the streets is welcome. The residents of the boxes are met by coaches, those of the pit by hackneys or chairs or maybe a house servant; gallery dwellers seek out link boys to light their way, or trust to themselves. Memory already begins to play tricks about just how the mime had moved or just when the orchestra accompanied the arias of *Artaxerxes*. The theatre servants return their costumes, stack their scenery, take a final count of the receipts, extinguish the candles and lamps. The fragile, evanescent experience of the theatre is gone, never to be played in quite the same way, never to be recaptured, even by the critic hurrying to file his copy for the *Morning Chronicle*, much less by the scholar two centuries later. On such stuff as these walking shadows are dreams made.

Notes

1 See M. S. Auburn, *Sheridan's Comedies* (Lincoln, NB, 1977), p. 36, p. 192.

2 The accounts of the nine actors subsequently discussed rely upon P. H. Highfill, Jr, K. A. Burnim and E. A. Langhans, *A Biographical Dictionary of Actors, Actresses,*

Musicians, Dancers, Managers & Other Stage Personnel in London, 1660–1800 (Carbondale, IL, 1973–93).

3 In *Sheridan's Comedies*, I show how a great number of new and older comedies bear correspondences to Sheridan's works.

4 C. Price sorts the evidence for Sheridan's play-doctoring and authorship of lost pieces in the second volume of his edition of *The Dramatic Works of Richard Brinsley Sheridan* (Oxford, 1973), p. 775ff.

5 Transcription of unpublished MSS, docketed RP 80/103 by the Victoria and Albert Museum, now in the Theatre Museum, Covent Garden, a gift on 16 May 1980 of May, May and Merriman, a firm lineal to Richard Wilson, recipient of some of these letters and attorney for Drury Lane.

6 C. Price lovingly discusses Sheridan's character in general terms in the Introduction to his edition of *The Letters of Richard Brinsley Sheridan* (Oxford, 1966), especially pp. xvi–xx.

7 Milhous, p. 22, in R. D. Hume, ed., *The London Theatre World, 1660–1800* (Carbondale, IL, 1980).

8 Q. Skinner, 'Sheridan and Whitbread at Drury Lane, 1809–1815', *Theatre Notebook*, xvii (1962/3), 40–6, 74–9, discusses this relationship. He thinks Sheridan's general financial operations were founded upon a 'mixture of credit and optimism', and he characterizes the relationship this harshly: 'Fickle, malicious, selfish, vain, Sheridan formed the worst complication in all Whitbread's work.'

2

'Future retrospection': rereading Sheridan's reviewers

RICHARD C. TAYLOR

The withdrawal of *The Rivals* after a disastrous opening performance at Covent Garden on 17 January 1775 is a well-established part of theatrical lore: a combination of sloppy acting and miscasting doomed the initial staging, and eleven days and some quick rewriting and recasting later, the play was successfully remounted, and it held the stage for fifteen nights. Since then it has become a mainstay of theatrical repertories, one of a handful of works representing the sprawling and diverse field of eighteenth-century theatre.

The responses of London newspaper critics to the first production suggest another possible reason for the initial failure of *The Rivals*: Sheridan had written a self-consciously novel play, one that set tradition and contemporaneity in conflict and satirized both. This theme is delightfully expressed by Mrs Malaprop in her muddled announcement: 'our retrospection will now be all to the future' (IV.ii.136–7). Theatrical and social convention run up against the romantic sentimentalism in vogue and the patriarchal challenges of the novel and its readers. To some extent, because of the novelty of the play in its setting, characterization, language and ideology, convention-bound critics and audience members essentially missed the point. Withdrawing it from production, ostensibly for revision, served another purpose: to let the novelty of the experience sink in, to allow a second reading by an audience not so stunned by its originality.

Mark Auburn argues that the play's 'pleasure derives from individual effects and not from a sophisticated overall informing aesthetic design'.[1] Yet it is this purposefully confused double gaze, forward and backward, that unifies the play – that informs its language, its characterizations, its plot conflict – and also helps explain the difficulties it presented to its first audience and reviewers. Critics and producers who conflate *The Rivals* with *The*

Man of Mode, or *The Way of the World*, or *The Beaux' Stratagem* are also missing the point: Sheridan did not write Restoration comedies. The play itself inscribes a theatrical tradition for satiric purposes, but its newness is its *raison d'être*, its structure, its language, its thematic centre. It is a rivalry of a triumphant present over a ridiculous past. John Loftis argues that Sheridan 'took promising dramatic materials' from Restoration comedy, 'reworking them in his own idiom'.[2] This new idiom – and not the well-rehearsed plot conventions that critics denounced – is the central dramatic vehicle, established in the opening dialogue between the Coachman and Fag:

FAG . . . none of the London whips of any degree of Ton wear *wigs* now.

COACH More's the pity! more's the pity, I say. – Odd's life! when I heard how the lawyers and doctors had took to their own hair, I thought how 'twould go next . . . believe me, Mr Fag: and look'ee, I'll never gi' up mine – the lawyers and doctors may do as they will.(I.i.71–8)

It is a new age to which all the characters respond: the enlightened have discarded their wigs; Bath, not London, is the centre of fashion and intrigue; young women pillage circulating libraries rather than plundering reputations at cabalistic card parties; the female protagonist conspires to lose her inheritance and marry a poor man – we are in a world turned upside down. Sheridan writes for an audience of novel readers, an audience familiar with Smollett and Mackenzie, the scandalous romances of mid-century, the idea of female quixotism. His audience must have been well aware, also, of the persistent Tory attacks against the novel as a threat to patriarchal control – attacks that are pilloried as mindless and dictatorial, just as the new 'romanticism' of the young is lampooned. The real rivalry is between those struggling awkwardly and pretentiously for novelty and those who would squelch it.

Two years later, audiences were ready to applaud, and critics to accept, Sheridan's novelty. *The School for Scandal* was 'admirably suited to the present aera' (*Gazetteer*, 10 May 1777). The reviewer for the *London Evening Post* announced: 'Under this *poetical St George*, we may expect to see the Dragon of *mere sentimental drama* entirely subdued, and the standard of *real comedy* once more unfurled' (8–10 May 1777). The propaganda war passed from Goldsmith to Sheridan had been won: while somehow becoming the new Congreve, as the *Gazetteer* proclaimed, Sheridan apparently captained the triumph of the new laughing comedy over sentimentalism.

The reviewer for the *Morning Chronicle* suggests that with some revision the new play might have been titled *The Man of Sentiment* (24 May 1777). Sentiment, though, was not a dragon to be slain, but the conceptual embodiment of modernity. It was the vortex around which swirled ideological confusion, hypocrisy, and misjudgement – a rivalry of competing definitions and sensibilities. Sheridan's triumph, here, lies not in his savaging the reigning genres of sentimentalism, but in offering a clarifying corrective: dropping the screen of ambiguity that veiled contemporary treatments of the sentimental ideal and offering his own comic vision.

Is *The School for Scandal* somehow a better play than *The Rivals*? Did Sheridan's dramatic abilities mature to such an extent that in less than two years he could develop from a clumsy hack to the greatest dramatist of his generation – as his reviewers would seem to have it? Attempts to explain the difference between the two plays have, by and large, followed a critical line established by Thomas Moore in his *Memoirs of Sheridan*: 'With much less wit, it [*The Rivals*] exhibits perhaps more humour than *The School for Scandal*.'[3] Such impressionistic analysis is almost completely unhelpful in revealing why one play succeeded and one failed upon their initial appearances. Perhaps the two plays are much more of a piece than critics have been willing to accept: both topical and colloquial, both structured around ideological rivalries, both offering linguistic inventiveness and new character types, rather than original 'fables', for comic effect.

The Rivals was the only new comic mainpiece mounted at Covent Garden in the 1774–5 season. Four days before its opening, the company revived *She Stoops to Conquer*, which had begun its initial run on 15 March 1773.[4] The revival might have been an attempt to prepare audiences for the new comedy – with the implicit message: *The Rivals* is the same sort of comedy as Goldsmith's hit. The character of Acres was easily recognizable as 'a second Tony Lumpkin' (*Public Ledger*, 18 January 1775). Jane Green, who had played Mrs Hardcastle, was cast as Mrs Malaprop. As a veteran performer of 'conspiratorial chambermaids, eccentric maiden ladies, and silly hostesses', Green appeared to be the perfect choice to create Mrs Malaprop.[5] Edward Shuter, a veteran of three decades on the stage and Goldsmith's first Hardcastle, seemed an equally apt choice for Sir Anthony Absolute.[6] Both casting choices reinforced the idea of *The Rivals* as the new *She Stoops*, a new 'laughing comedy' antidote for the ills of sentimental comedy.

Critics of the opening performance enumerated a series of damning flaws. 'This Comedy was acted so imperfectly, either from the Timidity of the Actors on a first Night's Performance, or from an improper Distribution of Parts, that it was generally disapproved' (*St James Chronicle*, 17–19 January 1775); 'Shuter was . . . shamefully imperfect' (*Morning Chronicle*, 18 January 1775). Reviewers barely noticed Jane Green's Mrs Malaprop until the play was returned. How is it that veteran cast members, many of whom had appeared in apparently similar roles, by all accounts botched the opening performance? In her study of experimental language in Sheridan's plays, Christine Wiesenthal provides a partial answer: 'in the inexperienced hands of an exuberant, young comic playwright, two essentially antagonistic discourses begin to compete against one another'.[7] What critics have identified as a structural ambivalence, reflected in the play's awkward diction, further reinforces the central conflict in the play: both the romantic excesses of novelty and the eccentricities and irrationality of the old order are exposed and placed in conflict – a confusion embodied in Mrs Malaprop's infectious verbal chaos. Incredibly, critics seemed to miss the Malaprop game so central to the play's comic inventiveness: 'The diction is an odd mixture of the elegant and the absurd. Some of the scenes are written in a very masterly stile; others in a low, farcical kind of dialogue' (*St James Chronicle*, 17–19 January 1775); 'in language it is defective to an extreme' (*Public Ledger*, 18 January 1775). Such is the result of the clashing cultural assumptions that Sheridan is recording, but for reviewers characters such as Malaprop were not 'copied from nature' and her language was a 'defect' in the playwright's skill (*Morning Chronicle*, 18 January 1775). The *Public Ledger* condemned the 'shameful absurdities in language' apparently without recognizing the source and satiric intention of these 'absurdities' (18 January 1775). While it is possible that the acting difficulties were a product of laziness on the part of Shuter and others, it is equally plausible that the performers were unprepared for the complex play of language and the demands of creating new character types.

For at least one observer, the language of the play was strikingly realistic, 'more natural, as coming nearer the current coin of ordinary conversation' than *The School for Scandal*.[8] The younger characters employ a contemporary jargon replete with allusions to the social milieu of the mid-1770s. Such a commitment to contemporaneity was another breach of decorum.

Also singled out for critical condemnation was John Lee's Sir Lucius O'Trigger. Irish stereotypes and social prejudice against the Irish generally were so commonplace that the sanctimonious objections to Lee's O'Trigger are somewhat surprising. Lee was another well-established performer who had acted in Ireland in the early 1770s and who had also managed at Bath, ideal credentials, one might assume, for the role.[9] And yet response to his character was universally hostile: 'What the Devil Business can he have with the Part of a mere Irishman?' (*St James Chronicle*, 17–19 January 1775); 'This representation of Sir Lucius is indeed an affront to the common sense of an audience, and is so far from giving the manners of our brave and worthy neighbours, that it scarce equals the picture of a *respectable* Hotentot' (*Morning Chronicle*, 18 January 1775); 'the casting Mr Lee for the part of *Lucius O'Trigger*, is a blunder of the first brogue' (*Morning Chronicle*, 20 January 1775). This latter review pointed to inconsistencies in dialect and the fact that Lee was not 'Irish enough' to pull off the role. A correspondent to the *Morning Post* claimed never to have seen 'a portrait of an Irish Gentleman, permitted so openly to insult the country upon the boards of an English theatre' (*Morning Post*, 21 January 1775). The revised and recast O'Trigger is largely stripped of ethnic identity: he is an old fool, whose function is to articulate antiquated ideas about honour and courtship – most notably realized in his promoting the ludicrous duel between Acres and Absolute. His interference, like that of the other old fools in the play, invites the possibility of a murderous outcome to the various romantic intrigues.

The objections to the original O'Trigger anticipate a serious problem in producing Sheridan: the racist and anti-Semitic epithets mouthed by fools and heroes alike. 'I hated your poor dear uncle before marriage as if he'd been a black-a-moor,' proclaims Mrs Malaprop (I.ii.174–5); 'the lady shall be as ugly as I choose . . . she shall have a skin like a mummy, and the beard of a Jew' (II.i.361–4); 'though I were an Æthiop, you'd think none so fair' (III.ii.65–6). The anti-Semitism that runs throughout *The School for Scandal* produces palpable discomfort in contemporary audiences, and no amount of directorial cutting easily eliminates it. Ironically, London audiences now seem less sensitive – or perhaps more accustomed – to Irish stereotypes than to these other forms of bigotry.

Another moral objection to the play was to its 'numberless *oaths*' (*Morning Chronicle*, 27 January 1775). For Sheridan, though, cursing is more than an isolated technique for character development or a means of achieving shock value; it is a means of underscoring his theme: new-fangled cursing versus ludicrously outdated cursing, both of which add to a delightful bewilderment that interferes with communication and causes further generational separation. For reviewers, though, cursing was a violation of decorum and delicacy, and 'One of the Pit', writing to the *Morning Chronicle*, threatens the author on this subject: 'the English are not sudden, but strong in their resentments, and if he persists in such scandalous negligence of his duty, he may one day experience it' (27 January 1775). Absolute remarks that Acres' 'Odds whips and wheels' and 'Odd's Blushes and Blooms' and 'Odds Crickets' represent 'an odd kind of a new method of swearing' (II.i.258–9). Acres blunders, as do his cohorts in foolishness, in trying to modernize himself. His efforts are foiled by a comic duality: he opposes the modern system of '*sentimental swearing*' (II.i.268) and is tradition-bound. Of oaths he declares that 'nothing but their antiquity makes them respectable . . . the "oath should be an echo to the sense"' (II.i.263–7). He is a perverse upholder of the 'old learning', of the Augustan aesthetic, and so his own attempts at novelty are hopelessly outmoded, another instance of 'future retrospection'.

Reviewers also complained about the excessive length of the play: 'insufferably tedious' (*Morning Chronicle*, 18 January 1775); 'lulled several of the middle gallery spectators into a profound SLEEP' (*Public Ledger*, 18 January 1775); 'a *full hour* longer in the representation than any piece on the stage' (*Morning Chronicle*, 20 January 1775). This response is most puzzling given the almost invariable sprightliness of Sheridan's plays in performance. Was his first audience asleep? Some of those attending the first revival apparently hissed when they noticed that a comic scene involving Lydia had been cut (*Morning Post*, 30 January 1775). Audiences had, indeed, been accustomed to shorter pieces designed to accommodate the double-billing that was typical at both Drury Lane and Covent Garden.

Another possible solution concerns the novelty of the plot. Novel-readers in the audience might have recognized a structural looseness and digressiveness typical in the fiction of the period. In the plot and language of *The Rivals* and in its patterns of allusion, Sheridan inscribes a rivalry between the drama and the novel. The relationship between late-eighteenth-century theatre and the novel was roughly analogous to the current one between the novel and television: one medium overtaken in popularity and influence by another; a form of entertainment struggling for currency and relevance while acutely aware of the cultural ascendancy of another form. Much like the self-reflexive concern with novel-reading and readers in the novels themselves, Sheridan's play, in another act of 'future retrospection', lampoons the theatrical tradition while pillorying the influence of the novel on custom and language.

If the opening conversation about wiglessness signifies a struggle between the old and new in fashion, the dialogue that opens Scene ii between Lucy and Lydia establishes the female protagonist as a woman of the moment, a devourer of novels and a denizen of circulating libraries. The items on her latest novelistic menu were all recent publications, two, *The Fatal Connection* (1773) and *The Tears of Sensibility* (1773), published only a year before the play was written. Like Charlotte Lennox's Arabella, Sheridan's Lydia had been nursed on the romance; but unlike Arabella, who had educated herself on bad translations of old French romances, Lydia's preferences were strictly modern. She is the embodiment of a Tory nightmare: a young woman scorning paternal authority, hell-bent on an improper alliance, devoid of common sense. Arcane and serious tomes such as *The Whole Duty of Man* (1659) are useful only for hair-pressing – a moribund ideology impressed into the service of modishness.

At the same time, Lydia functions to mock the outmoded manner of courtship preferred by her aunt, Mrs Malaprop, who assumes the hackneyed pastoral pseudonym 'Delia', and who has chosen as her object of affection a 'tall Irish baronet' – presumably an equal affront to fashion (I.ii.49). When her aunt and Sir Anthony Absolute approach, the trappings of modernity must be hidden and the furnishings of propriety displayed: James Fordyce's sermons and *Lord Chesterfield's Letters* conceal Smollett and Mackenzie and Lydia's volumes of scandalous memoirs (I.ii.137–46). Sir Anthony then harangues against 'teaching girls to read' (I.ii.186), while his rhetorical partner Mrs Malaprop insists that Lydia 'illiterate' her lover from her memory (I.ii.154). By the time Mrs Malaprop speaks out against serious education for women, Sheridan's audience should have learned to read her ironically. Clearly, Mrs Malaprop's charm-school view is as empty a system as Lydia's education-by-novel.

Another obvious influence of the novel in *The Rivals* is its 'sentimentalism', evidenced by its characterizations, by overt textual treatment of the idea, and by the critical reaction to the play. The principals are novelistic protagonists to the extent that they conceive of romance and of themselves as lovers. Even the relatively pragmatic Julia describes her lover Faulkland as a typical romantic hero: 'being unhackney'd in the passion, his affection is ardent and sincere; and as it engrosses his whole soul, he expects every thought and emotion of his mistress to move in unison with his' (I.ii.103–6). Captain Absolute, too, is a self-described sentimentalist. Like Malaprop's diction, Lydia's romanticism is contagious, and her lover admits: 'Am not *I* a lover; aye, and a romantic one, too? Yet do I carry every where with me such a confounded farago of doubts, fears, hopes, wishes, and all the flimsy furniture of a country Miss's brain!' (II.i.74–6). Like Lydia, the Captain sees duty and obedience as a dusty veneer concealing passion and independence. The idea of arranged marriage is an anachronistic fraud – his father, after all, 'married himself for love' (II.i.397) – to be defeated by ingenuity. Yet when his scheming goes awry, he blames his lover's sentimental inclinations: 'Lydia is romantic – dev'lish romantic, and very absurd of course' (V.ii.49–50). Sentimentalism, as a code-word for modishness, is a satiric target – 'sentimental swearing' or the 'sentimental elopement' Lydia had planned – and the antithesis of a 'Smithfield bargain' view of courtship that is equally ridiculous.

Reviewers of *The Rivals* did not know what to make of this theme: 'the characters of Faulkland and Julia are even beyond the pitch of *sentimental* comedy, and may be not improperly stiled *metaphysical*' (*Morning Chronicle*, 18 January 1775). Clearly, if the play had indeed been marketed as a successor to *She Stoops to Conquer*, Sheridan had been positioning his work in opposition to sentimental comedy. In 'An Essay on the Theatre' for *Westminster Magazine* (January 1773), Goldsmith advocated 'laughing comedy', in which category theatre historians have subsequently placed Sheridan's works, as a sort of antidote to sentimentalism. However, Sheridan's reviewers almost unanimously accused him of outré sentimentalism, without recognizing his satiric aim.

Among critics, however, the word *sentimental* was not entirely pejorative. Responding to the revised production, the *Morning Chronicle* extols 'some of the most affecting sentimental scenes I ever remember to have met with' (*Morning Chronicle*, 27 January 1775). On the other hand, the tenor of the *Morning Post* reviewer's comments of 31 January 1775 more or less reflects the play's subsequent reputation: 'sentimental blockheads, so much admired by the gaping multitude of our century, were not a little disappointed at the success of Mr Sheridan'. The play, then, lives as a triumph over sentimentalism. Sheridan's comedy survives, and rival offerings such as Isaac Bickerstaff's *Love in a Village*, Ambrose Phillips' *The Distress'd Mother* and Thomas Francklin's *Matilda* are forgotten.

John Loftis casts Sheridan as a social conservative: 'His authorial judgments . . . reveal a reverence for English social institutions as marked as that of Henry Fielding.'[10] Yet *The Rivals* was in many ways a risky undertaking, an attack levelled on both the ancients and moderns. There is no Alworthy among Sheridan's aristocrats: they have hollow notions of honour, their authority is suspect, their language gibberish, their education vapid. If, as reviewers complained, the plot conflicts and resolution of *The Rivals* are wildly implausible, and its structure loose and digressive, Sheridan is responding satirically to the influence of a fashionable sentimentalism inscribed in the novel. The important rivalry, here, is not between suitors but between the foolishness of the old and the absurdities of the young. The result is miscommunication, malapropism, a purposeful clash of styles which critics, bound by absolute notions of decorum, could only describe as the flaws of an inexperienced playwright. Loftis describes the world of *The Rivals* as one 'of social and financial practicality familiar in Restoration and eighteenth-century comedy, in which a rich and repulsive suitor such as Bob Acres might be rejected in favour of a rich and attractive suitor such as Jack Absolute, but in which misalliances do not occur except as a form of punishment, outside the absurd fantasies of a girl whose head has been turned by reading novels'.[11] What separates the play from its comic predecessors and situates it in mid-1770s London is its novelty, its idiomatic contemporaneity, its confusion of language and cultural identity. Mackenzie has met Lord Chesterfield; Smollett is duelling with 'the learned and pious author of *The Whole Duty of Man*'; the 'deep play' has moved from London to Bath and – more ominously – from the theatre to the novel.

By 1777, when Drury Lane introduced *The School for Scandal*, critics were prepared to overlook the playwright's derivative plotting and linguistic 'awkwardness'. They recognized the topicality of Sheridan's moral concern and that Sheridan was targeting hypocrisy, one of the 'prevailing vices of the times' through which many 'assume the appearance of men of virtue and sentiment' (*Morning Chronicle*, 9 May 1777). Beyond its titular concern with gossip and its archaic Wycherley-like plot, the play is an arena for competing visions of modernity – specifically, for defining a moral ideal, the idea of sentiment that dominated late-eighteenth-century discourse. Hypocrites and debauchees, young and old – all appropriate and misappropriate the term in their efforts to make moral judgements. The rivalry in this play is not so much a generational one, but a semantic one between competing visions of the sentimental ideal.

Sheridan's first scene establishes the social problem or challenge that unifies the play: distinguishing the 'man of Sentiment' from the 'Sentimental Knave'. The audience must recognize that the scandal school has corrupted the virtues of 'sensibility' and 'sentiment': Surface speaks of

Mr Snake's 'sensibility and discernment'; and Surface is 'moral' because he is '*a man of Sentiment*'; he mistrusts Snake because he 'hasn't Virtue enough to be faithful even to his own Villainy' (I.i.73–122). Scandal is the machinery that has circulated this ethical perversion.

In the National Theatre's 1990 production at the Olivier, Peter Wood's visual metaphor for this process was newsprint, which covered the flat surfaces of the set; even the furniture was papered over by scandal. If the 'country wife' plot has recognizable seventeenth-century roots, the implicit attack on the ascendant print culture is distinctly late Georgian, when the threat, as Sir Peter puts it, of being 'paragraph'd – in the news-Papers' is a prevailing trope for loss of reputation (I.ii.13–14).

Like *The Rivals*, *The School for Scandal* has its 'old fools': Mrs Candour, a variation of the Mrs Malaprop character, asks Lady Sneerwell, 'how have you been this Century' (I.i.165–6); Sir Peter is essentially a 'Pinchwife'. Their principal fault, though, is in either distorting or failing to comprehend the modern idea of sentiment. Sir Peter mistakes Joseph Surface as 'a man of Sentiment' (I.ii.51). For Lady Sneerwell, sentiment is merely an affectation to 'study' (I.i.351–2). For Joseph, 'sentimental' is little more than the characteristic of his favourite French plate (V.ii.106–7). The young lovers Maria and Charles represent true sentiment, Maria for her discernment, Charles for his generosity and honesty. The importance of this theme lies not only in Sheridan's verbal insistence upon it throughout the play but also in the climactic comic moment. When Charles throws down the screen – arguably one of the most sublimely funny moments in all of comedy – hypocrisy is unveiled, and virtue revealed. The punchline, here, is Charles's mocking echo of Sir Peter: 'there's nothing in the world so noble as a man of Sentiment!' (IV.iii.385–6). The stage directions then suggest a long silence: the point has been made; nothing further remains to be said.

If Goldsmith had established a self-serving critical rivalry between laughing comedy and sentimental comedy, Sheridan weaves this rivalry into the fabric of his two best-known plays. Sentimentalism becomes a comic theme, a pivotal issue that separates generations and divides the virtuous and the fraudulent. Further confusing the rivalry between an antiquated and paternalistic older generation and an absurdly 'romantic' younger one is the obscuring medium of gossip – private conflict made public. Newsprint becomes the metaphor for 'future retrospection': language used to distort and deceive, past values and current fashions jumbled. Clarity of vision and expression become heroic acts.

While bad acting probably contributed to sabotaging the initial performance of *The Rivals*, the evidence of critical response suggests that audiences and reviewers were unprepared for a new play about newness. Strategically linking the production to Goldsmith's *She Stoops to Conquer* failed because, quite obviously, Sheridan is not Goldsmith. Unlike Goldsmith's comedy, Sheridan's plays attempt to inscribe a historical present: where clear communication has become nearly impossible, where equally absurd new and old systems of thought compete, where deception is fashionable. Given the thematic and linguistic complexity of his plays, it is hardly surprising that Sheridan's work needed to 'sink in'. Even the critical reception of *The School for Scandal* involved a sort of 'future retrospection': Sheridan captures the modern era because he is a new Congreve – *The Way of the World* in 1777. Needless to say, Sheridan is not Congreve either.

Notes

1 M. S. Auburn, *Sheridan's Comedies: Their Contexts and Achievements* (Lincoln, NB, 1977), p. 36.
2 J. Loftis, *Sheridan and the Drama of Georgian England* (Oxford, 1976), p. 43.
3 T. Moore, *Memoirs of the Life of the Right Honourable Richard Brinsley Sheridan* (London, 1815), i, p. 141.
4 C. B. Hogan, ed., *The London Stage, 1660–1800, Part Five, 1776–1800* (Carbondale, IL, 1968).
5 P. H. Highfill, Jr, K. A. Burnim, and E. A. Langhans, *A Biographical Dictionary of Actors, Actresses, Musicians, Dancers, Managers and Other Stage Personnel in London, 1660–1800*, vi (Carbondale, IL, 1978), pp. 328–35.
6 *A Biographical Dictionary*, xiii (1991), pp. 370–84.
7 C. S. Wiesenthal, 'Representation and Experimentation in the Major Comedies of Richard Brinsley Sheridan', *Eighteenth-Century Studies*, xxv(3) (Spring 1992), 311.
8 Moore, *Life*, i, p. 141.
9 *A Biographical Dictionary*, ix (1984), pp. 201–9.
10 Loftis, *Sheridan and the Drama of Georgian England*, p. 46.
11 Ibid., pp. 46–7.

3

Sheridan, Congreve and *The School for Scandal*

ERIC RUMP

In the long summer days of June 1776, Sheridan might well have felt that life was particularly sweet. In the opening months of 1775, he had established his name as a new and successful playwright with *The Rivals*; the end of the same year had seen the start of the record-breaking run of *The Duenna*. In the November of 1775, just before *The Duenna* had opened, his wife had borne him a healthy son,[1] and the negotiations with Garrick for the purchase of his share of Drury Lane had, by the June of 1776, been successfully completed. This made Sheridan not only a successful playwright and happy father but also the manager and part owner of a great London theatre. In consequence, his future activities would directly involve him in that theatre's artistic success or failure. It was no doubt a challenging prospect; equally it must have been an exciting one.

The most daring innovation that Sheridan made in the opening months of his first season at Drury Lane was the revival of three of the four comedies of Congreve. Although these revivals were important both in terms of Congreve's reputation and as an artistic statement about comedy on Sheridan's part, their importance has largely been overlooked or played down by Sheridan's earlier biographers. Moore, Rae and Sichel pass over them with barely a mention and their comparative lack of significance either for Sheridan or comedy in general may have been finally established by R. Crompton Rhodes and W. A. Darlington in the 1930s. Rhodes, in *Harlequin Sheridan*, states boldly – but totally inaccurately – that the Congreve revivals '. . . were not appreciated',[2] a statement more or less confirmed by Darlington when he says that '. . . nothing of particular importance was produced during the early months of the new management's regime'.[3] Understandably, given such categorical statements, subsequent biographers and commentators have, in the main, either said nothing about these revivals or accorded them the briefest of sidelong glances in their rush to get to the opening night of *The School for Scandal.*

The boldness of Sheridan's move in reviving the 'licentious' plays of Congreve can be better appreciated by a review of the depths to which Congreve's reputation had fallen during the 1760s and early 1770s, a collapse that can be most readily grasped by comparing two commentaries from the 1750s with three from the early 1770s. In 1754, Arthur Murphy contributed a thoughtful essay on characterization in comedy to *The Gray's Inn Journal* (31 August 1754), in which Congreve is portrayed as one of the masters:

An *Old Batchelor*, for instance, is very common, but he must pass thro' such an Imagination as *Congreve's* to support several scenes in the Drama with the most exquisite pleasantry. Though the character was not new, yet his management of it has all the Graces of Novelty, and the Situations in which we see him are all exquisitely ridiculous. Personages of this Class, unless artfully conducted, may very soon tire an Audience, but in this excellent Poet's Hands nothing suffers a Diminution. The same, I think, appears in his Sir *Paul Plyant*, in which character there is perhaps as much comic Force as in any one piece on the stage.

No concern about Congreve's 'immoral' or 'licentious' tendencies is at any point suggested in this piece. Such a concern, it is true, is fleetingly touched upon in a review of *Love for Love* in *The London Chronicle* (20–2 January 1757) but with its enthusiastic praise of the play's 'Wit, Plot, Humour, and Character' and its appeal to Garrick to undertake some of Congreve's comic roles in the future, there is no suggestion whatsoever that the plays were in any way unsuitable for public (or private) consumption.

Such enthusiasm wanes rapidly in the 1760s and has almost entirely disappeared by the early 1770s. The commentators still acknowledge, even praise, certain aspects of Congreve's art – his characterization, the regularity of his plots, even his wit – but virtues such as these are weighed in the balance against his 'licentiousness' and are found wanting. For instance, the writer for *The Dramatic Censor* (1770) openly praises Congreve's 'pleasing delineations of life', his 'brilliant wit' and his 'amazingly regular and pleasingly intricate plots' but virtues such as these are not sufficient to rescue his plays from overall condemnation:

. . . a most abominable vein of licentiousness runs through the whole; virtue reluctantly peeps in, while vice with brazen front bolts forward unblushing, unrestrained . . . His pieces must give great pleasure either in action or perusal, but are like the sweet scented rose, with prickles beneath, which while it gratifies one sense wounds another; it is with reluctance we pronounce the sentence of moral justice which condemns his four comedies, as pernicious . . . (ii, p. 468)

Much the same combination of praise for certain aspects but overall condemnation is found in a review of the 14 November (1771) performance of *Love for Love* at Drury Lane where the reviewer notes that the characters are 'strongly drawn' and that the plotting displays 'great ingenuity' but nevertheless, because of its '. . . vein of licentiousness . . . it is the wish of Humanity, and of Virtue, that this Play was consigned to oblivion, with all its merits, on account of this particular' (*The Theatrical Review*, i, p. 190). An almost identical note is struck in a review of the 4 April (1772) performance of *The Way of the World* at Covent Garden where, whatever the play's virtues, it is the '. . . abominable vein of Licentiousness' that makes it one which is '. . . scarcely fit to be exhibited at this time, when the public virtue of the age has so commendably laid the Stage under restrictions with respects to this particular' (*The Theatrical Review*, ii, p. 162).

While commentators such as these were attacking Congreve on the fairly general grounds of his 'licentiousness', others were more specific in their objections. One grave cause for concern was that the 'wit' in these plays was often uttered by characters that could be considered morally vicious or corrupt, thus lending such figures a spurious glamour. 'Philo-Virtutis', a letter-writer to *The Gazetteer and New Daily Advertiser*, complains in general terms of those plays where the 'vicious characters' are 'so brilliant' (4 October 1765), a theme given specific application to Congreve and Restoration comedy by *The London Magazine*, where 'those glittering compositions of wit and licentiousness' (July 1768) are expressly condemned and where the pronouncement is made that, in times as morally chaste as the present, no audience can any longer be 'charmed with obscenity because it may be brilliantly expressed' (February 1768). One possible consequence of having such brilliant but vicious characters portrayed on stage, *The Theatrical Monitor* suggests, is that they might well provide corrupting models for some members of the audience, a point the writer illustrates – though scarcely proves – by pointing to Congreve's plays:

Sharper in the *Old Batchelor*, has made many a pick-pocket; *Careless* in the Double Dealer has made many a worthless young fellow, if not worse; *Valentine* in Love for Love has made many a spendthrift; *Maskwell* has made many a villain.

(14 November 1767)

If the men in the audience must be protected from such pernicious influences, so, it seems, must the women, for their 'women of virtue' are 'libels upon the very idea of delicacy' (*The London Magazine*, May 1771) and, in consequence, there surely can be no 'men of understanding who would choose to put the most celebrated of these writers into the hands of their daughters, or their wives . . .' (*The London Magazine*, March 1768). A final solution to all this moral contamination is thunderously proposed by *The London Magazine*, where total theatrical darkness is seen as preferable to any performance of a Restoration comedy:

> . . . it is much better utterly to abolish the theatre, than to keep it open by authority to give us a contempt for every thing which we ought to esteem, and a passion for every thing we ought to view with detestation. (July 1768)

Although there are remarkably few voices raised in defence of Congreve or Restoration comedy in the journalism of the 1760s – there is one letter in *The General Evening Post* (23–6 November 1771) in support of *Love for Love* – the fact that a few stubbornly unreformed playgoers still exist is tacitly acknowledged by some writers, even if such acknowledgement is only given in an attempt to silence them. For instance, *The Public Ledger* (25 September 1765) admits that there still exist some 'minor critics' who find the wit of Restoration comedy attractive, but the heavy-handed sarcasm employed by the writer is an obvious attempt to portray them as fatuous beyond measure:

> . . . we have a number of minor critics in this metropolis, who have such a prejudice in favour of wit, that with all their faults, the writers . . . hold an unrivalled degree of excellence in their estimation. 'What (cry these elaborate judges of the drama) is all the merit of the present hour to that single stroke of Congreve's, in the Way of the World, where Witwou'd says that Petulant and he sputter at each other like a pair of roasting apples. – Ah! – that's a flight of genius, infinitely beyond anything which our authors now-a-days can possibly pretend to; and worth every thing that has been produced since the beginning of the present century.

Likewise, *The London Magazine* (May 1771), while claiming that the country's 'taste' in dramatic literature has remarkably improved, nevertheless admits that there are still some who have a 'superstitious veneration' for writers such as Congreve, and, in the July 1768 issue, significantly links such 'critics' with those who are less than enthusiatic about sentimental drama, a dramatic vogue *The London Magazine* was especially keen on promoting:

If therefore the public mind is so well disposed as to prefer them [sentimental dramas] to those glittering compositions of wit and licentiousness, which formerly gave so much satisfaction, he must be an enemy to virtue who speaks of them with disapprobation on account of their gravity. – By condemning sentimental pieces, we reason against the sense of our own convictions, and nothing can be a stronger argument of a bad heart, than a willingness to be entertained at the expense of morality.

This link between a distaste for sentimental drama and a wholehearted enthusiasm for earlier comic writers like Congreve is what makes 1775 something of a turning point in the evaluation of Congreve's plays. In the October of that year, Drury Lane mounted a revival of *The Way of the World* and those writers appreciative of Congreve's art, writers whose voices had been more or less mute since Murphy in the 1750s, started to be heard again. In *The Gazetteer*, for instance, it is not only the return of Congreve to the stage that is celebrated but also the reappearance of a type of drama that can provide a welcome relief from the sentimental dramatists:

Sentimental Comedy has so vitiated the taste of the town that it ceases to be a matter of surprise why Congreve's pieces are not more frequently laid before the public. This great Master of the Drama, were he to rise, and take a view of our modern *sermon-like pieces*, would blush for his countrymen, and scarcely desire to exist (if not to reform) among the play makers that infested the stage since Murphy's abdication. (9 October 1775)

Much the same connection is made by *The Morning Chronicle*:

Congreve has given as much wit and spirit in one act of this play as would serve to set up twenty such moral spinning poets as Cumberland, etc . . . Elegant as the theatre now appears, the performance of the *mighty genius of the stage* would give it such attractive powers that not the genius of other artists can equal. (9 October 1775)

The Morning Post, however, still had concerns about the play's 'indelicacy', but instead of condemning it out of hand, as might well have been the case in the 1760s or early 1770s, had an interesting suggestion to make as to how that obstacle might be overcome:

As much as this Comedy is admired for its wit and humour, it is in its present state, severely reprehensible for that indelicacy, which the author has made prevail, even in preference to some essentials of the drama. If we look back indeed, to the corruption of the stage, in those days, the licentious taste of the times, may stand forth in its defense; – but at this more refined era, there will hardly be found a man, however libidinous in private, who will be bold enough to patronize this ribaldry, on the public stage. If we are to have this play performed, (and indeed, it would be high treason against wit to lay it on the shelf,) let the delicate and critical taste of a *Garrick*, or some other dramatic writer, root out these poetical excrescences, without destroying the fruit; then will *The Way of the World* stand the severest test of criticism, and be acknowledged by the most polished hearers, to be an ornament to the British stage. (9 October 1775)

Garrick was by now approaching retirement but it was clearly a challenge that Sheridan, the new manager of Drury Lane, was only too ready to accept.

Sheridan may well have been first introduced to Congreve's plays by his father, for Congreve had played a significant role during his years as manager of the Smock-Alley theatre in Dublin. Thomas Sheridan had played Maskwell in *The Double Dealer*, Valentine in *Love for Love* and Fondlewife in *The Old Batchelor* and though he never appeared in *The Way of the World*, he put it on each season from 1748 to 1754 and in 1757 and 1758.[4] In addition to mounting individual plays of Congreve, he also offered them as a 'series', as he had done with a number of Shakespeare's plays, thereby suggesting that he may have seen Congreve's achievement as falling not far short of Shakespeare's. On his last return to the London stage at Covent Garden in the 1775–6 season, he appeared in plays such as *Cato*, *Venice Preserved* and *The Fair Penitent*, but for his benefit he chose to play Maskwell in *The Double Dealer*. The advertisement for this performance in *The Gazetteer* (5 March 1776) claims, a little inaccurately, that the play had not been performed 'these twenty years'; the same advertisement also claims that the play has been 'carefully revised and corrected by expunging all the exceptionable passages'. If the text published in *The New English Theatre* (vol. 9, 1777) is the text of this performance, as seems quite likely, then what Thomas Sheridan cut out were specific sexual and religious references. For instance, Mellefont's remark in Act 1 that '. . . hell is not more busy than her [Lady Touchwood's] brain, nor contains more devils, than that imaginations' disappears, as do Maskwell's solitary ruminations on Lady Touchwood in Act 3:

. . . yet I know what she means by toying away an hour well enough. Pox I have lost all appetite to her; yet she's a fine woman, and I lov'd her once. But I don't know, since I have been in a great measure kept by her, the case is alter'd; what was my pleasure is become my duty; and I have as little stomach to her now as if I were her husband.

However, such deletions apart, Sheridan in no way attempts to reformulate or rewrite the play, and it was given a single performance on 5 March, with

Sheridan in the role of Maskwell. The one review of this performance in *The Gazetteer* notes the reappearance of this play without hostility, but without much enthusiasm either:

Last night Mr Congreve's comedy of The Double Dealer was revived at Covent-garden for the benefit of Mr Sheridan. This comedy, like most pieces wrote by the same author, abounds with wit, character and fable. It originally contained several expressions too loose and indelicate for the present times, which have very properly been expunged . . . Mr Sheridan in Maskwell by attempting ease (which is far from being natural to him) hurts the proper consequence of the character . . . (6 March)

However, as this was a single performance given under the special circumstances of a benefit for an ageing actor, it was scarcely sufficient to establish a re-exploration and revitalization of Congreve's plays; that was to be left to his son later in the year.

Garrick may have suggested to Sheridan that he 'reform' Congreve's plays;[5] even if he did not, Sheridan could readily have found in Garrick's long career as an adaptor two somewhat different approaches to Restoration comedy. The first of these is represented by the alterations Garrick made to Vanbrugh's *The Provoked Wife* in 1744. Garrick, in this case, deleted some of the sexual and religious references and dropped some of the exchanges between Belinda and Lady Brute, such as the one in v.ii where Belinda confesses that she might yet 'pick up some odious man of quality' for her husband but retain Heartfree as her 'gallant'. The net effect is to represent both Belinda and Lady Brute in a marginally more proper light. Overall, these alterations – as opposed to the more extensive alterations made by Garrick in the 1770s[6] – are relatively minor and the play is thereby allowed to remain intact and to speak for itself in its own voice. A far different approach to Restoration comedy, however, is represented by Garrick's transformation, in 1766, of Wycherley's *The Country Wife*. The play is revealingly described in the advertisement to the published version as 'this wanton of Charles's day', and the task Garrick set himself was to transform this 'wanton' into something more suitably 'innocent'. To accomplish this, Garrick had to rewrite about half of the play. He was understandably able to keep Wycherley's 'high' plot, since Alithea, in Wycherley's play, is seriously concerned that her honour forces her to keep her promises to Sparkish, but something far more lethal than a pruning knife is unsparingly used on the rest. All those splendidly duplicitous upper-class women, such as Lady Fidget, are axed; the famous 'china' scene, of course, disappears without trace, and the sceptical rake Horner is replaced by the shy and modest Belville who is pursuing the unmarried country girl Peggy (Wycherley's Margery), in order to rescue her from the clutches of her surly guardian Moody (Wycherley's Pinchwife). At the end of the play, instead of Wycherley's darkly ironic 'dance of cuckolds', there is a comforting double marriage and a reassuring epilogue from Peggy in which the joys of 'loving always'[7] are duly celebrated. Garrick's version has a certain bland charm about it but the dark, sardonic and unsettling aspects of Wycherley have entirely disappeared.

Whether it was Garrick or his own father who motivated Sheridan, he undoubtedly threw himself vigorously into the revival of Congreve's plays, mounting productions of *The Old Batchelor*, *Love for Love* and *The Way of the World* in the short space of six weeks. It is difficult to determine exactly what alterations to the original texts were made, but if the text of *Love for Love* published in *Bell's British Theatre* (London, 1777, vol. 8) is Sheridan's version, as the advertisement for it claims (*The Morning Post*, 29 November 1776), then Sheridan kept as much of the original as he thought possible. Overt sexual suggestiveness or directness is cut out or played down, as in the following speech of Prue where the first sentence is kept but the remainder deleted:

> For now my mind is set upon a man, I will have a man some way or another. Oh! methinks I'm sick when I think of a man; and if I can't have one, I would go to sleep all my life; for when I'm awake it makes me wish and long, and I don't know for what – and I'd rather be always asleep than sick with thinking.

Likewise, the overnight liaison between Scandal and Mrs Foresight is quietly dropped and whereas in Congreve Tattle asks Prue to show him where her 'bed-chamber' is, in Sheridan this becomes the slightly more decorous 'dressing-room'. Religious references are deleted and some passages seemingly have been cut on grounds not of 'licentiousness' but simply to shorten the play. There are a few brief additions which serve to link scenes where something has been deleted. Although some of the earthiness or robustness of Congreve's characterization disappears, in the main the play remains very much Congreve's rather than Sheridan's. The reviewer who described Sheridan's alterations as 'very trifling' (*The Morning Post*, 30 November 1776) probably got it about right.

However, it was not with *Love for Love* but *The Old Batchelor* that Sheridan started his Congreve revival which after '. . . such alterations as the taste of the times rendered necessary' (*Morning Chronicle*, 20 November 1776) he put on at Drury Lane on 19 November. If there were any doubts in Sheridan's mind about the advisability of reviving a Congreve comedy that had virtually been banished from the stage for the last fifteen years, then the reception it received must have been very gratifying. Praise was given to the play and, with the exception of Reddish, who had failed to learn his part, to the performers. *The Gazetteer* was delighted by the success of the revival, especially as such a success represented a triumph over all those 'modern Colliers' and 'sentimental scribblers', and Sheridan himself is duly given praise for his 'judgment' in bringing back to the stage '. . . one of the most capital plays' (20 November). This connection between Sheridan, Congreve and the opposition to sentimental comedy is forcefully made a month or so later in *The Morning Post* where the writer expresses the hope '. . . that every person would occasionally assist in expelling a species of entertainment, so useless, so unpleasing, so unclassical, and so utterly inconsistent with the genius, and purposes of the drama, as *sentimental comedy*. – Much, very much is due to the judgment of Mr *Sheridan* for reviving some of that admirable writer Congreve's comedies . . .' (28 December).

Although this revival of *The Old Batchelor* was warmly received, some troubled voices can still be heard. In *The Morning Post*, the reviewer thought Sheridan had been somewhat too sparing with his 'pruning knife' (20 November) and *The New Morning Post* doubted – wrongly as it turned out – whether the '. . . taste of the town will again relish that male libertinism, which accompanied the masculine genius of Congreve . . .' (23 November). A letter writer to *The St James Chronicle* (14–17 December) thought it was '. . . the highest Dishonour to the present age' that a play like *The Old Batchelor* should be 'revived with success' and another letter writer, although portraying himself as '. . . a devilish impudent fellow . . .' was nevertheless '. . . greatly shocked at the many indelicate speeches still remaining in the Comedy of *The Old Batchelor*' (*The Morning Post*, 11 December).

Although such voices, typical of the 1760s and early 1770s, can still be heard, Sheridan must have been relieved that they had now become fairly marginal, as he opened his second revival, *Love for Love*, only ten days after presenting *The Old Batchelor*. Fortunately, the reactions to this revival were as positive as they had been to the earlier play. *The Gazetteer* (30 November), after praising Congreve's work for providing 'rational entertainment', went on to single Sheridan out by name and to congratulate him for paying the public the 'highest compliment' in reviving Congreve's comedies. *The Morning Post*, after describing, as previously noted, the alterations to *Love for Love* and *The Old Batchelor*, as 'very trifling', went on to warn its readers that for some – though presumably not for the reviewer himself – the play might remain somewhat too 'strong':

> Indeed the dish, even in its present state, is served up in a style, savory enough, to prevent the most high-fed glutton from starving! – Tho' the bed-chamber of Miss *Prue* is now converted into a closet, the manner in which *Tattle* and she enter it, and remain in it, till the nurse comes, who is at first refused admittance – is rather too strong for some modern stomachs. (30 November 1776)

Even *The London Magazine*, veering perhaps with the wind, found itself able to extend to the revival of these two plays its 'hearty commendations' (December 1776). Nor did the revival of *The Way of the World*, the final play in Sheridan's Congreve cycle, draw forth any new dissenting voices. Although commentary on this revival is less extensive than on the previous two, it is laudatory throughout. For *The Morning Chronicle* (1 January 1777), the revival was 'worth the attention of every lover of drama' and *The Gazetteer*, after once more praising Congreve for his 'rational entertainment', went on to congratulate Mrs Abington for her performance as Millimant and to award to King (Witwoud), Smith (Mirabell), and Yates (Sir Wilfull Witoud) 'the highest applauses' (1 January 1777). A summing up of Sheridan's bold experiment may be left to *The London Magazine*:

> The Managers of Drury Lane in particular have shown an earnest disposition to deserve the attention and encouragement of the town. They will, we hope, recollect, as no doubt they have already felt, the advantages to be derived from industry, when accompanied by perseverance and judgment. The circumstance we chiefly allude to was the revival of Congreve's plays, the strength with which they were brought out, and the judicious, nay, masterly manner the parts were cast, as far as the insolence and caprice of a few capital performers would permit. (1 January 1777)

With such a magazine now on his side, Sheridan might well have thought that a gamble that could have proved disastrous in the early days of his management had handsomely paid off.

The effectiveness of Sheridan's successful restoration of Congreve can, in part, be seen in the reviews of *The School for Scandal* which opened on 8 May 1777, only a few months after Sheridan had completed his Congreve series with *The Way of the World*. With one or two exceptions, the reviews were all glowingly congratulatory and, significantly, some of the reviewers displayed their enthusiasm for the play by expressly linking Sheridan to Congreve. For reviewers such as these, clearly Congreve was no longer a playwright to be vilified and condemned but, instead, had become someone whose work now represented a highpoint in a tradition of great comic writing that Sheridan, with *The School for Scandal*, was reintroducing to the English public. The most prominent of those taking such an approach is the reviewer for *The Gazetteer*:

> The piece abounds with manly sentiments, intirely divested of affectation, and which are conveyed to the heart through the purest channels of wit. In this particular Congreve eclipsed the fame of all his predecessors, no nation excepted; for the wit of Aristophanes most generally lies in puns, Greek jingles, and local allusions, we know very little of, Plautus' *sales* [witticisms] are too low; – nor were *les bons mots* the real forte of Molière. They who have a sufficient knowledge of literature will not offer to contest that Congreve sits unrivalled on the throne of dramatic wit; – and if any author has the right to dispute Congreve's royal supremacy, it is the writer of The School for Scandal. (10 May 1777)

The reviewer for *The London Evening Post* also invokes the name of Congreve and sees this return of 'wit' not only as praiseworthy in itself but also as a means of mounting a successful challenge to sentimental drama:

> Mr Sheridan, who, at the same time he indulges his Muse in all the flights of *wit* and *fancy*, restrains it within the pale of *decency* and *morals*. Under this *poetical St George*, we may expect to see the *Dragon* of *mere sentimental drama* entirely subdued, and the standard of *real comedy* once more unfurled. (8–10 May 1777)

An interesting retrospective assessment undertaken by *The Universal Magazine* some seven years later sees this 'Dragon' as not only challenged by *The School for Scandal* but effectively defeated:

> By *The School for Scandal* the style of Congreve was again brought into fashion, and sentiment made way for wit, and delicate humour. That piece has indeed the beauties of Congreve's comedies, without their faults; its plot is deeply enough perplexed, without forcing one to labour to unravel it; its incidents sufficient without being too numerous; its wit pure, its situations truly dramatic. The characters however are not so strong as Congreve's, which may be regarded as the principal fault of this excellent piece. (lxxvii, 1785)

While the reviewers of *The School for Scandal* are generally united in their praise for Sheridan's wit and timely satire, and while some of them specifically invoke the name of Congreve to suggest an historic continuity between the two playwrights, this connection between Congreve and

Sheridan is always made in general rather than specific terms. The composition of *The School for Scandal*, as is now known,[8] was a long and complicated process, and far more went into that process than Sheridan's revival of Congreve's plays in the autumn of 1776. It is possible, however, that even before the Congreve revivals, Sheridan had Congreve's plays at the back of his mind and *The Way of the World* in particular. For instance, in the opening scene of *The Way of the World*, Fainall describes to Mirabell the 'cabal' nights organized by Lady Wishfort:

> . . . last night was one of their cabal nights; they have 'em three times a week, and meet by turns at one another's apartments, where they come together like the coroner's inquest, to sit upon the murdered reputations of the week.

In Congreve's play, however, the operations of the 'cabal' remain very much in the background; in Sheridan, the operations of the 'school' are much more front and centre. Comparisons can be made between Charles Surface and Mirabell, but if Charles is a 'Libertine', to use Lady Sneerwell's term (I.i.63), then Mirabell has been far more 'libertine' in the past than Charles appears to have been. Joseph and Fainall can likewise be compared, but as Joseph's 'feigning' is chiefly concerned with his adoption of the role of a man of sentiment, his thematic function in the play is markedly different from that of Fainall. Waller's poems are mentioned in both plays and this may well be more than just coincidence.

It should be pointed out, however, that even those reviewers who invoke Congreve's name, do not view Sheridan's achievement in *The School for Scandal* as primarily a successful recreation of a vanished Restoration world or a detailed reworking of a particular Congreve play, but as a work whose appeal in part lay in its timeliness, especially in terms of the object of its satire. *The Morning Chronicle*, for instance, is quite clear about this:

> *The School for Scandal* is the production of Mr Sheridan, and is an additional proof of that Gentleman's great abilities as a dramatic writer. The object of the satire is two-fold – Detraction and Hypocrisy, which are the prevailing vices of the times; by the first the good are reduced to a level with the worthless, and by means of the second the latter assume the appearance of men of virtue and sentiment. Nothing therefore, could have been more seasonable than this comedy, which, in point of execution, is equal, if not superior, to most of the plays produced for the last twenty years.
>
> (9 May 1777)

The Gazetteer, while admitting that scandal-mongering may be as old as human history, likens its current virulence to a 'horrid monster' (10 May

1777) and for *The London Magazine* those who practise it are no better than a 'brotherhood and sisterhood of modern mohawks' (xlvi (1777), p. 228).

If, however, Congreve is never mentioned in terms of the subject matter of the play, significantly he is seen by some as the touchstone by which Sheridan's incisively witty treatment of the subject can be justly and properly judged. Of course, the wit displayed, in line with Sheridan's alterations of Congreve, eschews the overtly sexual and thereby contains itself within the bounds of 'decency and morals' (*London Evening Post*, 8–10 May 1777). However, its presence in *The School for Scandal* is uniformly praised and is seen as a welcome relief from what *The London Magazine* terms 'the disgusting sermonic stile' (xlvi (1777), p. 230). It is as though an aspect of comic writing or comic vision, for some time regarded with suspicion or distaste, had been revitalized by Sheridan, and the links to older comic writers – Congreve in particular – that had been severed, were now rejoined. In the view of many of his contemporaries, a tradition had been successfully revitalized by the new manager of Drury Lane.

Notes

1 J. Morwood, *The Life and Works of Richard Brinsley Sheridan* (Edinburgh, 1985), p. 56.

2 R. C. Rhodes, *Harlequin Sheridan* (Oxford, 1933), p. 69.

3 W. A. Darlington, *Sheridan* (London, 1933), p. 66.

4 E. K. Sheldon, *Thomas Sheridan of Smock-Alley* (Princeton, 1967), 473–4.

5 T. Davies, *Memoirs of the Life of David Garrick* (London, 1808), 2, p. 351.

6 For a fuller discussion, see H. W. Pedicord and F. L. Bergmann, eds., *The Plays of David Garrick* (Carbondale, 1982), v, pp. 341–5.

7 Pedicord and Bergmann, eds., *The Plays of David Garrick*, vii, p. 254.

8 For a thorough discussion of this, see C. Price, ed., *The Dramatic Works of Richard Brinsley Sheridan* (Oxford, 1973), i, pp. 287–303.

4

Sheridan, Molière and the idea of the school in *The School for Scandal*

JAMES MORWOOD

Save in the most general terms, the influence of the plays of Molière on Sheridan, observed by nineteenth and early twentieth-century commentators,[1] appears to have slipped out of notice as scholars have concentrated on tracking down Anglo-Irish analogues for his comedies.[2] This is a matter for regret since Sheridan – as this volume seeks to show elsewhere – is part of a broader dramatic tradition. Just as his work harks back through Restoration to Shakespearean comedy,[3] so he looked across the Channel to the plays of France's greatest comic genius.

We need not be surprised at this. His father, Thomas Sheridan, had written *Captain O'Blunder* (1759), a one-act curtailment of Molière's three act comédie-ballet, *Monsieur de Porceaugnac* (1669), while his mother, Frances Sheridan, made clear use of *Le Tartuffe* (1664), IV.vii – in which Orgon tells the unmasked hypocrite to leave his house, only to realize that it is his house no longer – in her comedy, *The Dupe* (1764):

MRS ETHERDOWN . . . I desire you will leave my house directly.

SIR JOHN WOODALL *Your* house!

MRS ETHERDOWN Yes, *my* house, Sir . . .

SIR JOHN WOODALL Get you out of my doors, thou fiend!

MRS ETHERDOWN . . . yes, I *will* quit your house, and leave you to the scorn and laughter of mankind. When next you hear from me, it shall be with an authority that neither you nor your friend there . . . shall dare to dispute; and so, with the utmost contempt, I turn my back upon you both. (IV, pp. 53–4)[4]

In *A Journey to Bath*,[5] the character of Champignon is manifestly derived from Molière's M. Jourdain in *Le Bourgeois Gentilhomme* (1670). The degree to which Sheridan knew – and pillaged – his mother's work remains insufficiently appreciated.

Molière had found his way into much English Restoration comedy.[6] As Voltaire observed in 1734, 'Les Anglais ont pris, ont déguisé, ont gâté, la plupart des pièces de Molière'.[7] Among many examples, Henry Fielding adapted two of his plays; and it seems likely that Vanbrugh had M. Jourdain in mind when he wrote Lord Foppington's dressing scene in *The Relapse* (1696) (I.iii). Sheridan himself was to adapt this play in *A Trip to Scarborough* (1777). He had in the meantime made his own use of M. Jourdain when he made his Acres dress up foppishly and practise his dancing in *The Rivals* (III.iv.1–33).

TARTUFFE

Many an auditor of *The School for Scandal* (henceforth *SforS*) will have sensed the presence of Molière's Tartuffe behind the character of Joseph Surface, whose surname, borrowed from Mrs Surface in Frances Sheridan's *A Journey to Bath*, is in itself an indication of hypocrisy.[8] (Joseph himself speaks of 'the sentimental *French* Plate' he uses (my italics) instead of the 'silver ore of pure Charity' (V.i.105–7).) In the spring of 1670 there appeared Matthew Medbourne's *Tartuffe* or *The French Puritan*.[9] John Wilcox scathingly remarks that this comedy 'is bad enough as translation or as English verse to merit any amount of abuse, but it is the first attempt made during Restoration times to transfer the high seriousness of the French comic master to the English stage'.[10] (In point of fact, it was pre-dated by Thomas Shadwell's unpublished *The Hypocrite* which was first performed at Lincoln's Inn Fields on 14 June 1669.) Medbourne also lays down some very specific stage business, adding to Molière's directions (given below in French where they exist), e.g.:

Enter Tartuffe, *and passes over the Stage in a demure posture With b[o]oks as going to Church.*

Then, in Tartuffe's attempted seduction of Elmira (Medbourne's version of Elmire):

[*They seat themselves.*
[*He presses her hand.* (*Il lui serre le bout des doigts* – Molière)
[*She cries out.*
[*Puts his hand upon her knees.* (*Il lui met le main sur le genou* – Molière)
[*Draws back her Chair, and he approaches his.* (*Elle recule sa chaise, et Tartuffe rapproche la sienne* – Molière) (III.iii, pp. 29 and 30)

and in the following scene:

[*Damis comes out of the Closet where he was retir'd.* (*DAMIS, sortant du petit cabinet où il s'était retiré.* – Molière) (III.iv)

In 1717, Colley Cibber adapted Medbourne's translation as *The Non-Juror*[11] (the title referring to a priest who refused oaths to the government and royal family and was thus under suspicion of being Roman Catholic and pro-Pretender). Tartuffe becomes Doctor Wolf, Orgon and Elmire Sir John and Lady Woodvil (cf. Frances Sheridan's *The Dupe* with her Sir John Woodall – see above, p. 71). The daughter Mariane becomes Maria. Witty and droll and a self-professed '*Coquette*' (I, p. 12) – thus looking forward to Sheridan's Lydia and Lady Teazle rather than to his Maria –, she is the comedy's central character. Cibber builds up the relationship between the young lovers (Maria and her suitor Mr Heartly) to a vast degree.

Two passages from *The Non-Juror* are of particular interest for Sheridan scholars. In one of them, Maria playfully advocates a bill against coquetry:

You had best advise your friend *Heartly* to bring in a Bill to prevent it: All the discarded Toasts, Prudes, and superannuated Virgins, would give him their Interest I dare swear: (I, p. 13)

This may be a source for *SforS* II.ii.147–56. Secondly, in the play's last act, Lady Woodvill explains Doctor Wolf's alert powers of invention to her husband:

. . . he saw you listning, and at the Instant turn'd his Impious barefac'd Love to me, into Equivocal Intercessions pretending to *Maria*. (V, p. 82)

There comes to mind Joseph's ready adaptability when found by Lady Teazle on his knees before Maria (*SforS*, II.ii.198–209).

Following Medbourne and Molière, Cibber makes Sir John conceal himself '*under the Table*' (V, p. 83) to listen to Doctor Wolf – who enters '*with a Book*' (p. 83) – as he talks with and attempts to seduce Lady Woodvill. Later Sir John refers to Dr Wolf as a Viper and cries, 'out of my House' (both p. 88). Before long '*A Pistol is heard from within*' (p. 90) and we hear from Betty the maid:

The Doctor, Sir, and Mr *Charles* [a former victim of the Doctor's] were at high Words just now in the Hall, and upon a sudden there was a Pistol fir'd between them: Oh! I am afraid poor Mr *Charles* is killed.
SIR JOHN How!
BETTY Oh! here he comes himself, Sir, he will tell you more. (pp. 90–1)

Here we may have the germ of Sir Peter's unwounded entrance and of Rowley's 'I heard high Words' in *SforS* v.ii.136 and 169.

There follows (p. 92) Charles's explanation for what has happened: 'at this, grown desperate, [Doctor Wolf] ran with Fury to some Pistols that hung above the Chimney, to revenge him: I in the Instant as he reached one, seiz'd upon his Wrist, and as we grappled, Sir, the Pistol firing to the Ceiling, alarm'd the Family . . .' This may be the source for the fantastic variations played by Sir Benjamin Backbite and his uncle Crabtree on the supposed duel in *SforS* (v.ii.43–95).

After doing good service on the London stage for half a century, *The Non-Juror* was superseded in 1768 by *The Hypocrite*, 'Taken from Moliere and Cibber' by Isaac Bickerstaff.[12] In his Preface (p. ii), Bickerstaff asserts that he is going back to Molière's Tartuffe for the character of Dr Cantwell, a fraudulent Methodist.[13] The Elmire character is now Lady Lambert, her husband Sir John Lambert, and his daughter Charlotte. Slimmed down from 'Cibber's admirable Maria' (p. ii), she retains the latter's teasing coquetry. She was performed by the first Lady Teazle, Mrs Abington, to whom Bickerstaff pays a handsome tribute: 'There is a natural ease and vivacity in her manner, and, in this part particularly, a fashionable deportment . . . which gives a brilliancy to every thing she says . . .' (p. iii). Dr Cantwell was played by King and Sir John Lambert by Packer, the creators of Sir Peter Teazle and Snake respectively.

For the great scene of attempted seduction, Molière put his Orgon – and Cibber his Doctor Wolf – under a table. Perhaps taking his cue from the last act of Goldsmith's *She Stoops to Conquer* (1773), Bickerstaff hides his Sir John Lambert behind a screen (Lady Lambert: Behind that screen you may easily conceal yourself. (v.ii, p. 80)).[14] Soon (p. 81) Doctor Cantwell enters '*with a book*' (cf. *SforS* iv.iii.103–4 where Lady Teazle '*Goes behind the Screen*' and Joseph Surface says to his servant, 'Give me that – Book! –').

Lady Lambert later expresses her misgivings in the following exchange, where Bickerstaff adds his own touches as he shuffles Molière and Cibber:

my reputation is dearer to me than my life.

DOCTOR CANTWELL Where can it find so sure a guard? the grave austerity of my life will dumb-found suspicion, and yours may defy detraction.

LADY LAMBERT Well, Doctor, 'tis you must answer for my folly.

DOCTOR CANTWELL I take it all upon myself. Heaven, 'tis true, forbids certain gratifications; but there are ways of reconcilement, and laying the fears of a too scrupulous conscience.

LADY LAMBERT Every way, I perceive, you are determined to get the better of me; but there's one thing still to be afraid of.
DOCTOR CANTWELL Nothing, nothing.
LADY LAMBERT My husband, Sir John. (pp. 83–4)

Here surely is the basis for the glorious sophistries of Joseph's attempt upon Lady Teazle's virtue (*SforS* IV.iii.33–94).

Before long (p. 85) Sir John steps forward to tell Cantwell to 'leave my house' (cf. Sir Peter with the scandal-mongers (*SforS* V.ii.158–9,162,164)) and later (p. 86) he tries to explain Cantwell's hypocrisy to his mother:

The Doctor is a villain, Madam; I have detected him; detected him in the horrible design of seducing my wife. (Cf. *SforS* IV.iii.424 and 429)

Soon (pp. 87–8) we have the passage with the 'high words', the pistol shot, the healthy appearance of a character supposedly dead and the explanation for the shot, all minimally adjusted from *The Non-Juror* (see above, pp. 73–4).

The very strong presence of Bickerstaff's *The Hypocrite* – and through it of Molière, Medbourne and Cibber – in Sheridan's *SforS* is, I trust, extremely evident by now. Sheridan staged his play in May 1777, towards the end of his first season as manager of Drury Lane. It is scarcely surprising that Bickerstaff's frequently performed comedy was taken out of the repertoire after 15 November 1776 and not re-staged until 11 November 1779 ('not acted these three years'). On that evening it was performed with *The Critic* as endpiece. Having produced a major new play, Sheridan could afford to be candid about the important debt of his previous comedy to the Tartuffe tradition.

We have now to consider how Sheridan makes use of this tradition in his *SforS*. My own feeling is that he exploits it to give to his Joseph Surface an aura of menacing evil which is in fact altogether absent from his characterization. The whiff of sulphur clings to Molière's Tartuffe. He is, of course, a figure in a comedy and his desire for Elmire renders him up to a point ridiculous. Religion, however, is a serious matter and the total ruthlessness with which he uses his hypocrisy as a means to his acquisitive and lustful ends brings to mind the Machiavels of the Elizabethan drama. Tartuffe is lethally dangerous and it is only by the miraculous intervention of royal clemency that the menace which he embodies is neutralized and Orgon is saved.

Joseph is quite otherwise. Of course he is a 'smooth tongue Hypocrite' (IV.iii.424 – cf. 'Good Mr Hypocrite' (line 407), V.ii.226, V.iii.107), but

Sheridan ensures that his fraudulent sentiments are entertaining, not threatening (e.g. at I.i.100–6). Engaging, poised and adroit, he wins the audience's sympathy with his frequent asides. His inability to control the development of his plotting renders him ultimately harmless and he foresees his exposure as early as Act II in a self-aware and humorous soliloquy (ii.230–5). Maria finds him repellent (II.ii.190, III.i.139–41), but so appealing is Sheridan's presentation of him that we must surely believe that he wishes us to view her reaction as a matter of intuition rather than reasonable judgment.

Yet *SforS* would lack dramatic tension if there were no sense of threat and danger. In order to care about their situation, an audience must feel that Maria is in grave peril, not only of having her love for the good-natured Charles irretrievably undermined, but also of falling into the hands of a vicious rogue; that Lady Teazle is genuinely endangered by the attempt of a sophisticated 'Mr Logick' to seduce her (IV.iii.101–2); that Sir Peter, a 'too credulous Friend' (IV.iii.425), is seriously at risk from a hypocrite's deceit.

Simply on its own terms, Sheridan's characterization of Joseph will not supply the menace or the deep-dyed villainy necessary for that. To see this in clear relief, one need only compare him with Arthur Murphy's exactly contemporaneous portrait of a truly vicious hypocrite in his Malvil (whom one of the characters tauntingly calls Monsieur Tartuffe at his unmasking [v, p. 92]) in *Know Your Own Mind* (1777).[15] Sheridan's comic strategy in *SforS* is not to set good against bad, but complication against simplicity. However, he is able to hint at another scenario – in which virtue, good nature and innocence stand in deadly peril – through his striking exploitation of the dramatic tradition fathered by *Tartuffe*, which had been constantly before the eyes of the London public. Joseph can remain Joseph while a sense of Tartuffe's evil hangs suggestively in the air.

As a footnote to this discussion, I suggest that the traditional stage business for Tartuffe's first attempt to seduce Elmire, largely indicated by Medbourne in his adaptation (see above, pp. 72–3), should be borne in mind for the staging of the scene between Joseph and Lady Teazle in *SforS*, IV.iii. Medbourne, building on Molière, makes effective use of chairs and directs the physical action expressively. The famous James Roberts painting of the Screen Scene (1777) (see Plate 4) includes a settee on the stage; a slightly later mezzotint, published by Sayer in 1789, shows two chairs. Medbourne's stage directions for *Tartuffe* may prove of value to producers of *SforS*.

LE MISANTHROPE

The scandal scenes in Sheridan's comedy take their origin from another Molière play, *Le Misanthrope*, specifically from its great scene of character assassination (II.5). As Van Laun remarks, 'au lieu de Célimène et d'Arsinoé [Sheridan] nous donne trois dames, lady Sneerwell, lady Teazle et Mrs Candour, tandis que Crabtree, Sir Benjamin Backbite et Sir Peter Teazle sont probablement des réminiscences d'Acaste, de Clitandre et d'Aceste'.[16] The English play in which the influence of *Le Misanthrope* is most evident is William Wycherley's reworking of Molière's play in *The Plain Dealer* (1677).[17] In II.i of Wycherley's comedy, Olivia, the equivalent of Molière's Célimène, presides over a salon of scandal-mongers which is later invaded by the plain-speaking Manly (Molière's Alceste). This scene looks forward to the scandal scenes in *SforS* (I.i.123–352, II.ii (the latter complete with the incursion of the plain-speaking Sir Peter) and V.ii.1–167).

In 1766 Isaac Bickerstaff altered *The Plain Dealer*, remarking in his Preface (p. v)[18] that the 'licentiousness of Mr Wycherley's Muse, rendered her shocking to us, with all her charms'. In this version the scandal scenes are II.i–v. Their spirit is very much that of Lady Sneerwell's salon, evoked by Sheridan some eleven years later. Olivia, played by Mrs Pope, the first Mrs Candour, delivers these lines about the absent Lord Plausible, played by Dodd, the first Benjamin Backbite:

> Hold, cousin! I hate detraction: but I must tell you he is a tiresome, insipid coxcomb; without either sense to see faults, or wit to expose them; in fine, he is of all things my aversion, and I never admit his visits beyond my hall; (II.iii, p. 25)

Six lines later, Lord Plausible makes a welcome entrance. Earlier (p. 23) Novel, acted by King, the first Sir Peter Teazle, has complained about Olivia's engrossing the scandal (cf. *SforS* V.ii.82).

The flavour of Bickerstaff's Wycherley adaptation comes across pungently in the following exchange in which he abbreviates and then elaborates on his original:

NOVEL Then there's Miss what d'ye call her –
OLIVIA As sluttish and slatternly as an Irish woman bred in France.
LORD PLAUSIBLE She has a prodigious fund of wit; and the handsomest heel, elbow, and tip of an ear, you ever saw.
NOVEL Heel and elbow! Ha, ha, ha!
ELIZA I find you see all faults with lover's eyes, my lord.

LORD PLAUSIBLE Oh, Madam, your most obliged, faithful, very humble servant! to command! –

NOVEL Pray, my lord, are you acquainted with lady Sarah Dawdle?

LORD PLAUSIBLE Yes sure, Sir, very well; and extremely proud I am of the great honour; for she is a person whose wit, beauty, and conduct, nobody can call in question.

OLIVIA No!

NOVEL No! – Pray, Madam, let me speak.

OLIVIA In the first place, can anyone be called handsome that squints?

LORD PLAUSIBLE Her eyes languish a little, I own.

NOVEL Languish! Ha, ha, ha!

OLIVIA Languish!

ELIZA Well, this is to be borne no longer: cousin, I have some visits to make this morning, and will take my leave. (II.iv, p. 27)

This is surely very much in the spirit of Sheridan's scandal scenes. However, Wycherley seems to have given the author of *SforS* some hints which are not in Bickerstaff. His Lord Plausible, who, like Mrs Candour, 'libels everybody with dull praise, and commonly in the wrong place; so makes his panegyrics abusive lampoons', rebukes his fellow gossips:

Oh, madam, seriously, you are a little too severe . . .
Nay, i'faith, i'faith, you are both too severe. (II.i.311–13, 324, 338)

Compare *SforS* I.i.161–3 and II.ii.70–1 and 93.

Another Bickerstaff passage is of interest. Olivia's cousin Eliza remarks:

> I find, cousin, one may have a collection of all one's acquaintances pictures, at your house, as well as at Mr Reynolds's,[19] with this difference only, that his are handsome likenesses: to say the truth, you are the first of the profession of portrait-painters, I ever knew without flattery.

OLIVIA I draw from the life, cousin; paint every one in their proper colours. (II.iii, p. 24)

This passage provides us with a helpful link between the scandal scenes and the portrait scene (IV.i) in *SforS* – which it may well have suggested. Lady Sneerwell's salon puts on display the scandal-mongers' malicious vignettes, the hall-of-mirrors portraiture of humorous gossip. Of one exponent of the art, Snake remarks that 'she generally designs well . . . but her colouring is too dark and her outline often extravagant' (I.i.21–3).[20]

Charles Surface's house, on the other hand, contains the portraits of 'the family of the Surfaces up to the Conquest' (IV.i.1–2). Far from being from the glamorizing brush of Reynolds, 'your Modern Raphael, who gives you the strongest resemblance yet contrives to make your own Portrait independent of you' (6–7), these paintings are 'all Stiff and Aukward as the Originals' (9). In Charles's house, the surface provides an accurate guide to the reality of the characters on the canvas. It is in this context that Careless raises doubts about the accuracy of the painting of Sir Oliver, the only original who is in the room with his portrait:

> . . . that ill looking little Fellow over the Settee . . . That now to me is as Stern a looking Rogue as Ever I saw – an Unforgiving Eye, and a damn'd disinheriting Countenance! an Inveterate Knave depend on't . . . (85, 91–3)

It is surely all part of a splendid joke that the one painting over which doubts are raised – by what we must take to be a decidedly merry and no doubt teasing art critic – is the one which Charles in his devotion to his uncle resolutely decides not to part with. In a heart-stopping moment, Charles Surface, present in the room with his uncle (a Surface too), finds the genuine benevolence of the authentic (if unrecognized) Sir Oliver a far more urgent reality than the careless pessimism of Careless's art criticism. As the scene develops, the surface becomes irrelevant in comparison with the heart's instinctive grasp of the truth.

And what else can we learn from Sheridan's inclusion in *SforS* of the Molière-Wycherley tradition? This will have been far less well known to a contemporary audience than that spawned by the iconic figure of Tartuffe, and Sheridan does not fall into the trap of trying to play on more or less subconscious reminiscences here. Even so, the use he makes of Molière-Wycherley-Bickerstaff is instructive.

The first point to make is that in *SforS* Sheridan expands his predecessors' scandalous material to an enormous degree, allocating it to three separate scenes instead of reproducing their single continuous bursts. (Compared with Bickerstaff's 407 lines, Sheridan has 764, after adjustment has been made for the relative size of print.) Since nothing that the gossipmongers say on stage advances the action one whit, Sheridan's play must mark time as they divert themselves – and us – at this considerably increased length. Sheridan is certainly aiming to underscore the time-wasting frivolity of their scandal, but in order not to alienate his audience as he stretches out their spinning of chatter, he must lay emphasis on its amusement value as well.

Molière, Wycherley and Bickerstaff all use their scandal-scenes to sully their leading lady by showing her as an enthusiastic participant in a ritual which is as malicious and hypocritical as it is trivial and demeaning. Sheridan has two ladies to expose to his scandalous set. By stressing Maria's unease among them (e.g. at I.i.321–2) he is able to make a moral point about her goodness. His Lady Teazle has been corrupted by them – 'O! they have made you just as bad as any one of the Society,' growls Sir Peter (II.i.89–90) – but confirms her reformation by repudiating their company (V.iii.191–5). Here Sheridan builds on the possibilities for moral comment inherent in his predecessors' treatment of the scandal theme.

In Molière, Wycherley and Bickerstaff, the gossip-mongers also provide a foil for the misanthropic hero who, in his dedication to plain speaking as well as plain dealing, is uncompromising in his display of brutal scorn towards them. But Charles, Sheridan's exponent of 'plain Dealing' (III.iii.123), is kept completely apart from the scandalous company. Sir Peter (Van Laun's suggestion for Sheridan's equivalent to Alceste, Molière's misanthrope) certainly mingles with them and makes his rejection of their values extremely clear to them (II.ii.148–63). But like Charles, he is anything but a misanthrope. In II.ii he leaves the scandal-mongers with a genuinely witty acceptance of what they are ('but I leave my Character behind me. –' (line 172)), and even in V.ii when he expels them – and with them their world of complication and distortion – from his house, he is soon laughed out of his distress and accepts Rowley's advice to 'retort their malice only by shewing them [he is] happy in spite of it' (lines 246–7). By keeping Charles clear of the scandalous set and soft-pedalling Sir Peter's response to it – in fact by eliminating the misanthrope, so savagely indignant at human frailty – Sheridan mutes its potential for danger just as he has done in his characterization of Joseph. Frivolous and shallow complicators they may be; but they are not vicious or evil. They do not appal, they entertain. Their silliness is their salvation.

Like *The Hypocrite*, *The Plain Dealer* was taken out of the Drury Lane repertory for three years. After a performance on 3 May 1776, it was not revived till 15 May 1779 (again, 'Not acted these 3 years.'). By then the triumphant success of Sheridan's comedy was a matter of history. Even so, it was said that people 'used to annoy him about his plagiarisms from Wycherley, till he at last swore he had never read a line of [him]'.[21]

THE SCHOOL

The very title of *The School for Scandal* is a tribute to Molière. And the latter's 'school' plays, *The School for Women* and *The School for Husbands*, are clearly highly relevant to Sheridan's play. In fact it seems almost certain that these comedies of Molière became known to Sheridan through Arthur Murphy's *The School for Guardians* (1767).[22] This is made up of characters, situations and business from *L'école des Femmes*, *L'étourdi* and *L'école des Maris*. Its Prologue includes a handsome tribute to the great French dramatist:

MOLIERE, of old, and still with rapture seen,
Was legislator of the comic scene.

The small circumference of the world of Georgian literature is emphasized when Murphy renders the humorous name assumed by Arnolphe in *The School for Wives* (Monsieur de la Souche) as Mr Biddulph. This is an unequivocal reference to the best-selling novel of Sheridan's mother, *Memoirs of Miss Sidney Bidulph* (1761), a fact that in itself makes it hard to believe that Sheridan did not know Murphy's play.

As Durant has demonstrated, the education of women is a fundamental theme of *The Rivals*[23] and Murphy's comedy had a strong influence on that play. *The School for Guardians* is about the inadequacy of two educational methods – one to bring up a girl in ignorance and the other to bring her up with knowledge of the town. Both methods fail because youth calls to youth, brushing aside the absolutism of age. The opening argument, when Sir Theodore insists on his choice of bride for his son, is an important source for the conflict between Sir Anthony and Jack Absolute in II.i and III.i of *The Rivals* (e.g. 'a complection, a nose, and a lip!' – Murphy, I.i, p. 2; cf. *The Rivals*, III.i.55–8), and inevitably in view of Sheridan's subject and his knowledge of Murphy's play, there is much important source material (hitherto neglected) for Sheridan's first play in *The School for Guardians*. In addition, as Oldcastle's simple rustic education for his ward Mary Ann is held up against the town-education given her sister Harriet by Lovibond, we find here an exploration of one of the fundamental themes of *SforS*.

At one stage of the comedy Harriet shuts her suitor Belford in another room and plays a supposedly loving scene with her guardian and, as he thinks, husband-to-be, Lovibond, who gloatingly revels in Oldcastle's humiliation at his ward's behaviour to ironic effect:

LOVIBOND . . . the young gentleman – one Mr Brumpton – a wild fiery young spark – he was in the very house with her, and she [Mary Ann] hid him in the closet – ha! ha!

HARRIET In the closet! well! after that, I will never own her for my sister! – the wicked girl! – I am glad I have not visited her –

LOVIBOND Ha! ha! ha! – poor man [Oldcastle]! – he never suspected any thing – had it been my case, I should have smoked it in a moment –

HARRIET Without doubt! – there is no imposing upon you –

LOVIBOND Oh! no – no such thing – ha! ha! (v, p. 65)

Here we are very much in the world of the last two acts of *SforS*. As well as the theme of duping, we have concealment in a closet (*SforS* IV.iii.244, *s.d.*) and laughter in abundant measure (*SforS* V.ii.198–213).

There are further interrelations. Harriet says of Belford, 'He knows I like him; I have told him so a thousand times; that is my eyes have told him so –' (II, p. 19). And Mary Ann says to Oldcastle, 'And I am sure, I shall always be glad to see you, if you live these three years to come –' (V, p. 75). Compare *SforS* V.iii.235 and 196–7.

There are other 'school' plays from the period. Two of them appear to have left little or no mark on Sheridan's work. William Whitehead's *The School for Lovers* (1762),[24] based on Fontenelle's *Le Testament* (1758), was classified as 'a sentimental comedy' by Murphy, who went on to say of it, with justice, that those 'who expected laughter holding both his sides, were disappointed'.[25] Hugh Kelly remarks in the Preface of his *The School for Wives* (1774)[26] that, though 'he has chosen a title used by Molière, he has neither borrowed a single circumstance from that great poet, nor to the best of his recollection from any other' (p. 1). In fact Kelly's play seems to owe a debt to *The Rivals* and, if it looks forward to a Sheridan play, it is to *The Critic* (pp. 10–11, p. 71).

Elizabeth Griffith's *The School for Rakes* (1769),[27] however, (based on Beaumarchais' *Eugénie* [1767]) does appear to have influenced Sheridan. In Act I (p. 13) Lord Eustace and Frampton discuss the latter's 'sentiments' (cf. II, p. 16, lines 1–2). An exchange at II, pp. 21–2 looks forward importantly to *SforS* (see especially I.i.13–19):

SIR WILLIAM EVANS . . . I meant to give you joy, of your approaching marriage.

HARRIET Surely, my ears deceive me! (*Aside.*)

LORD EUSTACE You jest, Sir William!

SIR WILLIAM By no means, I assure you – I have it, from undoubted authority.

MRS WINIFRED Ridiculous!

SIR WILLIAM I tell you, sister, that it is in one of today's papers – I know what I read, sure – . . . The paragraph, I saw, ran thus – 'We hear there is certainly a treaty of marriage, on foot, between lord Eustace, and lady Anne Mountford, which will be concluded, in a few days' – and then, a great deal more, my lord, about both your accomplishments, which I have forgot.

MRS WINIFRED I never knew any thing come of a *We hear*, yet. – But I wish you had brought home the paper.

LORD EUSTACE Ha! ha! ha! – And is that your undoubted authority, Sir William? Why, at this season of the year, when occurrences are rare, the news writers couple half the nobility, in England, to fill up their papers – But, as there are no other papers fill'd up, by the parties themselves – your marriages, in print, are not allow'd good, in law.

MRS WINIFRED How can you be so easily, disconcerted, child? (*Aside to Harriet.*)

SIR WILLIAM I think it highly insolent in them, my lord, to take these liberties, without authority, as such reports may sometimes happen to be prejudicial, to one party or the other.

LORD EUSTACE The freedom of the press, Sir William, tho' sometimes injurious to individuals, must never be restrain'd, in this land of Liberty. 'Tis the very *Magna Charta* of freedom.

MRS WINIFRED So it is, my lord.

LORD EUSTACE However, there have been some slight grounds, for the report you mention.

In the Beaumarchais (I.ii) the source of the information is not the newspapers but valet talk ('Discours de valets'). Thus it is Griffith who brings journalism into play – a lead gratefully followed by Sheridan.

In III, p. 44 Robert, Sir William's servant, exclaims, '– such quarrelling, such high words!' (cf. *SforS* V.ii.169); in III, p. 50 Mrs Winifred asserts, 'I never was mistaken, in my life' (cf. *SforS* I.ii.50, V.ii.186–7). In IV, p. 60 Mrs Winifred confronts Lord Eustace:

Your lordship did not use to be at a loss for an answer.

LORD EUSTACE Have patience, madam; I confess that appearances, are against me.

MRS WINIFRED Aye, and realities, too, my lord.

Compare *SforS* IV.iii.387–8. Later Frampton urges Lord Eustace (V, p. 75), 'Continue to preserve your present bliss, my lord, and I am over-paid.' Compare Rowley in *SforS* (V.iii.246–7): 'but deserve to be happy – and you overpay me –'.

The School for Rakes has certainly made its mark upon *SforS*.

By far the more important influence, however, is that of *The School for*

Guardians with its two guardians and two wards. In *SforS* Sir Peter Teazle is the guardian of Maria (I.ii.34–5, III.i.154), he has been the guardian of Joseph and Charles (I.ii.47, IV.iii.169), and when he expresses his view to his wife that a husband should have some authority over her, she replies that if that was what he wanted he 'should have adopted [her] and not married [her]' (II.i.10). In all these roles, he is in some way ludicrous – as are Murphy's Molière guardians – as an authority figure.

Lady Teazle has had a country education like Murphy's Mary Ann, and this appears to have left her, like Murphy's Harriet, extremely susceptible to the attractions of a corrupting city education. Certainly before six months are out she is revelling in it as if to the manner born (I.ii.2–3, 10–12, II.i.91). She has learned her perverse lessons at least in part in the School for Scandal presided over by Lady Sneerwell (I.ii.32–3), a truly accomplished President, as Snake emphasizes at the play's outset (I.i.23–9). Here she has received a precipitate education in entertaining triviality, in futile complication – an education, one could say, in disinformation.

Joseph too takes her instruction in hand, offering her what one might call a sentimental education. In IV.iii she comes to his library where even the screen is a source of knowledge, hung as it is with maps (113–14). Here she receives from her 'Mr Logick' (101–2) a perverse tutorial in which he tries to convince her understanding (83–4) of a 'Doctrine' (79) which justifies adultery. Even before Sir Peter's entry, Joseph's 'Pupil' (194) is unimpressed (92–3). What she hears behind the screen enables her to recover her senses (418) and it is Sir Peter's Arts that have furnished her with the means (419). She has learnt the play's fundamental lesson – to trust no schooling but that of the Heart (420–3). Confident in this truth, she can now resign from the School for Scandal:

> . . . let me also request you to make my – Respects to the Scandalous College – of which you are President – and inform them – that Lady Teazle Licentiate – begs leave to return the Diploma they granted her – as she leaves off Practice and kills Characters no longer. (V.iii.191–5)

Unsurprisingly in view of its title, Sheridan's play constantly makes reference to education, always in a sceptical or ironical context. Lady Sneerwell suggests that Joseph should 'study Sentiments' (I.i.351–2) and it is by his sentiments that Joseph has edified Sir Peter, persuading him that he is 'a model for the young men of the Age' (I.ii.50–2, II.iii.59–60, V.ii.178–81). It is only the falling of the screen that reveals Joseph's fraudulent status as an educator. Moses gives Sir Oliver so impressive a lesson in usury ('learn', 'learning', 'Master', 'instructions', 'Tutor', III.i.83–122) that the latter feels that 'it must be my own Fault if I am not a compleat Rogue before I turn the corner' (123–4). Charles gives his friends a tutorial on the benefits of drinking (III.iii.1–23). As we have seen (pp. 78–9), he conducts an art lesson – which breaks down when Careless raises the question of the psychological truth of Sir Oliver's portrait (IV.i.1–128). And the scandalous set's ludicrous propensity to error is entertainingly underlined when they award Sir Oliver a Degree in medicine ('Faculty', 'Physician', 'Doctor', V.ii.107–19).

Education in *SforS*, it appears, is full of pitfalls. Good-hearted honesty is a more trustworthy guide, and that is why it is appropriate in this play that Sir Oliver should make a trial of his nephews' Hearts (II.iii.65). Yet it is important that the contrast the play draws between natural feeling and acquired artifice should not be seen as a battle between good and evil. Molière's 'school' plays are entirely free of the anger which informs his *Tartuffe* and *Misanthrope*. Their tyrannical guardians are impractical theorists, essentially ludicrous as events slip ever further from their control, and Molière appears to celebrate their folly, not to excoriate it. This fundamental benevolence of spirit, preserved intact in Murphy's version, is strongly felt in *SforS*. Earlier in this essay I have been anxious to argue that a comic principle is not necessarily a moral one and have suggested that, in suppressing Molière's savage, if comic indignation, Sheridan presents Joseph and the gossiping set in a largely benign light. In his treatment of the 'school' theme, on the other hand, Sheridan takes over the benignity of his sources and articulates his comedy, again not in terms of good and bad, but by setting the complexities of schooling against the simple dictates of the human heart.

Notes

1 E.g. H. Van Laun, 'Les Plagiaires de Molière en Angleterre', *Le Molièriste*, xxvi (May 1881), 56.

2 E.g. J. Loftis, *Sheridan and the Drama of Georgian England* (Oxford, 1976), M. S. Auburn, *Sheridan's Comedies, Their Contexts and Achievements* (Nebraska, 1977), *passim*.

3 See e.g. J. Morwood, *The Life and Works of Richard Brinsley Sheridan* (Edinburgh, 1985), pp. 37–41.

4 F. Sheridan, *The Dupe* (London, 1764). Soon we have the following: Sir John Woodall [*Walking about*] The fiends! – the vipers! – the monsters! (IV, p. 55). Cf. 'Fiends – Vipers! – Furies!' (*The School for Scandal* V.ii.166).

5 F. Sheridan, *A Journey to Bath*, ed. W. Fraser Rae (London, 1902).

6 See e.g. F. J. Kearful, 'Molière Among the English 1660–1737' in *Molière and the Commonwealth of Letters*, ed. R. Johnson, Jr, E. S. Neumann, G. T. Trail (Mississipi, 1975).

7 Voltaire, *Lettres sur les Anglais* in *Oeuvres complètes de Voltaire*, vi (Paris, 1869), p. 53.

8 See Morwood, *Life and Works*, p. 80.

9 M. Medbourne, *Tartuffe* (London, 1670).

10 J. Wilcox, *The Relation of Molière to Restoration Comedy* (Columbia, 1938), p. 60.

11 C. Cibber, *The Non-Juror* (Dublin, 1759).

12 I. Bickerstaff, *The Hypocrite* (London, 1769).

13 P. A. Tasch, *The Dramatic Cobbler* (Lewisburg, 1971), pp. 171–2.

14 Tasch, *Dramatic Cobbler*, p. 172.

15 A. Murphy, *Know Your Own Mind* (London, 1777).

16 Van Laun, *Le Molièriste*, xxvi (May 1881), 56.

17 W. Wycherley, *The Plain Dealer*, ed. J. L. Smith (London, 1979).

18 I. Bickerstaff, *The Plain Dealer* (London, 1766).

19 Master Lely in Wycherley's *Plain Dealer*, II.i.215–16 (quoted by C. Price in *Sheridan Plays* (Oxford, 1975), p. 266).

20 See C. S. Wiesenthal, 'Representation and Experimentation in the Major Comedies of Richard Brinsley Sheridan', *Eighteenth-Century Studies*, xxv (3) (Spring 1992), 321–2, 325.

21 *Memoirs, Journal, and Correspondence of Thomas Moore*, ed. Lord J. Russell (London, 1853), ii, pp. 297–8.

22 A. Murphy, *The School for Guardians* (Dublin, 1767).

23 J. D. Durant, *Richard Brinsley Sheridan* (Twayne, 1975), pp. 75–82.

24 W. Whitehead, *The School for Lovers* (Dublin, 1762).

25 A. Murphy, *The Life of David Garrick* (Dublin, 1801), p. 236.

26 H. Kelly, *The School for Wives* (Belfast, 1774).

27 E. Griffith, *The School for Rakes* (Dublin, 1769).

5

Satire and celebration in *The Critic*

DAVID CRANE

To begin at the beginning with Sheridan's *The Critic* means going back more than a hundred years before its composition. Although the play is intensely topical, intensely of the political moment in 1779, it is also the culmination and recreating of a theatrical tradition which began in December 1671 with the first performance of a play called *The Rehearsal* by George Villiers, Duke of Buckingham. The prologue of Sheridan's piece already refers to the earlier writer, to 'those gay days of wickedness and wit, When Villiers criticized what Dryden writ',[1] and by contrast the first lines of dialogue show Dangle at breakfast reading the letters page of the *Public Advertiser* on the subject of the state of preparedness of the army to meet the immediate threat from France in the autumn of 1779. A deeply instinctive feeling for the vitality of the theatrical tradition goes hand in hand, then, with a sense that life is to be lived most energetically in the contemporary theatre of politics, in this last of the three great plays Sheridan wrote before turning his main attention to politics when he was elected to Parliament, in the Whig interest, a year after *The Critic*, in September 1780.

Sheridan was a playwright turned politician; Buckingham in 1671 was the most important minister at the court of Charles II and was not above turning his hand to a play. He had had in mind for several years the possibility of a satirical piece on the bombastic, ranting fashion of heroic plays, so much cultivated in the Restoration theatre,[2] and by the summer of 1771 had fixed upon Dryden as the chief butt of his satire. *The Rehearsal*, like *The Critic*, is the theatre looking in upon itself, at the rehearsal of a play shortly to be offered to the public. The writer of the play being rehearsed, a spectacularly incompetent and vainglorious dramatist called Bayes (this an allusion to Dryden's poet laureateship), persists desperately with the final preparation of his heroic tragedy in the face of the mocking commentary of two cultivated gentlemen of leisure, Johnson and Smith, whose critical authority is never called into question. Bayes's tragedy finally expires under the assault of its critics, the intrusive and elaborate defence offered by its author, and the indifference of the players, and Bayes himself bids farewell to his endeavours in this sort:

> since they will not admit of my Plays, they shall know what a Satyrist I am. And so farewel to this Stage, I gad, for ever.[3]

Buckingham's attack is a simple one, and there is no doubt who is on the side of the angels. It has that characteristic of good caricature, ingenuity without subtlety, and this, together with its wide range of satirical attack (extending far beyond Dryden, so that in all nearly forty contemporary plays are alluded to), made it a favourite with audiences who relished as much the absurdity of many of the plays they went to see as the wit of this energetic attack upon them in the name of common sense. *The Rehearsal* was not only clearly a favourite with audiences, however, but also with players; and here begins the player-created theatrical tradition which was still alive in Sheridan's day. It was reported, right at the beginning, that Buckingham took great pains in coaching John Lacy, who created the part of Bayes, in Dryden's more laughable and recognizable idiosyncracies of manner,[4] and the fashion soon arose, becoming no doubt more important as the particular objects of attack were forgotten, for using the part of Bayes to allude to the oddities of fellow actors. In particular Garrick (Sheridan's immediate predecessor as manager of Drury Lane), who played the part of Bayes nearly fifty times, used this means of keeping an old piece fresh and topical.

So what Sheridan had as his source while he was writing *The Critic* was a long-running Restoration play whose chief intended focus was an entirely negative attack upon certain characteristics of the English theatre of its time, whose chief triumph was the victory of the cool, classical critic in the persons of Johnson and Smith. But he would also have felt that there was something a little more complex about the matter than that: even in *The Rehearsal* itself there are miscellaneous references to a longer theatrical tradition and presence which could not easily be satirized, that of Shakespeare; and certainly in the production tradition of the play the negative quality of its attack went with an in-group or club-like quality of comic reference to fellow players, who were after all in the same trade. In Sheridan's own play, the Shakespearean reference and the *amiable* twitting of fellow players are even more clearly marked characteristics, and these more strongly marked features may prepare us for a more complicated mixture in Sheridan of the amiable and the hostile than we find in Buckingham.

The Critic opens with the Dangles at breakfast, arguing about Mr Dangle's obsession with the theatre. The fundamental contours of the argument between husband and wife make it abundantly clear that Dangle, the enthusiast, is the one put down in the first exchange. He is, after all, an enthusiast but neither a performer nor a writer, nor indeed even sufficiently confident and well-informed to be a critic. More than this, he is laughably more concerned with the latest theatrical news than with vital information of the hour affecting the state of his country. As Mrs Dangle observes:

> No, no; you never will read any thing that's worth listening to: – you hate to hear about your country; there are letters every day with Roman signatures, demonstrating the certainty of an invasion, and proving that the nation is utterly undone. – But you never will read any thing to entertain one. (I.i.25–9)

Sheridan is playing tricks with his audience, however. As they laugh approvingly at Mrs Dangle's attack upon her husband, they are themselves open to the charge of being mere enthusiasts. Why else, in their country's hour of need, should they be in the theatre? And it may very well be that their own interest in the political events of the world outside the theatre is of a quality not unlike Mrs Dangle's: 'But you never will read any thing to entertain one.' The real energy of Mrs Dangle's charge against her husband is not that he is concerned with theatrical trivia, but that his wife finds herself not entertained by the theatre as she is by the world outside. She seeks entertainment as surely as he, is a marginal enthusiast as surely as he, but politics rather than plays are her theatre. If Buckingham's play relies on a steady background sense of the world outside the playhouse as more real and authoritative, Sheridan's by contrast crosses and recrosses the boundary, establishing an intimate network of relationship between the theatrical and the political world.

Shortly after the opening scene between the Dangles, Sheridan brings on Sneer the critic and Sir Fretful Plagiary the dramatist, this last character a caricature portrait of the contemporary playwright, Richard Cumberland (William Parsons, who created the part, mimicking Cumberland's appearance and manner as John Lacy had Dryden's). We see again something more complicated happening, however, than in *The Rehearsal*. There is satire there for sure, more energetically than with the Dangles; but again as with Mr and Mrs Dangle, Sheridan allows the vital distinction and difference between the opposing characters to disappear in the audience's mind, so that a complex amalgam replaces a simply binary opposition. Sneer the critic is as foolish as Sir Fretful, and every bit as dependent upon illusory and self-regarding notions. For Sneer the theatre should be devoted to something morally infinitely more worthy than mere entertainment (I.i.122–5), and for Sir Fretful it is the arena only for self-advancement. We are a very long way from the cool and authoritative distance of unquestioned critic from satirized playwright of *The Rehearsal*, and in the falling together of Sneer and Sir Fretful in our common dislike, the sense that the theatre is indeed for entertainment, not for moral instruction nor for reputation, becomes curiously authoritative. The audience begins perhaps, thus early in the play, to sniff the idea in the air of celebration, even to value the Dangles, as they had not at first, for their various enthusiasms. To be alive, to be enthusiastic, comes to seem very positive by contrast with Sneer and Sir Fretful.

And so the stage is set for Puff, one of the great comic creations of the English theatre, appropriately introduced by a scene with Italian musicians singing trios, with Dangle beating rapturously out of time (I.ii.1–43). If Sir Fretful is the playwright as helpless butt of satire, in the manner of Bayes, then Puff is playwright as transformer of reality, a creator both of himself and of a world he surrounds himself with, who exploits and triumphantly transforms the satiric energy directed against him. At an early stage in our acquaintance with Bayes in *The Rehearsal* we are, as it were, given a peep behind the scenes as he reveals to Johnson and Smith the rules by which he writes, 'some certain helps, that we men of Art have found it convenient to make use of',[5] Bayes's 'rules', of Transversion, Record and Invention, turn out to be no more than plagiarizing devices which eke out his own inadequacy of wit, and what he does is to lay bare for the inspection of critics and audience how little he, the creation of Buckingham's wit, can himself create.

With Puff's 'rules', a conscious reference by Sheridan to *The Rehearsal* (I.ii.148–9), all is different. Behind the scenes Bayes has nothing whatever to offer, whereas Puff comes to the writing of his play, *The Spanish Armada*, with a kind of exuberant overspill of an abundance of creative energy already displayed in his chief activity of life. He is not, in the sense that Bayes and Sir Fretful are, a playwright by profession; he is a creator of things out of nothing by profession:

I make no secret of the trade I follow – among friends and brother authors, Dangle knows I love to be frank on the subject, and to advertise myself *vivâ voce*. – I am, Sir, a Practitioner in Panegyric, or to speak more plainly – a Professor of the Art of Puffing, at your service – or any body else's. (I.ii.55–9)

And when this exuberance is 'reduced to rule', the scientific reduction to rule quivers with an energy it points to but cannot enclose within a definition. One is reminded not of Bayes but rather of Touchstone's virtuoso performance at the end of *As You Like It* on the way to 'quarrel in print by the book':

Yes Sir, – PUFFING is of various sorts – the principal are, The PUFF DIRECT – the PUFF PRELIMINARY – the PUFF COLLATERAL – the PUFF COLLUSIVE, and the PUFF OBLIQUE, or PUFF by IMPLICATION. – These all assume, as circumstances require, the various forms of LETTER TO THE EDITOR – OCCASIONAL ANECDOTE – IMPARTIAL CRITIQUE – OBSERVATION from CORRESPONDENT, – or ADVERTISEMENT FROM THE PARTY. (I.ii.151–8)

Certainly there is satire here, a satiric recognition that the public prints are not in the business of soberly dispensing information, but are rather vehicles for personal and party advantage and gratification of all sorts. But the satire is overwhelmed by the joyous abundance with which the thing complained of is done. And as Puff, for instance, demonstrates the 'puff direct', Sheridan allows this insubstantial piece of fiction to curl back, envelop and elevate the real actor who is speaking the lines; so strong are insubstantial fictions:

A new Comedy or Farce is to be produced at one of the Theatres (though by the bye they don't bring out half what they ought to do). The author, suppose Mr Smatter, or Mr Dapper – or any particular friend of mine – very well; the day before it is to be performed, I write an account of the manner in which it was received – I have the plot from the author, – and only add – Characters strongly drawn – highly coloured – hand of a master – fund of genuine humour – mine of invention – neat dialogue – attic salt! Then for the performance – Mr DODD was astonishingly great in the character of SIR HARRY. That universal and judicious actor Mr PALMER, perhaps never appeared to more advantage than in the COLONEL; – but it is not in the power of language to do justice to Mr KING! – Indeed he more than merited those repeated bursts of applause which he drew from a most brilliant and judicious audience! As to the scenery – The miraculous power of Mr DE LOUTHERBOURG's pencil are universally acknowledged! – In short, we are at a loss which to admire most, – the unrivalled genius of the author, the great attention and liberality of the managers – the wonderful abilities of the painter, or the incredible exertions of all the performers! (I.ii.160–78)

Thomas King, the chief comic actor at Drury Lane, was playing the part of Puff and so speaking these lines of ecstatic praise about himself. James Dodd was also on stage at this point as Dangle, and John Palmer as Sneer; de Loutherbourg provided the much admired sets and scenes for Puff's play later here rehearsed, *The Spanish Armada*, which was itself an amiable reference to the 'unrivalled genius' of Tom King who was not only a playwright as Puff, but who also in real life, as manager of Sadler's Wells, probably put together *The Prophecy; or, Queen Elizabeth at Tilbury*, performed with great success in June 1779 at the height of the alarm about invasion by France and Spain. Everything is drawn in, even – especially? – Sheridan himself as the 'unrivalled genius' who actually wrote this speech and the greatly attentive and liberal manager who staged the play.

Before ever Puff's play comes to be rehearsed in *The Critic*, then, we have Puff himself established as a showman, a producer of glittering effects out of nothing which nevertheless hold enthralled real substantial people. We have him established, in short, as a true man of the theatre, the magic of which, as everyone who has had anything to do with it knows, consists of flimsy devices which yet somehow seem real and for the duration of the dream, however long that may be, not shadows.

Bayes, who abandons the stage at the end of Buckingham's play, never had any real sense of it, nor as a consequence any real fellow feeling with the players who put on his piece. For Bayes, the stage (sharply separated in his mind from a less significant real world) is a place where he may play the artist, a place he thinks of as sufficiently uninhabited by ordinary real human emotion and experience to be able capaciously to tolerate his devised nonsense. For Puff the stage is fundamentally the stage of life, and he understands that real human experience proceeds often by flimsy fictions and impossible beliefs; he has a Dickensian instinct about the degree to which real people walking the streets can be ludicrous or impossible acts of the imagination; so that before ever we come to Act II of *The Critic* and the opening of *The Spanish Armada* with the scene at Tilbury Fort, we have some feeling that whatever nonsense it is, and however much we are invited to laugh at it, it will somehow survive to entertain us and draw us in.

The very beginning of the rehearsal allows both these responses. Puff's play is so dreadful that the players have cut it massively, as the Under Prompter says:

> . . . I believe, Sir, you will find it very short, for all the performers have profited by the kind permission you granted them . . . you gave them leave to cut out or omit

whatever they found heavy or unnecessary to the plot, and I must own they have taken very liberal advantage of your indulgence. (II.i.42–8)

On the other hand, de Loutherbourg's set of Tilbury Fort is, as Dangle says, 'very fine indeed!' (II.ii.1) and, together with the pageant with which both *The Spanish Armada* and simultaneously *The Critic* end, attracted much admiration.

Puff's play as it proceeds is given virtually no chance of making any independent effect because it is so often interrupted; by Sneer and Dangle because they don't like it much, by Puff because he does. But whereas the interruption of Bayes's play in *The Rehearsal* causes it to disappear, the reverse happens in *The Critic*. *The Spanish Armada* begins to penetrate and occupy space everywhere. Perhaps because the three onlookers have already, in the exhibition of the 'puff direct', been identified and celebrated as the real people they were, they would now seem to the audience to be *playing parts* every bit as much as the players in Puff's tragedy. If it is ludicrous for the heroine of that play, Tilburina, to be 'inconsolable to the minuet in Ariadne' (II.ii.264) or to enter 'stark mad in white satin, and her confidant stark mad in white linen' (III.i.285–6), then so is it pretty odd for real grown men to be pretending to be characters called Puff, Dangle and Sneer. Sheridan makes sure that everyone on the stage is drawn into the conspiracy of pretending to be who they aren't, drawn into the conspiracy of a play made up of costumes, words, scenes, music to deceive an audience itself also drawn in because willing to be deceived, to forget Tom King, James Dodd, John Palmer. And the authority of this deception is yet more emphasized and established because it draws on Shakespeare as well. Tilburina stark mad in white satin and saying her wild words at III.i.292–301 must almost certainly be intended to recall to the audience Ophelia similarly mad in the performance of *Hamlet* which immediately preceded *The Critic* on its opening night, Sheridan's play being intended as an afterpiece, a pendant to the main theatrical fare of the evening. The point can be enforced, because a beefeater in Puff's play, no doubt for the occasion of the second night of *The Critic* where *Othello* was the main piece, has a familiar line: 'Perdition catch my soul but *I* do love thee' (III.i.105).

The Spanish Armada reaches out even further with Lord Burleigh, beyond Shakespeare, actors, playgoers. If Puff's play was the most remote of the fictions offered to the audience at Drury Lane in the autumn of 1779, taking place as it did on the main inner stage of the theatre, which in the eighteenth-century arrangement of things was the place for imaginatively distant spectacle, pageant and romance, we may nevertheless see in the example of Burleigh how that most remotely theatrical of worlds reached forward to the forestage where the spectating, commenting characters were standing, and from them into real life. Lord Burleigh, who says nothing, is Puff's 'principal character' (III.i.125–6). He enters at III.i.128, no doubt from an entrance giving directly on to the main inner stage, as would have been the case with all the other characters in Puff's play:

Enter BURLEIGH, *goes slowly to a chair and sits.*

He sits, no doubt, centre stage, on the one chair the scene movers have just left behind for that purpose. Nothing happens, and Dangle enquires whether Burleigh is going to speak at all. Puff responds indignantly:

Egad, I thought you'd ask me that – yes it is a very likely thing – that a Minister in his situation, with the whole affairs of the nation on his head, should have time to talk! – but hush! or you'll put him out . . . his part is to *think* . . . (III.i.132–7)

After this, Burleigh exits as wordlessly as he came, and the stage direction is interesting:

BURLEIGH *comes forward, shakes his head and exit.* (III.i.139)

He goes out not by an exit, as would have been said, 'within the scene', within the enclosed performance of *The Spanish Armada* taking place on the main inner stage, but by a forestage exit. He becomes a forestage character, like Dangle, Puff and Sneer. Exiting like this he makes a bid for a different kind of reality, and as Sheridan no doubt intended, two days after the first performance Burleigh was identified in the *Morning Post* as a reference to the prime minister, Lord North, who in the crisis of 1779 similarly did nothing.

Burleigh became Lord North, or alternatively Lord North became Burleigh. Dangle's dismissal, in the first lines of *The Critic*, of any interest in Lord North and his preference instead for Puff's new tragedy signals a turning to a theatrical world which has led us back to Lord North in a far more vivid and telling way than ever Mrs Dangle could have conceived might have arisen from her kind of interest in current affairs. The theatre and the world outside interpenetrate each other; and just as *The Spanish Armada* and *The Critic* become in the end the same play in the final pageant of Sheridan's (or Puff's) piece, so in this final part politics and the theatre marry together in a celebration of England. Puff introduces the show:

Now then for my magnificence! – my battle! – my noise! – and my procession! (III.i.313–14)

The Thames comes in with 'two gentlemen in green with him' (III.i.324), his banks. One can imagine the rocking delight of the audience as Thames and his two banks, 'one crown'd with alders and the other with a villa' (III.i.327) to signify the difference between the north bank and the Surrey side, enter at the head of a procession of 'all his tributary rivers to compliment Britannia with a fete in honour of the victory' over Spain (III.i.322–3). The thing is ludicrous, in the best style of Puff's play, but then even Shakespeare knew that the stage was ludicrous, constantly about to topple over into farce, especially if anything went wrong with the fragile arrangements; and it is the genius of a great showman like Puff not to lose his nerve at the approach of the ludicrous. Just pile on the effects, make a louder noise, engage the best scene painter of the day, persuade the manager of Drury Lane to give you his theatre for the show, cunningly calculate the timing so that the audience is already disposed for patriotism but also very easy about it because the main crisis of the summer is past, have close by your side the greatest dramatist of the day, at that moment in his life when his powers as playwright, showman-manager and political enthusiast flow most easily like tributary rivers into a single stream, and you have it, you have it:

Flourish of drums – trumpets – cannon, &c.&c. Scene changes to the sea – the fleets engage – the musick plays 'Britons strike home.' – Spanish fleet destroyed by fire ships, &c. – English fleet advances – musick plays 'Rule Britannia.' – The procession of all the English rivers and their tributaries with their emblems, &c. begins with Handels Water musick – ends with a chorus, to the march in Judas Maccabæus. (III.i.332ff.)

Notes

1 *The Critic*, prol. 5–6 (all quotation is from Cecil Price's edition of the *Plays*, as noted in the introduction to this volume; but I have also drawn on my own edition of *The Critic* (New Mermaids, 1989)).

2 *The Rehearsal*, ed. D. E. L. Crane (Durham, 1976), p. vii.

3 Ibid., v.i.411–13.

4 Ibid., p. viii.

5 Ibid., I.i.88–9.

6

Sheridan and language

JACK D. DURANT

Whatever his feelings about his father's close preoccupations with language, Richard Brinsley Sheridan came onto the literary scene immersed in similar preoccupations of his own. One of his earliest published works, a letter to the *Public Advertiser* for 16 October 1769, attacks a political opponent, an earlier correspondent named 'Novus', not for failings of logic but of language. 'I am afraid it will be necessary to examine the Performance itself a little,' writes young Sheridan (under the pseudonym 'Jockey'),

> not with an Intention to refute any Part of it . . . but merely to point out to the Author a few of those absurdities which . . . he may possibly have Understanding enough to perceive, when coolly held forth to his View, stript of their pompous Epithets, specious Metaphors, and all the dazzling Decorations with which the *conceited* Writer ever gilds his Ignorance.[1]

Then follow in the body of the letter, and in a second letter drafted but not published (*Letters*, i, 12–18), sardonic complaints against the stupid offences of poor Novus, not just his pompous epithets and specious metaphors but also his abuses of grammar, diction, tone, and decorum, his eagerness to sacrifice truth for 'prettinesses', his 'empty, blustering style', and his 'dismal tautology' (*Letters*, i, 8, 13). No solecism escapes notice.

To survey the life of Sheridan is to perceive at once that these preoccupations with language never desert him. If his comedies delight us as feasts of language, his letters and speeches focus us often upon issues of grammar and usage. If, as a young man, his correspondence runs comfortably to puns and conundrums – 'No Woman *in England* can [pro]perly be said to be *in Continent*,' he writes to his sister Elizabeth in 1772 (*Letters*, i, 43) – his speeches of thirty years draw him time and again to language as a medium of intellectual and behavioural analysis. He finds in language a reliable basis of judgement because (as his numerous references to it suggest) he establishes himself in a coherent theory of language.

Fundamental to this theory is his conviction that truth and justice as moral absolutes inhere in the human apprehension. Comments of his in 1785 and 1787 attest his belief that the private conscience functions on its own, that, perceiving what is unquestionably just, it knows the limits of mere political expediency.[2] Consequently, in attacking Warren Hastings in 1788, he can invoke justice, '*august* and *pure*', as a value in its own right, 'the abstract idea of all that would be perfect in the spirits and the aspirings of men' (*Speeches*, i, 424), or he can protect it from profanation by separating it from Hastings' villanous company (*Speeches*, i, 420). People have the innate equipment, he feels, to apprehend moral absolutes, and they have clear obligations to serve them.

What serves them best, in his view, is conduct that rests upon principle, and generates incontrovertible fact. 'On *that justice I rely*,' he declares (again against Hastings), 'deliberate and sure, abstracted from all party purpose and political speculations! not in words, but on facts!' (*Speeches*, i, 424–5). In championing truth, Sheridan tirelessly adverts to facts, gestures, demonstrable proofs, attestable conduct, actions (e.g. *Speeches*, i, 489, iii, 9–10, 225, 397; *Letters*, iii, 156, 312–13). To his mind, language, given its tonal and semantic ambiguities, its imprecisions and discolourations, never quite measures up (*Speeches*, i, 37, 100, 343–4; *Letters*, iii, 110, 165). He yet maintains, however, that there is 'sense in words' (*Speeches*, iii, 396), that words play a role in the service of truth, and his theory of language reflects in close detail his convictions about this role.

Surely his most sustained endorsement of language as a vehicle of truth emerges in 'To the Freeholders of England', an open letter he published, perhaps under his own editorial supervision, in *The Englishman* for 13 March 1779. Very much in the spirit of Swift's Drapier, he intends in this piece to communicate lucid and impelling information, and in doing so he commits himself to facts 'stated in plain language' (*Letters*, iii, 308), to '*plain* and *authentic information* of facts' (309), to 'the plainest narrative of facts, where the relation carries with it the stamp of truth' (310), to 'a regular and unornamented appeal' (312). Here he establishes himself in a conviction from which he never wavers, the conviction that the simplest, plainest, least emotional, and most fact-oriented language best serves the truth. In later declarations he reinforces the point by observing that wisdom dictates 'the straight path' (*Speeches*, ii, 149), that truth requires no eloquence (ii, 223,

545), that intelligibility must prevail over elegance of language (ii, 278), that urgency for truth overrides subtle nicety in diction (ii, 425), that plain speech sustains public credit (iii, 136).

Of course, simplicity and factuality assume for Sheridan precision and concision in grammatical and dictional usage. In a favourite parliamentary ploy, he discredits measures under debate by exposing grammatical lapses in them. 'To find the meaning of the different articles,' he remarks of the Articles of Peace in 1783, 'grammatical order was to be inverted; for it was impossible to come to the meaning of them, by adhering to the rules of grammar' (*Speeches*, i, 35), and in 1790 he finds of a bill to levy excise taxes on tobacco 'that it was full of clauses of an opposite and contradictory nature; that many of them were absolutely irreconcilable; and that the whole bill had been framed and put together by a man who could write, but who could not read' (*Speeches*, i, 523). Feeling concision to be a natural helpmate to precision, he similarly pillories parliamentary opponents who favour elaborate and evasive phrases over aptly chosen single words. For example, in responding to an opponent who had told the assembly that 'they were engaged in a war against an enemy who denied the existence of a Being, and who acknowledged nothing either divine or human', Sheridan suggests icily 'that he meant the French were a nation of atheists' (*Speeches*, iii, 122–3; cf. i, 451).

If simplicity and factuality in language thus imply for Sheridan accuracy and concision in usage, they also imply for him sound ethical character. Good character lies at the foundation of his theory of language. Consequently, his attacks upon Warren Hastings and eventually upon Bonaparte turn often upon the interrelationships of language and principle. In defending his treachery, says Sheridan, Hastings does not hold the language 'which manliness and conscious integrity would have dictated' (*Speeches*, i, 406); his conduct is not such as 'a *Christian* ought to perform, or a *man* to avow' (i, 419); having put his 'conscience into departments', he surrenders his language to '*commissioners*' by whom 'His words are to be strung – arguments spun – passages are to be woven' indifferent to the truth (i, 373–4). For his part, Bonaparte, self-appointed head of the 'Western family', simply plays out the role of Swift's Lord Peter (in *A Tale of a Tub*), who declares while dining with his brothers that 'this tough crust is excellent mutton'; thus casually, says Sheridan, do the unprincipled redefine language (*Speeches*, iii, 423). When he declares in 1785 that 'Accuracy of style and intelligence of expression' are 'as necessary parts of an act of parliament, as the soundness of its principle, and the salutary effects of its operation' (*Speeches*, i, 111), he acknowledges in a broad and summary way the interdependencies of language and principle.

In his view, then, language best serves innate human apprehensions of truth when it is simple in diction and statement, when it records and elucidates fact, when it is accurate in grammar and diction, and when it reflects the intentions of principled people. It may also serve the truth by applying rhetorical devices; but Sheridan warns, in his implied theory of language, that, if the truth is to be served, rhetorical elaborations must be practised with great scrupulousness.

One who applies rhetorical reinforcements must first of all discern the responsive capacities of the audience. By Sheridan's assessment, a parliamentary opponent, Colonel Fullerton, had failed of this discernment while discussing the debts of the Prince of Wales in 1795. He had 'so obscured his language with metaphor, and embellished it with coarse daubing, as to render it totally unintelligible to meaner capacities' (*Speeches*, ii, 505). Even Charles James Fox, Sheridan's closest political friend, too often disregards the capacity of his audience. He 'was apt . . . to spin a little too fine' although 'no man had more information to ground argument upon, more wit to adorn that argument, or logic to support it' (*Speeches*, ii, 150).

In a second rule of rhetoric, Sheridan insists that decorums be closely observed. He acknowledges himself highly sensitive to the 'style and tenour' of discourse (*Letters*, i, 144), and his comments on it rarely omit some reference to stylistic aptness: how to write a familiar letter (*Letters*, i, 63–5), how to write a thank-you note (*Letters*, i, 103), how to write a dedication (*Letters*, ii, 222), how to write an inscription (*Letters*, iii, 95), how to represent the sentiments of royalty (*Letters*, i, 203), how to frame a petition (*Speeches*, ii, 221–2), how to address an enemy (*Speeches*, ii, 205–6), how to criticize a pastoral poem (*Letters*, i, 185), how to show respect for female sensibilities (*Speeches*, i, 422). Little wonder, then, that in opposing Burke in 1793, on the matter of 'Traitorous Correspondence' during the war with France, Sheridan should snarl loudest against breaches of decorum. Burke had, 'as he usually did', said Sheridan, 'made a very eloquent speech; and, as usual also, employed his wit, his mirth and humour, upon subjects which did not perhaps call for either – war, treasons, murders, or massacres' (*Speeches*, ii, 188). To Sheridan's mind, decorums should obtain in all forms of written and spoken discourse.

In a subtle extension of this conviction, Sheridan holds, as a third principle of rhetoric, that language in discourse must provide a proper vestment for thought and sentiment. In debating the India Bill in 1784, for example, when he gives sardonic expression to an assurance that the minister 'would re-commit the bill, that it might be divested of its slovenly dress, and made conformable to common sense – even if the principles were to be divested of common justice' (*Speeches*, i, 89), he insists that the word provide proper vestment to the thought; and he does so again in 1797, when, in discussing the mutinies at Spithead and the Nore, he challenges a printed petition on grounds of style. '[I]t is evident,' he says, 'that it does not express the sentiments of British seamen. The language in which it is drawn up, is more like the language of a circulating library, than that of a forecastle. It is no more the production of a British seaman, than a British seaman is the enemy of his country' (*Speeches*, iii, 194). The language of the petition fails of truth because it fails to reflect the authentic sentiments of the petitioners: the word does not properly invest the thought.

In a fourth principle of rhetoric, Sheridan requires that figurative language be governed by logic and taste. An opponent who, in 1800, launches the formidable metaphor that 'the breath of the nostrils of administration lay in Mr Pitt's tongue', excites from Sheridan the jovial rejoinder that the gentleman is 'more remarkable for the pith and vigour of his expressions than for the neatness of them' (*Speeches*, iii, 365), and with similar astuteness Sheridan dogs other misconceived metaphors that afflict parliamentary debate. Quite early in his political career, in February of 1781, he pounces upon an ill-judged metaphor of Mr Courtney, who had accused the opposition of envying those 'who basked in court sunshine':

> He begged leave to remind the honourable gentleman, that though the sun afforded a genial warmth, it also occasioned an intemperate heat, that tainted and infected everything it reflected on. That this excessive heat tended to corrupt as well as to cherish; to putrify as well as to animate; to dry and soak up the wholesome juices of the body politic; and turn the whole of it into one mass of corruption.
>
> (*Speeches*, i, 4)

With comparable fervour, he anatomizes a storm metaphor in 1792 and a phalanx metaphor in 1793 (*Speeches*, ii, 128, 149); and in 1794, again immersed in the interminable proceedings against Warren Hastings, he comes to grief over one of his own metaphors (comparing the treasures of the zenana to an offering laid upon the altar of a saint), which has undergone merciless scrutiny by the defence. It is 'the first time in his life,' he says disingenuously, that he has 'heard of *special pleading* on a *metaphor*, or a bill of indictment against a *trope*' (*Speeches*, ii, 374), but he knows the tactic well enough. He evokes it all too readily when he perceives that ill-drawn or casually managed figurative elaborations have obscured the clarity and accuracy of discourse.

Similarly, in a fifth principle of rhetoric, he sets himself against emotional reinforcements in written or spoken discourse. He is quick to notice when feeling conflicts with argument (e.g. *Speeches*, iii, 104), or when clamour overwhelms reason and justice (e.g. *Speeches*, i, 106; 148), or, most particularly, when abundance of emotion covers poverty of thought. A comprehensive rendering of his sentiment occurs in 1792, when, in a series of earnest questions, he assails the ministry for surrendering reason to passion. 'Had there been any want of splendid and sonorous declamation to cover a meagreness of argument? Any want of virulence of invective to supply the place of proof in accusation? Any want of inflammatory appeals to the passions where reason and judgment were unsafe to be resorted to?' (*Speeches*, ii, 134). Again, as in the matter of figurative language, he occasionally opens himself to the very charges he makes (e.g. *Speeches*, iii, 384), but his attitude is none the less clear: he mistrusts emotionally charged language and expects feeling to emerge naturally from the subject under consideration, not to be superimposed upon it. In responding to one high-toned speaker, he states his suspicions succinctly: 'They knew that in proportion as he was lofty in his manner, he was sinking in his intention' (*Speeches*, ii, 551). To the mind of Sheridan, emotional utterance rarely befriends the truth.

As we have seen, however, he does feel that well-governed language – if simple, factual, grammatically accurate, dictionally precise, rhetorically tactful (in decorum, figure, and feeling), and established in sound character – can serve the purposes of truth. It can communicate the honesty and integrity of principled minds. Its deepest vulnerability, he further feels, is that it cannot separate itself from principle, that, to the unprincipled mind, it provides a supple medium of deceit; and, in commenting upon it, he certainly acknowledges this dark side.

Throughout his career as a parliamentary speaker, Sheridan takes fierce exception to opponents for whom 'misapprehension was wilful and misrepresentation useful' (*Speeches*, ii, 150), who attempt to lead their audiences 'agreeably astray in a blossomed wilderness of rhetoric' (iii, 185). He is never more intense and comprehensive in analysing and exposing these kinds of offences, however, than in his prosecution of Warren Hastings. In

Hastings himself, and in his lieutenants and defenders, Sheridan perceives every sinister abuse to which language might fall prey.

In the House of Commons in February of 1787, having savaged the mind of Hastings as 'shuffling, ambiguous, dark, insidious, and little: nothing simple, nothing unmixed: all affected plainness and actual dissimulation', Sheridan condemns his writing in similar terms: 'in his style and writing there was the same mixture of vicious contrarieties; – the most grovelling ideas were conveyed in the most inflated language; giving mock consequence to low cavils, and uttering quibbles in heroics; so that his compositions disgusted the mind's taste, as much as his actions excited the soul's abhorrence' (*Speeches*, i, 235).

In Westminster Hall in 1788, Sheridan pursues his theme with undiminished vigour. 'Whatever . . . could be done for the purpose of concealment,' he declared of Hastings, 'was done in that mixture of canting and mystery, of rhapsody and enigma' characteristic of him. He gave 'a solemn appeal to heaven for the truth of averments', but his pledge was broken 'both to God and man' (*Speeches*, i, 397). Keeping 'as clear as possible of the fact which he was to relate', his 'only study was to lay a foundation as *fanciful* and as ornamental as possible . . . Delighting in difficulties, he 'disdained the plain and secure foundation of truth' (*Speeches*, i, 398). He had 'pronounced black white and white black' (i, 400); 'with an insulting perversion of terms', he had called 'sacrifice *protection*' (i, 413). He had adulterated sworn testimony with 'false inference' (i, 402–3). He had demonstrated his commitment to 'the trick, the quibble, the prevarication, and the untruth' (i, 409). In his utterance, 'The most desperate intention was clothed in the mildest language' (i, 414). In short, he had shaped to treacherous ends Sheridan's most revered ideals of language. He had corrupted simplicity by affecting it; he had represented falsehood as fact; he had inverted the significations of words; he had subverted decorums; he had divorced thought from expression; he had called upon ornament to obscure truth rather than to elucidate it; he had made false appeals to feeling. He had bent the rich resources of language to the purposes of deception, and language had stood all too ready to serve him. Through the negative example of Hastings (and others), Sheridan demonstrates that language, while tenuously available to truth, can place a smiling face upon falsehood, just as Hastings grins in '*brutal jest*' over his defenceless victims (*Speeches*, i, 416).

In the matter of language, then, humankind struggles on the horns of a dilemma. If language stands equally ready to serve falsehood and truth, might silence be preferred to it? Sheridan gives a negative answer to this question because he feels that truth, however difficult its plight, cannot survive without language. Silence, which can only generate ambiguities, cannot function as a definitive champion of truth.

Sheridan's acknowledgement of this principle finds many forms in his speeches. When not trying to interpret the smiles of Mr Pitt (i, 190), he is disavowing his ability to read people's hearts from their countenances (i, 443), or trying to divine whether or not their silence means assent (ii, 365), or attempting to plumb 'that impenetrable mystery, and that magnificent silence which was to characterise the day' (ii, 40), or challenging the ministry to break silence, as it had promised, on a given day of discussion, so that its sentiments might be known (ii, 93), or, in the matter of the naval difficulties in 1797, pleading to ministers to speak out lest the sailors take false inference from their silence (iii, 191). In opposing the suspension of petition in 1795, Sheridan declares himself unworthy, should the measure succeed, to continue as the 'representative of a dumb and enslaved people', and, in rejecting silence, he celebrates as an absolute right the 'freedom of discussion' (ii, 525). Similarly, he speaks out against the suspension of *habeas corpus* because 'he would never so far forget his duty to the country as to allow it to pass in silence' (ii, 379), and he speaks to the regency issue in 1788 'merely to prevent any false conclusion being drawn from his silence' (i, 431). He everywhere asserts his conviction that silence generates ambiguity and that truth requires support through language. Silence, he knows, provides no alternative to the trying human dilemma, the frustrating realization that while language gives itself readily to falsehood, it is a necessary, if feeble and tenuous, agency of truth. Ordered civilization cannot exist without it.

To seek contexts for Sheridan's theories of language is to eliminate rather quickly any intimate associations with his father's linguistic projects. Richard's fascinating little early unpublished treatise called 'The Royal Sanctuary' suggests that, like his father, he saw education in language as a means of strengthening the efficiency of communication among people by stabilizing the meanings of words (*Letters*, i, 55), but he rejects his father's tendency to reduce rhetoric to pronunciation or to see in the levelling of dialects the definition and empowerment of society. As one commentator remarks, Thomas Sheridan, an actor-rhetorician, concerns himself principally with aural delivery and interpretation. Richard Sheridan, as writer-orator, must confront conceptual problems of invention, arrangement, and style.[3] His theory relates less to his father's than to that of such contemporary theorists as George Campbell, who concern themselves, as he does, with the practical exigencies of communicating the truth and who recruit to this effort all the resources of language – literal and figurative – even while knowing them to be facile agents of falsehood, agents 'able to be seduced by sophistry in the garb of reason', as Campbell puts it.[4]

In general, judging from the commentary of historians, Sheridan's views of language accord comfortably with those of respected professional theorists of his time. Like them, he clearly adopts the Lockean conviction that language, not simply an imitation of objects, reflects mental action, that 'all words lead back to the mind that made them'.[5] Consequently, theory, in the later eighteenth century, explores the 'relationship between language and its users'; it constructs a record of 'the habits and history of men speaking to men'; it focuses upon 'The ability of men to understand one another'.[6] Its tendency, then, is to minimize the importance of dead and remote languages, as Sheridan does in his 'Royal Sanctuary' (*Letters*, i, 55), and to examine the resources of the English language itself, 'of the nature and properties of words, of their relation to each other, and of their established connexion with the ideas to which they are applied'. Such inquiry must lead, as Sheridan would have it, to improved precision of usage and thus to greater efficiency in communication, to a keener understanding of our means to 'transfuse our sentiments into the minds of others'.[7]

The study of language, then, gives emphasis in the mid- and late-eighteenth century (as Sheridan's own theory demonstrates) to private and corporate social responsibility: language provides a means to and a measure of social order and stability.[8] In doing so, it equips young Sheridan, the playwright, with a powerful and comprehensive means to analyse and dramatize the human moral and social condition. To read his three main comedies – *The Rivals*, *The School for Scandal* and *The Critic* – in relation to his implied theory of language is to sense in them a depth of observation not otherwise readily perceived.

In *The Rivals*, where much comedy turns upon verbal vitality and surprise, Sheridan obviously finds a medium through which he can explore and explode many assumptions about language. Surely in the malapropism, which features words 'ingeniously *misapplied*, without being *mispronounced*' (1.ii.130–1),[9] he offers an answer to his father's large claims for pronunciation, the foundation, as Thomas Sheridan would have it, of a secure national identity.[10] Perhaps, too, the moments of false gesture in the play, when, for example, Jack prepares a 'penitential face' (III.i.16), Julia confesses a feigned 'countenance of content' (III.ii.39–40), and Faulkland designs to 'affect indifference' (III.ii.104), reflect the playwright's response to his father's boasts about the reliability of extra-verbal communication.[11] Anyway, the play brings both theories under stress. Moreover, as a comprehensive exploration of language, it even seems to challenge the most widely received and deeply entrenched explanations of verbal communication, those labelled by William P. Alston, in his *Philosophy of Language*, the referential theory, the ideational theory and the behavioural theory.[12]

The referential theory, which champions for language a one-to-one correlation between the word and the thing, comes under examination in *The Rivals* through the '*oath referential*' (II.i.268) of Bob Acres. With amazing resourcefulness, Bob has schooled himself to reduce every experience, however complex and emotional, to a selection of aptly chosen objective analogies – whips, wheels, blushes, blooms, crickets, minnums, crotchets, etc. – usually acknowledged, through the prefatory word 'odd's', to be God's creation. While suitable tangentially to the situations evoking them, these oaths excite laughter because they represent experience in over-simplified, wholly extrinsic terms; they thrust it outside the mind, ignoring its complex affective, intellectual, and psychological dimensions. Consequently, they deceive Bob as to the urgency of his own situations, dulling his awareness of earnest and even life-threatening realities, and they display the deficiencies of the referential theory of language, a theory touted in the seventeenth century by Thomas Sprat, who, like Bob Acres, values language as a means of labelling God's creation, of returning to 'a primitive purity, and shortness, when men deliver'd so many things, almost in an equal number of words', as Sprat puts it in his *History of the Royal Society*.[13] As echoes of the referential theory, Bob Acres' oaths evoke pre-Lockean misconceptions of language.

The ideational theory, a thoroughly Lockean concept, comes under examination in *The Rivals* through the malapropism, the linguistic centrepiece of the play. In arguing that words reflect ideas in people's minds, this theory finds classic expression in Locke's *Essay Concerning Human Understanding*, book 3, which explains that since society finds 'comfort and advantage' in 'communication of thoughts', it accepts words as signs of ideas and agrees 'by a voluntary imposition' (not by any 'natural connexion' between word and idea) what idea a given word will signify.[14] In larding her language with malapropisms ('progeny' for 'prodigy', 'contagious' for 'contiguous', 'orthodoxy' for 'orthography', to mention just a few), Mrs Malaprop aggravates comic disquiets on many levels. (1) She deprives society of the 'comfort and advantage' it expects and deserves through communication. (2) She violates the symbolic covenants by which the English language defines itself. (3) She demonstrates the frail foundations on which these covenants stand, since her own symbols intrude quite aggressively upon the generally received ones. (4) She evokes the need for some means of stabilizing the language. (5) She dramatizes the ultimate futility of these means. Sheridan accepts Locke's conviction that language reflects mental action, but he demonstrates through the malapropism that the action thus reflected bodes ill for language. He perceives that the imperatives of efficient communication call for intellectual and social vigilance of the most rigorous kind, since malaproprisms blight every mind to some degree.[15]

The behavioural theory looks to sentiment and feeling as the major stimuli of communicative response. According to Deborah Baker Wyrick, in her study of Swift's language, words to the behavioural theorist 'mean the desire of the author and the response of the audience, and their purpose is to precipitate action in a particular language situation'.[16] In *The Rivals*, Julia Melville brings the behavioural theory under scrutiny. In coping with the sentimental malady of her beloved Faulkland, who, 'not feeling why he should be lov'd to the degree he wishes . . . suspects that he is not lov'd enough' (I.ii.108–9), she certifies her affection with powerful emotional fervour. 'Then on the bosom of your wedded Julia,' she protests in one speech, 'you may lull your keen regret to slumbering; while virtuous love, with a Cherub's hand, shall smooth the brow of upbraiding thought and pluck the thorn from compunction' (V.i.21–4). By reinforcing logic with feeling she hopes to dissuade Faulkland from his folly, to assure him of his worth and of her willingness to risk every worldly comfort for it, but her agenda fails, and her words, which excite no response, achieve no real meaning. Like the referential and ideational theories, the behavioural one thus displays its insufficiencies. *The Rivals* demonstrates at every turn that language declines to lend itself to system.

In some of its best comic situations, furthermore, it aggressively betrays Sheridan's ideals for language. When, for example, the womenfolk of the play appeal to Fag for information about the crisis developing on King's Mead Fields, he entangles them in elaborate circumlocutions, obscuring in rhetoric the facts they so urgently seek (V.i.165–82). So much for the playwright's own commitment to factuality as an agency of truth. Lucy advances her stratagems throughout the play by affecting (i.e. corrupting) simplicity, the principle so much revered by Sheridan (II.i.266), and Sir Lucius presumes an affront from silence, the domain of ambiguity, on the ground that 'a man may *think* an untruth as well as *speak* one' (IV.iii.23–4).

In other marked ways Sheridan causes the language of *The Rivals* to betray his own linguistic ideals. In explaining their presence in Bath, when Fag commits Jack Absolute to an elaborate system of lies, his compunctions turn not on the lies themselves but on the fear of being discovered in them: 'it *hurts* one's conscience, to be found out' (II.i.48). Later, Sir Anthony, perplexed by Jack's feigned indifference to the beauty of Lydia Languish, takes refuge in the hope that Jack is indeed lying: 'I'll never forgive you, if you ha'n't been lying and playing the hypocrite,' he says (III.i.95–6). With the same casual morality he urges Jack earlier to forswear his vows to his 'Angel' (not yet known to be Lydia herself) because they are 'not worth redeeming' (II.i.345–6). Language thus fails in the play to engage truth and commitment. It also fails to achieve precision, largely because of the miseducated minds of Lydia, the romantic, Mrs Malaprop, the linguistic pretender, and Sir Anthony, the intractable absolutist, who cannot be trusted with the truth (II.i.396). It fails to invest significant abstract terms, such as '*honour*' (IV.i.10–28), 'cowardice' (V.iii.127–33), and 'modesty' (II.ii.56), with appropriate contexts, leaving them to wallow in vagueness and confusion. It awards persuasiveness to falsehood ('How persuasive are his words,' says Lydia to the palaver of Beverley [III.iii.141].), and it generates false and dangerous passions ('Your words are a grenadier's march to my heart,' says Bob Acres to Sir Lucius [III.iv.79]).

Language in *The Rivals* reflects a world fractured by ignorance, arrogance, confusion, deception, and caprice. People perhaps capable of communicating the truth, such as Jack Absolute and Julia Melville, surrender themselves to whimsy and irresoluteness, and no one even attempts the intellectual and moral rigour on which efficient communication depends. In her bemused declaration at the end of the play – 'Oh! Faulkland, you have not been more faulty in your unkind treatment of me, than I am now in wanting inclination to resent it' (V.iii.223–4) – Julia acknowledges the prevailing irony of this world, a world shaped not by logic and reason, the bedrock of sound communication, but by instinct and feeling. Perhaps these vague affective impulses bring some tentative and arbitrary resolution to the romantic conflicts of the play, but they bring no order to the larger world of the action, which continues unstable even after the final curtain has fallen.

In composing *The School for Scandal*, Sheridan again finds in language a major index to moral and social disarray. Since, as Sir Peter Teazle implies, character and reputation live or die through language – 'a character dead at every word I suppose' (II.ii.75) – scandal usually takes form as an illicit linguistic power play. It follows, then, that *The School for Scandal*, an elaborate anatomy of scandal, preoccupies itself with abuses of language, most of them instantly recognizable as departures from Sheridan's linguistic ideals.

In the elaborate false details with which Sir Benjamin and Crabtree describe the after-effects of the Screen Scene (V.ii.11–95), Sheridan dramatizes the vulnerability of facts, the valued underpinnings of accurate communication. In the malice and exaggeration of the similes by which the scandal cabal lacerates its victims (II.ii.29–69), he displays the corruption and misapplication of figurative language. The convoluted logic by which Joseph Surface, in the Screen Scene, subverts the word 'honor' (IV.iii.68–93) violates Sheridan's treasured principle of simplicity, and from Joseph's hypocritical sentiments emerge the same dark linguistic offences that Sheridan would one day charge against Hastings: 'the most groveling ideas . . . conveyed in the most inflated language; giving mock consequence to low cavils, and uttering quibbles in heroics' (*Speeches*, i, 235). As a 'smooth tongue Hypocrite' (IV.iii.424) with sentiments 'at his Tongue's end' (V.i.29), Joseph demonstrates that his 'speculative Benevolence' (V.i.24) rises to nothing more than a facile and pernicious management of language.

Actually, every word uttered by the scandal cabal aggravates some kind of linguistic outrage. To the instances already cited we should add Mrs Candour's destructive words of good will and the forged letters, specious news items, and practised mendacity that provoke Sir Peter's final judgement (in linguistic terms) against Snake: 'There's a precious Rogue – yet that Fellow is a Writer and a Critic!' (V.iii.226–7). Early in the play, Lady Teazle, who eventually learns otherwise, defends scandal as 'the freedom of speech' (II.i.88), but the proper posture upon it is taken by Maria, who rejects summarily Joseph's idle defence of his associates. To his comment 'They have no malice at heart', she replies, 'Then is their conduct still more contemptible for in my opinion – nothing could – excuse the intemperance of their tongues but a natural and ungovernable bitterness of Mind' (II.ii.183–7). She endorses, with Sheridan, the Lockean view that 'all words lead back to the mind that made them'.[17]

In doing so, they reveal in the world of *The School for Scandal* a dangerous whirlpool of sinister mentalities. Maria promotes as best she can her crusade for verbal honesty: 'his conversation is a perpetual Libel on all his Acquaintance,' she complains of Sir Benjamin (I.i.133–4); 'she does more Mischief than the Direct malice of old Crabtree,' she protests of Mrs Candour (I.i.159–60); 'in my opinion those who report such things are equally culpable,' she insists of the scandal mongers (I.i.196–7). So weak a voice as hers, however, cannot stem the tide of malice in the play. Even Charles Surface, whose energy and spontaneity generally recommend themselves over the subtle cunning of slander, shows a ready skill at duplicity when, during the screen scene, he redirects the comments overheard by Sir Peter about Joseph and Lady Teazle: 'Ah! you would have retorted on him,' says Sir Peter, while Joseph is out of the room. 'Aye – aye – that was a Joke,' says Charles, disempowering his good old friend (IV.iii.327–8). Language declines to provide a place of haven in *The School for Scandal.*

Neither, of course, is haven available in silence, the domain of ambiguity. When, in Act V, Sir Oliver attempts to 'construe' the blush of Maria, he thoroughly misconstrues it, attributing it to her affection for Charles rather than to her chagrin over his presumed relationship with Lady Sneerwell. 'Heydey – what's the mystery now?' asks Sir Peter, entering the confusion (V.iii.149–56). Confusion results again moments later when Charles declares that Maria has 'look'd yes' to his request for her hand. 'For shame – Charles,' she says; '– I protest Sir Peter there has not been a word –'; and to her protestation Sir Oliver quickly remarks, 'Well then the fewer [words] the Better – may your love for each other never know – abatement' (V.iii.235–9). As he had done in resolving *The Rivals*, Sheridan again lifts his conflicts above the realm of language. 'But Here shall be my monitor,' says Charles of Maria, '– my gentle Guide – ah! can I leave the Virtuous path those Eyes illumine?' (V.iii.251–2). Love and virtue, as extra-verbal values, secure his reformation and confirm his joys, but the clatter of language continues to pollute his world. The scandal cabal talks on.

In his last comedy, *The Critic*, Sheridan provides no respite from the clatter of language.[18] To be sure, he plants in the dialogue of his play some standards to which responsible speakers and writers might turn: when Dangle laments the loss of vitality in comic language ('No double entendre, no smart innuendo admitted' [I.i.133]) and when Sir Fretful Plagiary listens to a sharp discourse upon his own stylistic failings ('your bombast would be less intolerable, if the thoughts were ever suited to the expression; but the homeliness of the sentiment stares thro' the fantastic encumbrance of its fine language, like a clown in one of the new uniforms!' and 'your occasional tropes and flowers suit the general coarseness of your stile, as tambour sprigs would a ground of linsey-wolsey' [I.i.333–6; 338–9]). The standards implied in these speeches, however, function in the play as faint echoes of what ought to be. They represent a sanity nowhere apparent in fact or fiction.

What actually defines the world of fact in *The Critic* is, of course, the elaborate 'Art of Puffing', in which language, while abrogating all responsibility to the truth, promotes civility and security among people. It is, says Puff, an art 'of the highest dignity – yielding a tablature of benevolence and public spirit; befriending equally trade, gallantry, criticism, and politics: the applause of genius! the register of charity! the triumph of heroism! the self defence of contractors! the fame of orators! – and the gazette of ministers!' (I.ii.247–52). In all walks of life, it supplants ethics and substance with mere sound.

Language as abused in the world of fiction emerges in *The Critic* through the dialogue of Puff's tragedy, *The Spanish Armada*. Puff claims to accommodate 'much matter of fact' in his first scene by choosing 'plain and intelligible' language, but he actually chooses for this scene the same level of bloated fustian that dominates the remainder of his play, for which he claims 'trope, figure, and metaphor, as plenty as noun-substantives' (II.ii.148–50). Furthermore, since he is 'not for making slavish distinctions, and giving all the fine language to the upper sort of people' (III.i.35–7), he declines to distinguish character through language. From beginning to end, he sets his play awash in empty and florid verbal excesses.

If language actually heard in Puff's play descends thus in torrents, the unheard language, the language cut by the actors but promised for print, vastly multiplies the deluge. It includes a descriptive reminiscence upon the first meeting of Tilburina and Don Whiskerandos, an account of his courage in a sea fight, an elaborate simile of a canary bird, a series of mutual protestations upon the parting of Tilburina and Whiskerandos (reduced by an actor to the single line 'The less is said the better' [II.ii.462]), and numerous passages in which Queen Elizabeth is 'to be talked of for ever' (II.ii.489). Whether heard or imagined, abused language takes full possession of *The Spanish Armada*.

In two celebrated scenes, moreover, Puff demonstrates that silence serves him no better than language does. One of them, which places several characters at a ridiculous impasse of swords and daggers, purports to show that 'the greatest applause may be obtained without the assistance of language, sentiment or character' (III.i.165–6). Instead, the scene simply brings down derision upon itself. The other, which presents Lord Burleigh troubled and muted by the affairs of state, evokes without success the dramatic claims of silence. Puff intends, by a shake of Burleigh's head, to send the elaborate message that while the English 'had more justice in their cause and wisdom in their measures – yet, if there was not a greater spirit shown on the part of the people – the country would at last fall a sacrifice to the hostile ambition of the Spanish monarchy' (III.i.144–7). As Sneer's response indicates, however (148), the audience perceives no such message; as always, in fiction and fact, silence remains steadfastly ambiguous.[19]

Unlike *The Rivals* and *The School for Scandal*, *The Critic* offers no romantic extra-verbal resolution to its actions. In both the play itself and the play within it, it dramatizes through language (and through silence) a world unhinged by madness. Puff's pageant at the close gives graphic form to this madness, but it finds its principal index in language: in the idiot babblings of the deranged Tilburina (III.i.292–301), in the verbal pretensions and excesses of *The Spanish Armada*, in the noble art of puffing, in the polyglot confusion of mixed languages (when Mrs Dangle must communicate with foreign entertainers [I.ii.1–43]), in the arrogant linguistic offences of Sir Fretful Plagiary. The mad comic world of *The Critic*, which appeals for nothing so much as sanity in language, dramatizes a conviction basic to Sheridan's theory, the conviction that truth cannot prevail without language and that language, a most tenuous and vulnerable human resource, cannot often be trusted.

To assess Sheridan as a playwright of language is certainly to admire the energy and sparkle of his dialogue and to marvel at his amazing mind for sound, rhythm, and verbal nuance. A full appreciation of his gift, however, must also take into account his extensive commentary in non-dramatic sources upon language and its properties. From this commentary emerges the theory that language, if governed by a morally responsible mind, can communicate truth, the truth innately perceived by conscience. While truth fares best when expressed by simple, reserved, precise, grammatical and fact-based language, it can profit, in Sheridan's view, from careful and tactful rhetorical reinforcements. Many resources of language stand ready to serve it.

An irony basic to Sheridan's comic strategy, however, is that these same resources of language also stand ready to serve falsehood. If, when responsibly managed, language promotes moral and social stability, it foments chaos and treachery when carelessly or ignobly abused. It functions both as a cause of instability and an index to it. No assessment of Sheridan as a playwright of language, then, can properly exclude the penetrating and persistent views that constitute his theory of language. As the foregoing analyses indicate, he finds in this theory a ground of situation, of character, of moral and social analysis, and of expansive comic ambience. It adds density, complexity, depth, and urgency to his themes; and, without compromising his instincts for hilarity and delight, it engages keen interpretative challenges. It complements his celebrated wit and verbal dexterity, and with them it goes far to explain the delight long taken in his comedies as feats and feasts of language.[20]

Notes

1 R. B Sheridan, *The Letters of Richard Brinsley Sheridan*, ed. C. Price (Oxford, 1966), i, 7. References to Sheridan's letters, all drawn from this edition, are hereafter cited parenthetically in my text.

2 R. B. Sheridan, *The Speeches of the Right Honourable Richard Brinsley Sheridan* (London, 1842; rpt. New York, 1969), i, 101, 225. References to Sheridan's speeches, all drawn from this edition, are hereafter cited parenthetically in my text.

3 W. S. Howell, *Eighteenth-Century British Logic and Rhetoric* (Princeton, 1971), p. 228.

4 Quoted in Howell, *British Logic and Rhetoric*, p. 589.

5 M. Cohen, *Sensible Words: Linguistic Practice in England, 1640–1785* (Baltimore, 1979), p. 39.

6 Ibid., pp. 103, 136, 120.

7 Ibid., p. 104 (quoting Lindley Murray).

8 Ibid., pp. 80, 95, 119.

9 Sheridan, *Sheridan's Plays*, ed. C. Price (Oxford, 1975). All references to Sheridan's plays, provided parenthetically in my text, cite this edition.

10 W. Benzie, *The Dublin Orator: Thomas Sheridan's Influence on Eighteenth-Century Rhetoric and Belles Lettres* (Leeds, 1972), p. 29; Cohen, *Sensible Words*, p. 126.

11 Benzie, *Dublin Orator*, pp. 35–6.

12 W. P. Alston, *Philosophy of Language* (Englewood, 1964), pp. 11–31.

13 T. Sprat, *History of the Royal Society*, ed. J. I. Cope and H. W. Jones (St Louis, 1958), p. 113.

14 J. Locke, *An Essay Concerning Human Understanding* (Chicago, 1952), Book III, Chapter ii, Section 1.

15 In discussing techniques of artistic representation in Sheridan's comedies, C. S. Wiesenthal demonstrates that language in *The Rivals* claims identity as a character in its own right. As the comic dialogue explores the 'structures of language' (p. 314), it also has the effect of parodying the language of the sentimental dialogue, and just as the malapropism satirizes 'the figurative ideal of language', so the referential oath 'may be seen as a similar travesty on an old-fashioned linguistic ideal of "Lockean literalism"' (p. 317). See 'Representation and Experimentation in the Major Comedies of Richard Brinsley Sheridan', *Eighteenth-Century Studies*, xxv (3) (Spring 1992), 309–30.

16 D. B. Wyrick, *Jonathan Swift and The Vested Word* (Chapel Hill, 1988), p. 2.

17 Cohen, *Sensible Words*, p. 39.

18 Wiesenthal (pp. 327–8) notes Sheridan's movement away from arbitrary resolutions in the major comedies.

19 Looking at the Burleigh scene from a dramaturgical perspective, Wiesenthal remarks that while language is 'fraught with its own difficulties, the dangers of lapsing into absurdity through "dumbshew" appear yet greater' (pp. 319–20).

20 I adapt the closing phrase from O. Reinert, *Drama* (Boston, 1964), p. 386. In 'Plot, Character, and Comic Language in Sheridan', R. Hogan comments upon the 'language of humor', found primarily in *The Rivals*, in which 'the audience laughs at language faultily used', the 'language of wit', found primarily in *The School for Scandal*, in which 'the audience laughs at language cleverly used', and the 'language of parody', found primarily in *The Critic*, which 'satirizes presumptive excellence by exaggerating its faults'. See *Comedy from Shakespeare to Sheridan*, ed. A. R. Braunmuller and J. C. Bulman (Newark, Delaware, 1986), pp. 274–85.

7

Foiling the rival: argument and identity in Sheridan's speeches

CHRISTOPHER REID

To contemporary observers the House of Commons in the late eighteenth century was a theatre of great personal confrontations. At a time when the majority of members were, at best, occasional speakers, and when by nineteenth-century standards party organizations were undeveloped, the role of the relatively few regular participants in debate was heightened, and their contests sharpened. In April 1794 Philip Francis warned the House that the practice of 'confining every discussion, on subjects of importance, to three or four individuals' was a threat to the freedom of debate.[1] Surviving reports of the period tend to confirm the dominance of the same handful of speakers. In the confined and intimate space of St Stephen's Chapel, where the House then sat, the assembled members witnessed a clash of rhetorical opposites: Burke, Dundas, Pitt and Windham on one side of the Chamber, and Fox, Grey and Sheridan facing them on the other. In the parliamentary memory such repeated confrontations establish precedents and, in turn, excite expectations. They cohere into a kind of plot which, though not entirely predictable in its outcome, tends to select and position its key players in advance.

These pointedly adversative exchanges foreground what classical rhetoricians, following Aristotle, called *ethos*, the construction of character through the medium of speech. In his *Rhetoric* Aristotle classes ethos, together with *pathos*, the raising of emotions, and *logos*, rational argument, as one of the three primary means of persuasion or rhetorical proofs. In fact in an early comment he goes so far as to suggest that character 'is almost . . . the controlling factor in persuasion'.[2] In order to gain the audience's approval and trust, the speaker is required 'to construct a view of himself as a certain kind of person'.[3] The speaker cannot rely on the persuasive authority of an existing reputation for virtue. Aristotle insists that the right to such a reputation must be won in and through acts of address. Whilst it may be objected that in a political and print culture as highly developed as that of late eighteenth-century Britain an established reputation probably counted for a good deal in the minds of an audience, Aristotle's insight none the less points valuably to the dynamics of character: to character as established through verbal interaction and hence to character as a process of rhetorical unfolding rather than as a realization of a pre-existing political self.

In the course of the *Rhetoric* Aristotle catalogues both the topics of praise from which a favourable ethos might be derived and the topics of blame which might form the basis for a hostile construction of a political adversary. Significantly, he argues that given attributes of character may be made to serve either end. If, for example, we wish to condemn those noted for their caution we should call them 'cold and designing' rather than, say, prudent and responsible. If, on the other hand, we wish to praise 'those given to excess' we should speak of 'the rash one as "courageous," [and] the spendthrift as "liberal"'.[4] Such prescriptions – which, as we shall see, are closely applicable to the constructions and counter-constructions of character exchanged between Sheridan and Pitt – alert us to the double-sidedness of early rhetorical theory and its links with sophistical models of argument. If, as the leading sophists maintained, every question can be argued on contrary sides, the persuasive process necessarily involves the discovery of the opposite case. Every argument develops out of a dialogue and a critical engagement with this experienced or anticipated other.[5]

I

It is evident from contemporary reports that these principles, which might be thought of as constituting the deep structure or conditions of possibility of parliamentary discourse, were strikingly realized in Sheridan's speaking. When, very early in his parliamentary career, he for once crossed swords in debate with his ally Fox, the latter observed that 'his honourable friend Mr Sheridan had so much ingenuity of mind, that he could contrive to give an argument what turn he pleased'.[6] This was to prove an enduring image of Sheridan as a speaker. More than a decade later the rebuke that was perhaps concealed within Fox's compliment was made explicit when Pitt remarked that Sheridan, in his view a rhetorical opportunist, 'is possessed of such ingenuity as to bring together every argument, however incongruous, that may suit his purpose, and give it an appearance of connexion with the question'.[7] Throughout his parliamentary career he was regarded with a mixture of apprehension and respect (but also, frequently, of disdain) for his skill in finding the other side of an argument, in turning an adversary's metaphors in a new direction, and in applying another speaker's allusions and citations in an unexpected way.

As much as from statements of principle, it is out of such rhetorical contests that the speaker's ethos emerges. In a broad sense these practices may be understood as forms of quotation. The interactive character of eighteenth-century parliamentary discourse, where every member of the addressed audience is in theory a potential interlocutor, necessarily involves speakers in repeatedly citing, paraphrasing, and summarizing the words and arguments of other members. Even an opening statement introduced by a speaker moving a motion may embody quotation in the sense of voicing the known or anticipated arguments of an adversary in order to refute them in advance or to 'discover' one's own position. *Replies* more obviously embrace quotation, at once echoing and contesting a rival's utterance, perhaps by means of a counter argument or, as so often in Sheridan's case, through techniques of diminution such as ridicule and parody.

Sheridan's work as a playwright is clearly relevant here. John Loftis has argued that Sheridan's major plays are best understood as belonging to the genre of burlesque,[8] a mode of comedy which, so to speak, 'quotes' and enters into an ironic dialogue with a precursor text, and by so doing measures its difference from its predecessor. Many of Sheridan's replies to his parliamentary opponents are constructed in similar ways. In the tense and distrustful political atmosphere of the 1790s he typically mixed high seriousness and burlesque in his assaults on Pitt's campaign of repression against organized radical opinion. Sternly denouncing Pitt's 'system of terror' (ii,548), as he came to call it, as an encroachment upon English liberties, Sheridan also ridicules it for lacking any foundation in political reality. Where the Commons Committee of Secrecy, chaired by Pitt, claimed to have unearthed an elaborate plot against the constitution, Sheridan found only 'fabulous plots and forged conspiracies . . . originating solely in the foul imagination of his Majesty's ministers' (ii,401). On 5 January 1795, following the acquittal of the accused radicals at the recent treason trials, he ridiculed the evidence brought forward by the prosecution to prove the existence of a conspiracy:

On the first trial one pike was produced, that was afterwards withdrawn from mere shame. A formidable instrument was talked of to be employed against the cavalry; it appeared upon evidence to be a tee-totum in a window at Sheffield. There was a camp in a back shop, an arsenal provided with nine muskets, and an exchequer containing nine pounds and one bad shilling; all to be directed against the whole armed force and established government of Great Britain. (ii,446)

In *The Camp* and *The Critic* Sheridan had satirized the atmosphere of rumour and alarm which had been excited by the intervention of France on the American side in the War of Independence. In his speeches of the 1790s, following this precedent, he travesties the ministerial narrative of conspiracy and insurrection, reproducing it as mere bombast and hearsay. Pitt and his fellow alarmists are cast as the Puffs, or perhaps the Snakes, of the political world, authors of a bad tragedy of plot and counter-plot which Sheridan reworks and returns to its originators in the form of a political burlesque.

Burlesque of this sort exhibits on a large scale Sheridan's characteristic practice of finding the other side of, and then turning, an opponent's position. When he engaged in a point-for-point reply to a speech he often sought to undermine an argument by deconstructing his rival's metaphors. The possibilities of such an approach were shown as early as his third recorded speech in the Commons, when, in an exchange with John Courtenay, he ironically uncovered an alternative set of meanings in his opponent's figures of speech (i,4).[9] In the more urgent debates of the 1790s he entered into similar contests, often enough with erstwhile allies such as Burke and Windham, whose implacable hostility towards the French Revolution and its sympathizers in Britain was to culminate in a schism in the ranks of the parliamentary Whigs. On 30 April 1792 Charles Grey raised the issue of parliamentary reform on behalf of the Society of The Friends of the People, a recently established group of Whig reformers to which Sheridan belonged. Those opposed to Grey's proposals (the vast majority of the House) argued that the present time of crisis, with France apparently in turmoil and with growing discontent at home, was hardly an appropriate one at which to risk such an experiment. In the course of his speech Sheridan took up some of the metaphors in which this opposing case had been put:

one gentleman had talked of their nourishing a young lion, and another of a storm. Those metaphors might be applied either way. If they were at sea in a ship, and were to see a storm rising, it would be more natural for a good seaman to say of the vessel, 'there is a storm coming, let's examine the tackle, and see that her bottom is sound;' than to say, 'the ship is going on her regular course; let her proceed, without any fears for her safety.' (ii, 128)

We might think of this kind of rejoinder as a dispossession or 'capture' of a rival's voice which is at once quoted in order to be appropriated. It is an assertion of mastery over discourse comparable to repartee in conversation or scripted dialogue. In January 1795 William Windham referred to Sheridan's practice of making a 'watch-word' or 'party catch-words' out of his rivals' speeches. Sheridan, he complained, had turned his own phrase, 'acquitted felons', which he had used to describe the radicals unsuccessfully prosecuted for treason in 1794, and Burke's notorious words, 'a swinish multitude', against their originators.[10]

Such dexterity in reply, a core element, I would suggest, of Sheridan's political identity, is not well represented in published collections of his speeches. It emerges more clearly, though no doubt still in a diluted form, from reports of entire debates. Read in this context it becomes easier to understand why Sheridan's ripostes should have moved a rueful Burke to say that 'He admired and feared that gentleman's talents, and regretted that he should meet with opposition from him'.[11] On 8 April 1794, two days before Burke made this remark, the former allies clashed during a debate on a motion to impose a war-time tax on placemen and pensioners. Burke denounced the motion in typically uncompromising terms: not only would the revenue gained be paltry, the proposal itself was an infringement on the Crown's right to dispense patronage. In putting this last point Burke drew an interesting analogy: 'Let any person reflect within himself, whether he would give the same wages to his game-keeper as to his footman, to his footman as to his groom. Does any gentleman give the same wages to a boy in his stable as to his cook, who entertains his friends when they join in festivity with him?'[12] Rather than rejecting this analogy as simply invalid, Sheridan in his reply turned it to his own ends. By disputing the terms of Burke's comparison he showed how it might be used to support quite different, and more radical, conclusions:

does the right hon. gentleman mean to assert, that the crown possesses the sole right of judging what rewards were to be bestowed upon public servants? Then he would ask him who it was that is obliged to pay those rewards? He had put the case of a private family, and asked whether the master was not the proper judge in the distribution of reward; and if those rewards should be the same to all classes of his servants? He was ready to adopt the principle of his comparison, and to agree, that in both cases, those who pay were the proper judges of what should be paid. (ii, 349)

Within the framework of his rival's analogy Sheridan undermines Burke's complacent patriarchy and puts what in 1794 was an especially pointed political question: who are the masters?

The styles of reply I have been discussing involve Sheridan in quotation in an extended (and I think valuable) sense of the term. It encompasses the various means by which he seizes power over the other side's language, subjecting rival voices to his coolly monological control. Quotation in the more orthodox and restricted sense was also much favoured by eighteenth-century parliamentarians. The textual functions and cultural meanings of quotation of this sort are worth considering. To some extent they would depend upon the nature of the quoted source. The contemporary commentator, Nathaniel Wraxall, suggests that some speakers (including Pitt) were sparing in quotation from classical sources for fear of losing the attention of less learned members. Yet as Wraxall himself concedes, other leading figures (including Burke) quoted frequently and liberally from classical texts.[13] More frequent still were citations from English poets and dramatists, although speakers did not confine themselves to 'polite' sources: lines from comic songs and popular tags were also occasionally recited.

Quotation of the more serious sort, involving an appeal to textual precedent and an assertion of cultural authority in support of a particular case, is of special importance in a relatively closed political culture. In the late eighteenth-century House of Commons, for instance, the ability to cite an approved authority at once signified one's right to belong to an élite group and solicited the cultural sympathies of its members. Quotation was a demonstration of a special kind of knowledge, and of the ability to apply it; it was an affirmation of the cultural identity of the polite class and by the same token a cultural exclusion of the unenfranchised mass 'out of doors'. Within the Commons Chamber contemporary speakers saw that to quote accurately and, more to the point, appositely, was to wield a certain kind of power. If a test of the poet's skill in the eighteenth-century genre of imitation was to find in contemporary life a close equivalent to the classical original, then in political discourse the worth of a quotation would be judged by the quality of the correspondence established between the context of the original and the argument of the 'host' text. Like other parliamentarians of the period Sheridan often quotes in this strongly positive sense. When the coalition between Pitt's supporters and the Portland Whigs in July 1794 left the Foxites, who continued to oppose the war with France, isolated in the House, Sheridan paid a tribute to Fox as the leader of a principled minority. Quoting from the ironically warlike *Coriolanus* (v.iii. 73–4) he figures the embattled Fox as 'a man who, at this very moment, . . . did not to the public eye appear less for being more alone; on the contrary, who seemed to stand on higher ground from being less surrounded. To him, in the stormy hour, the nation would turn, and they would find him, "Like a great sea-mark, standing every fl[a]w, / And saving those that eye him."' (ii, 421)

That quotation of this sort was understood as a bid for prestige, and therefore for power, is evident from the efforts made by speakers to cap, challenge, or otherwise turn quotations made by their opponents. This kind of contest is well illustrated by surviving reports of the debates on Fox's East India Bill in November and December 1783. According to Wraxall, 'History, ancient and modern, poetry, even Scripture, all were successively pressed into the service, or rendered subservient to the purposes of the contending parties.'[14] He singles out Sheridan as the most resourceful of the textual combatants and his speech of 8 December, though imperfectly reported, was by all accounts a *tour de force* of contested quotation. The sketch in Sheridan's *Speeches* describes how he 'took up the several quotations from Shakespeare, Milton, and the book of Revelations; of Mr Wilberforce, Mr Arden, and Mr Scott, foiling them each with their own weapons, and citing, with the most happy ease and correctness, passages from almost the same pages that controverted their quotations, and told strongly for the bill' (i, 59). When Fox and the seven commissioners appointed by his bill were caricatured by Scott as Revelation's Beast with seven heads, Sheridan returned the text in kind by quoting 'three more verses from the Revelations, by which he metamorphosed the beast with seven heads, with crowns on them, into seven angels, clothed in pure and white linen'.[15] As Puff remarks in the context of another kind of debate, 'the *pro & con* goes as smart as hits in a fencing match'.[16]

The point that Sheridan challenged his adversaries on their own and chosen ground, quoting 'from almost the same pages', is important. Although he apparently managed to consult some pages of the book of Revelations in the course of the debate, he could not have known in advance the authorities which would be cited against the bill. His achievement in successively capping his rivals' quotations was as much a triumphant demonstration of his presence of mind as of his knowledge. He was to display the same resourcefulness on many other occasions: in January 1789, for example, when he disputed the accuracy and applicability of a quotation from Demosthenes made by Lord Belgrave (i, 438), or in April 1794 when he aggressively capped Burke's quotation from the political songwriter, Charles Morris, with another from the same source (ii, 345). The presence of mind and apparent spontaneity he displayed at such moments were susceptible to antithetical constructions. If interpreted as signs of sincerity, the unfeigned indicators of true feeling, they might contribute to the formation of a positive ethos. In turn, if interpreted as signs of shallowness and theatricality, they might offer materials from which his opponents could construct a more hostile image. Obviously there were times when Sheridan was able to undertake extensive and careful preparation (when he was introducing a motion, for example), and there were many others when his stance was studied, collected, and responsible: when he presented himself as an advocate for millions rather than an ingenious debater. Yet his practice as a speaker – and also, it would appear, as a playwright – seems to embody improvisation and spontaneity as important cultural ideals. In the course of his celebrated oration on the Begums of Oude, he gives an indication of his respect for the truth value of unpremeditated speech. Warren Hastings's counsel had explained that certain deficiencies in the defence Hastings had delivered to the House of Commons were owing to hasty preparation. 'I do not suppose it to be taken for granted', mocked Sheridan, 'that, when Mr Hastings speaks in a hurry, he necessarily speaks falsehood; as if the truth lay deep, but the falsehood came of course; as if to shape a truth required labour, pain and caution, but when he is off his guard, the falsehoods float on the surface and come of themselves all at once.'[17] His own favoured self-image as a spontaneous speaker, impassioned or witty, is played off again and again in his confrontations with Pitt.

II

In parliamentary discourse the speaker's character, potentially a powerful instrument of persuasion, is never possessed with absolute security. It emerges from exchanges with an adversary who is cast as the political and ethical opposite against whom the speaker may be positively defined. These constructions, however, rarely go uncontested: the adversary's character is discovered and projected as part of the same process, through counter-constructions of rival and of self. Such struggles over identity, in which real ideological and cultural differences are involved, are of signal importance in the period under review.

At the age of twenty-one William Pitt delivered his maiden parliamentary speech, just three months after Sheridan had delivered his, and made an immediately favourable impression. For the next twenty years they were to be commonly regarded as political and temperamental opposites. In their frequent exchanges in the Commons they certainly tended to project themselves as such, whatever the truth of the biographical record may have been. In their early confrontations Sheridan adopted the unflappable demeanour of a man experienced in social intercourse and public affairs, in contrast to the youthful Pitt, whom he represented as petulant, callow and unworldly. Thus, in the most celebrated of these incidents, he figured his rival as Ben Jonson's '*Angry Boy* in the *Alchymist*' (i, 38) in retaliation for allusions Pitt had made to his theatrical connections, then still regarded in polite circles as 'low' and vaguely disreputable.

An otherwise forgettable debate of May 1785 on Pitt's proposal to levy a tax on female servants further illustrates the argumentative ends to which such a contrast could be put. Sheridan objected to Pitt's plan, seeing it as a threat to the integrity of the family itself. If the proposal were to be accepted, he argued, then the tax 'ought at least to be balanced with a tax on single men, who certainly were a description of persons less useful to the community than men who were married, and had families . . . the tax on female servants could be considered in no other light than as a bounty to batchelors, and a penalty upon propagation' (i, 126). The assembled members would certainly have understood this as a personal allusion to Pitt. Unattached when Sheridan spoke, he was to remain unmarried throughout his life. More importantly, perhaps, he reputedly betrayed few signs of a sexual interest in women.[18] Contemporary reports indicate that his reputation for chastity could be made to serve quite different rhetorical ends, confirming Aristotle's insight that the same elements of character can be made to support opposing conclusions in an argument.

Pitt's reputed celibacy was interpreted by his opponents as a sign of his unnaturalness rather than of his purity. 'The immaculate continence of this British *Scipio*, so strongly insisted on by his friends, as constituting one of the most shining ingredients of his *uncommon* character, is only alluded to here as a received fact, and not by any means as a reproach' was a typically sly observation made by an anti-Pittite commentator during the

Westminster campaign of 1784.[19] As James Morwood has shown, Pitt's adversaries, including Sheridan, sometimes suggested, through innuendo and allusion, that Pitt was homosexual.[20] In the Commons the scope for introducing personal allusions of this sort was necessarily constrained by the conventions of parliamentary decorum, yet references to Pitt's sexuality – or the alleged lack of it – were nonetheless made. Nathaniel Wraxall records an incident when Pitt's temporary absence from the Chamber prevented opposition members from moving an adjournment at a time when their eagerness to see Sarah Siddons perform her celebrated role as Belvidera in *Venice Preserved* made them particularly anxious to suspend business for the day. 'As soon as the door opened and he made his appearance,' recalled Wraxall, 'one of them, a man of classic mind – it was Sheridan – exclaimed, "Jam redit et virgo!"'[21] Wraxall's text interestingly indicates how Pitt's sexual character was susceptible to both positive and negative constructions. On the one hand Wraxall argues that 'the correctness of his deportment and regularity of his private life . . . which, under Charles II . . . would have counted for little in the scale, operated with decisive effect in his favour under a prince such as George III'. Yet by the same token he goes on to concede that 'He was not . . . attached to the commonwealth by those endearing ties which blend the statesman with the husband and the father, thus giving a species of compound pledge for exemplary conduct to the country'.[22]

Sheridan may have had little personal interest in Pitt's private character but his speeches show that he understood how to exploit it in political argument. In his repeated contests with Pitt, but with special urgency in their debates of the 1790s, he produces a critical construction of his opponent as one who is chaste, chilly, and austere, whose haughtiness and remoteness from the world and its ordinary sympathies render him incapable of understanding the people, and consequently disqualify him from governing them wisely. The favoured image of Sheridan and his Foxite allies was this construction's other side: they represented themselves as sociable, gregarious, spontaneously good-natured, and bound to the people, whose parliamentary spokesmen they considered themselves to be, by unbreakable bonds of sympathy and concord. In turn Pitt and his lieutenants sought to contest this image, producing a different version from similar materials: in place of sociability, they found dissoluteness; in place of patriotism they found a bid for 'popularity' in the narrow and negative eighteenth-century sense: a factious appeal to the people, motivated by self-interest and ambition alone. And finally the Pittites saw in the chastity of their leader a positive image of moral correctness, incorruptibility, self sacrifice, and unusual dedication to public duty.

As I have argued elsewhere, in the 1790s this rhetorical context within Parliament was part of a larger struggle for national identity.[23] The remote and unsociable Pitt of Sheridan's speeches was also represented as somehow un-English: he was so out of touch with the current of national feeling that he had erroneously come to suspect the people of harbouring sentiments of disloyalty. In an important speech of 5 January 1795, Sheridan alluded to Pitt as 'a haughty and stiff-necked minister who never mixed in a popular assembly' and concluded that 'such a minister can have no communication with the people of England, except through the medium of spies and informers; he is unacquainted with the mode in which their sentiments are expressed, and cannot make allowance for the language of toasts and resolutions adopted in an unguarded and convivial hour' (ii, 452). To reverse this picture is to discover Sheridan's ideal political self-image. The Foxites, for whom he was a leading spokesman, prided themselves on being the one reliable channel between Parliament and the people; their very conviviality and the breadth of their social contacts made them in their own minds the authentic representatives of the mass of the people 'out of doors'. When a petition for parliamentary reform was presented to the House in 1793 by the Sheffield Constitutional Society, Sheridan was one of the very few members to defend its artisan authors against those who objected to the supposed indecency and lowness of its address.[24] Pitt, according to the counter-image industriously disseminated by Sheridan, could only communicate with the people through intermediaries. Personally aloof and austere, he did not understand their language, their customs, or their political culture.

In this respect, Sheridan alleged, Pitt's conduct as first minister was decidedly unfilial. On hearing the younger Pitt deliver his maiden speech, Burke is supposed to have remarked that 'He is not a chip of the old block: he is the old block itself!' In his speeches Sheridan did much to counter this impression. Whereas his plays generally sympathize with the young in their struggle to resist the tyranny of the old, in his speeches against Pitt Sheridan reverses these conventions of plot and invokes the example of the father against the ideologically wayward son. To quote the elder against the younger Pitt became a favoured strategy of Foxite argument. Thus in the speech of 5 January 1795 Sheridan cites the authority of Chatham against his son's support for the suspension of habeas corpus, declaring that 'he would say with the father of the right hon. gentleman . . . who, when he was asked whether he would submit to a tyranny of forty days, answered – "No; he would not consent that the people of England should be fettered and shackled even for an hour."' (ii, 439).

III

As we have seen, Sheridan complained that Pitt's aloofness rendered him incapable of understanding how people behave 'in an unguarded and convivial hour'. Whatever other faults they may have committed, Sheridan and the Foxites could not have been charged with lacking conviviality. Sheridan's election to Parliament in September 1780 was followed shortly after, and almost as significantly, by his election as a member of Brooks's, the fashionable London club favoured by the Whig élite. Membership of Brooks's assured him access to Fox's social circle which, as L. G. Mitchell points out, was also a political network.[25] Foxite social life, in which Sheridan was by all accounts an enthusiastic participant, had a distinctive, not to say notorious, style, the principal characteristics of which were sociability, prodigality, infidelity, exuberance, recklessness and debt. Fox himself was the very embodiment of this culture of aristocratic excess. The younger son of an exceptionally wealthy peer, he was a spectacularly extravagant gambler who was reputed to stake a thousand pounds on the turn of a single card.[26] Yet, like Sheridan, he also fostered a reputation as a man of the people: not only as one who was a defender of popular rights and causes in the parliamentary arena but also, and just as importantly, as one who had a special sympathy for, and understanding of, the temper of the people at large. The fact that in Parliament he represented Westminster which, with about 12,000 eligible voters, was one of the largest electorates in the country, lent support to this popular self-image.

Although he is now often described as a political failure, Fox seems to have carried off with considerable aplomb what may strike us as an exacting rhetorical task: to claim to serve the true interests of the people while continuing to enjoy a lifestyle of immense privilege and indulgence. Doubtless there were some among the crowds he courted who took exception to his conspicuous prodigality. Yet as Sheridan's generally positive, if not entirely uncritical, characterization of Charles Surface suggests, for much of the eighteenth century prodigality could also be read, and projected, as generosity of spirit and an invigorating freedom from restraint. As such, it could also play a part in the shaping of a popular political identity. In this context Ronald Paulson sees Fox as the true heir of John Wilkes, the foremost eighteenth-century practitioner of a politics of excess.[27] Foxite triumphs such as the Westminster campaign of 1784 certainly lend themselves to such an interpretation. Contemporary representations of the election depict it as a carnivalesque event which occasioned an extraordinary, if temporary, breaking down of the barriers which separated the popular from the polite. Fox's ally, and Sheridan's intimate friend, the Duchess of Devonshire, was lampooned in the prints for canvassing for the votes of the tradesmen of Westminster, while the carriage conveying the Prince of Wales, the Foxites' royal supporter, was reportedly prominent in a triumphal procession headed by twenty-four butchers bearing marrowbones and cleavers.[28]

The gregariousness for which Fox was famous was evidently an important ingredient of his political style. According to one of his biographers, 'wherever he went he was as much at ease in the company of domestics and tradesmen as he was in conversation with lords and ladies'.[29] To some extent this distinctly aristocratic style of easy sociability can be said to have shaped Foxite political practice. Unlike Pitt, the Foxites placed a high value on the mode of direct address to popular assemblies. In late 1795, for example, their campaign against the Two Acts, introduced by Pitt with a view to checking the circulation of radical opinion, was pursued almost simultaneously within Parliament and outside it in nearby Westminster Yard where they addressed large public protest meetings. Earlier that year in a speech at the Whig Club (itself a place of convivial resort for the leading Whigs) Sheridan had commended the public meeting as

> the best, the safest, and the most rational means of collecting and ascertaining the public feeling and decision. This had ever been and would continue to be his opinion, in spite of the authority of those whose principles, corrupted by the early possession of power, had imbibed a solitary disdain of all popular assemblies, and whose practices but too truly justified their dread of the effects of them.[30]

In often adverse political circumstances Sheridan did more than any other Foxite (Fox himself excepted) to shape a distinctive parliamentary character for his party as the Friends of the People. That character, however, proved difficult to sustain convincingly. In the 1790s it was being exposed on two fronts. In the Commons the remote and frigid Pitt of

Sheridan's construction was successfully inventing himself as incorruptible and purposeful, as one whose ethos of administrative efficiency, financial rectitude, and public service was arguably more attuned to the temper of the times.[31] If in one sense the Foxites seemed ideologically 'progressive' (in their support for parliamentary reform, for example), in cultural terms they were perhaps beginning to look outmoded. Outside Westminster their essentially aristocratic conception of their role as Friends of the People was being challenged by the development of radical organizations and societies representing the interests of tradesmen, artisans, and dissenting professionals who did not want the assistance of such 'friends' or who at any rate did not trust them.[32]

Sheridan's contacts with the members of such groups as the London Corresponding Society and the Society for Constitutional Information were unusually wide for a parliamentarian; he would have been fully apprised of the suspicion and even disdain in which his own organization, the Society of the Friends of the People, was held by extra-parliamentary reformers. In his speech of 5 January 1795 he illustrates the extent of artisan disillusion with the parliamentary establishment by referring revealingly to an incident he had witnessed during the recently concluded treason trials:

> When one of the Sheffield witnesses . . . was asked why his society declined communicating with the Friends of the People, he answered that he would tell them very plainly, that they did not believe them to be honest; that there were several of them members of parliament; that they had some of them been in place; and that they conceived the ins and the outs, however they might vary in their profession, to be actuated by the same motives of interest. I, who might be as little implicated in such a charge as any man, felt rebuked and subdued by the answer. (ii, 453)

Considered against this background, the stance of the Foxites, articulated so ably by Sheridan in his contests with Pitt, seems a precarious one. In such circumstances it is perhaps not surprising that Sheridan's political identity and parliamentary voice were commonly regarded as unstable.

Sheridan's acquaintance, the young George Canning, was an astute and unforgiving critic of such instability. In June 1795 he recorded his impressions of the most recent in a series of parliamentary debates on the Prince of Wales's debts. The debate, he noted in a somewhat garbled entry in his journal, 'was somewhat livelier than usual – being diversified by a speech from Sheridan, the strangest and most incongruous and unconstruable that ever fell from the mouth of man – toading, republican, full of economy and of generosity, and in short a medley of sentiments irreconcilable in themselves, but which it was business to court the Prince and keep well with the people by endeavouring to reconcile.'[33] Although Canning found the speech entertaining, it was evidently in his view a serious rhetorical failure. And that failure, we might infer from his analysis, was the consequence of contradictions within Sheridan's political self.

During the Regency Crisis of 1788–9 Sheridan had been closer to the Prince of Wales personally and politically than any other parliamentarian and despite a subsequent cooling in their relations, his association with the Prince was still widely regarded as the key to his fortunes. Yet, as we have seen, Sheridan's political stance as a Foxite Whig was that of an upholder of the rights and interests of the people at large against the encroachments of Crown prerogative. Canning's commentary demonstrates how difficult it could be to reconcile these roles. Sheridan the intriguer and habitué of the royal closet was always potentially at odds with Sheridan the reformer and self-proclaimed Friend of the People. His rhetorical dilemma was especially acute in June 1795, for the crisis of the Prince's debts coincided with a period of severe scarcity in the country. To have rewarded the Prince for his profligacy when the high price of provisions was causing real hardship would have been impolitic and, one might think, distasteful. In this context the logic of an amendment moved by Sheridan in the debate of 5 June becomes clear. Arguing that the sum required to pay off the Prince's debts should not be taken from the public purse, Sheridan moved that 'it becomes the house to consider whether this additional provision may not be made without laying any additional burden on the people, by the reduction of useless and inconvenient places' (ii, 499). Canning read this revival of the old opposition cry against Crown patronage as Sheridan's cynical attempt to reassert his popular credentials. It appeared to him to confirm the impression that Sheridan's political conduct was unusually duplicitous and self-serving. According to the analogy that was predictably drawn by hostile commentators, there was as at least as much of Joseph as of Charles Surface in his political composition.

The debate on the Prince's debts, while of no great importance in itself, allows us a glimpse of a complex and elusive political identity. Sheridan's theatricality, his tendency to shift between different roles, and his capacity to invent himself rhetorically were much noted by contemporary observers, and were generally ascribed to some deep-seated defects of personality. Yet ultimately such explanations seem reductive. In many ways Sheridan's instability was also that of his chosen party, the Foxite Whigs, and of a political style of which he was both a producer and a product.

Notes

1 *The Parliamentary History of England, from the Earliest Period to the Year 1803*, comp. W. Cobbett. 36 volumes (London, 1806–20) xxxi, 206. Hereafter cited as *PH*.
2 Aristotle, *On Rhetoric*, trans. G. A. Kennedy (New York and Oxford, 1991), p. 38.
3 Ibid., p. 120.
4 Ibid., p. 83.
5 For extended discussion of the issues touched on in this paragraph, see M. Billig, *Arguing and Thinking: A Rhetorical Approach to Social Psychology* (Cambridge, 1987), especially pp. 31–50, and *Ideology and Opinions: Studies in Rhetorical Psychology* (London, 1991), pp. 1–56; D. Leith and G. Myerson, *The Power of Address: Explorations in Rhetoric* (London, 1989), pp. 79–113.
6 *The Speeches of the Late Right Honourable Richard Brinsley Sheridan*. Three volumes (London, 1842; rpt. New York, 1969), i, 17. As in this instance, the *Speeches* sometimes cites Sheridan's interlocutors. Unless otherwise stated all subsequent references to Sheridan's speeches are to this edition.
7 *PH*, xxxi, 640.
8 J. Loftis, *Sheridan and the Drama of Georgian England* (Oxford, 1976), pp. 6–7.
9 For Courtenay's speech, see *PH*, xxi, 1277–83.
10 Ibid., xxxi, 1077, 1080–1.
11 Ibid., 381.
12 Ibid., 174.
13 *The Historical and Posthumous Memoirs of Sir Nathaniel Wraxall*, ed. H. B. Wheatley. Five volumes (London, 1884), iii, 12.
14 Ibid., iii, 169.
15 For the full debate, see *PH*, xxiv, 10–61.
16 *The Critic*, II.ii.374–5.
17 *Speeches of the Managers and Counsel in the Trial of Warren Hastings*, ed. E. A. Bond. Four volumes (London, 1859–61), i, 491. This shorthand transcription is the most reliable report of Sheridan's Westminster Hall speeches.
18 See J. Ehrman, *The Younger Pitt: The Years of Acclaim* (London, 1969), pp. 108–9.
19 *History of the Westminster Election*, 2nd edn (London, 1785), p. 280.
20 J. Morwood, *The Life and Works of Richard Brinsley Sheridan* (Edinburgh, 1985), p. 110.
21 Wraxall, *Memoirs*, iii, 219. Sheridan's allusion is to the predicted return of Astraea in Virgil's fourth Eclogue.

22 Ibid., iii, 232–3.

23 C. Reid, 'Patriotism and rhetorical contest in the 1790s: the context of Sheridan's *Pizarro*' in *Comedy: Essays in Honour of Peter Dixon*, ed. Elizabeth Maslen (London, 1993), pp. 231–50.

24 *PH*, xxx, 775–85. See A. Goodwin, *The Friends of Liberty: The English Democratic Movement in the Age of the French Revolution* (London, 1979), pp. 276–80.

25 L. G. Mitchell, *Charles James Fox and the Disintegration of the Whig Party 1782–1794* (Oxford, 1971), pp. 251–62.

26 See L. Reid, *Charles James Fox: A Man for the People* (London, 1969), pp. 122–4.

27 R. Paulson, *Representations of Revolution (1789–1820)*, (New Haven and London, 1983), pp. 140–1.

28 Reid, *Charles James Fox*, p. 204.

29 Ibid., p. 346.

30 W. Cobbett, *The Political Proteus. A View of the Public Character and Conduct of R. B. Sheridan, Esq*. (London, 1804), pp. 363–4. Cobbett usefully collects 'Extracts from Mr. Sheridan's Speeches at the Whig Club, and other Public Meetings' at the close of this vituperative work (pp. 345–88).

31 On this point, see L. Colley, *Britons: Forging the Nation 1707–1837* (New Haven and London, 1992), pp. 189–93.

32 See P. J. Brunsdon, 'The Association of the Friends of the People', unpublished MA thesis, University of Manchester (1961).

33 *The Letter-Journal of George Canning*, ed. P. Jupp (London, 1991), p. 265.

8

The political career of Richard Brinsley Sheridan

CHRISTOPHER CLAYTON

When Thomas Moore was preparing his biography of Sheridan he was told by Lord Thanet that Sheridan never liked any allusion to his being a dramatic writer.[1] Outstanding success as a playwright eased, and arguably enabled, Sheridan's introduction to the society of the Westminster political world, but his theatrical work, both as writer and manager, was a potent reminder that Sheridan had to work for a living and did not spring from a background of landed wealth and aristocratic leisure. This background remained the most powerful qualification for political leadership amongst the Whig élite – far more powerful than the recommendation of talent by itself. Charles James Fox could offer both talent and aristocratic pedigree, and in that fact lies the single most important explanation of why Fox could lead the Whigs, in spite of his manifest lack of judgement on occasion, and why Sheridan could never be seen as a legitimate Whig leader. Not only did allusions to Sheridan's theatrical background carry a clear message of his status as a parvenu on the political stage, but association with the theatre carried with it a distinctly disreputable aura. As the young George Canning explained to his mother, an actress: 'there is perhaps no subject on which public opinion decides more positively than on the respectability or *dis*respectability of different pursuits and occupations . . . the world is capricious and unjust – but it is peremptory – and to explain myself fully – need I do more than ask you – to what cause is Mr Sheridan's want of success and popularity to be attributed?'[2]

Had Sheridan been prepared to sacrifice his views on matters connected with the constitution, the problems of Ireland, the removal of religious disabilities and the plight of the poor and politically unenfranchised, he too, by joining his talents to those who served Pitt, might, like Canning, have achieved high office, but at the cost of sacrificing political principles and political friendship. Refusal to sacrifice either tied Sheridan's political fortunes to a set of politicians whose prejudices were aristocratic and exclusive. Sheridan's political career can thus be seen as a demonstration of the limited opportunities available to a non-aristocratic 'man of talent' in the Whig party of the late eighteenth and early nineteenth centuries. This has wider implications concerning both the development of political parties in this period and the progress of liberal reform. In particular, the weakness of the Whig party in the first decades of the nineteenth century can be explained by the deflection of ambitious, talented non-aristocrats of liberal temperament into the Tory camp, where their liberal aspirations were frustrated, often by monarchical prejudice. Sheridan's experience in politics at the hands of the Whig leadership can help to explain why this happened. This essay seeks to show why Sheridan's political career was a failure in comparison with his brief, glittering success as a playwright in the 1770s. It is also contended that his was not a dishonourable failure; he did remain loyal to political friendships and principles.

Sheridan's political career can be divided into four, broadly distinct, chronological periods. During the first decade of his parliamentary career Sheridan rose steadily to a position of considerable prominence in the House of Commons, making his mark as a notable exponent of the Rockingham/Foxite Whig thesis that the events of these years demonstrated an alarming growth of executive power. There were occasional flashes of independence, as when he disagreed with Fox on the latter's Bill to replace the existing Marriage Act on 15 June 1781,[3] and when he objected to Pitt's Irish commercial propositions in 1785 from a perspective that was specifically defensive of Irish constitutional rights rather than of British manufacturers' rights. Speaking in the debate of 30 May 1785 he declared that 'he was the mouth of no party . . . nor was he the tool of any party'.[4] This was perhaps to protect his arguments from the odium in which the Foxites were then held as a result of Pitt's victory in 1784. But that he *was* a party man was acknowledged by his sister, Betsy Sheridan, who commented 'he acts on this occasion from his own feelings, totally independent of any wish *his party* may have to harass the Minister' (my italics).[5]

The second period dates from 1789–90, when the impact of the French Revolution began to be felt on British politics. Sheridan acquired an unjustified reputation for dangerous radicalism and acted as a catalyst in the process which led to the break-up of the Whig party in 1794. During the 1790s Sheridan steadfastly supported Fox in his stand against the war with

France and in his belief that the real danger to British liberties derived from the growth of executive power and not from popular radicalism. But from 1797, the third period of his career, Sheridan appeared to follow a much more independent line, refusing to join the Foxite secession from Parliament in 1797 and calling for a united, patriotic resistance to the danger of a French invasion. During Addington's ministry he was in open disagreement with Fox's parliamentary tactics, although after 1804 he appeared to be reconciled again with his political colleagues. The fourth period encompasses the years 1806–12. The disappointment of Sheridan's political ambitions when the Ministry of All the Talents was formed in 1806 produced the final estrangement from the Whigs, led after Fox's death by Grey and Grenville. From 1807 he owed his seat in Parliament to the Prince of Wales's patronage. From 1809 he seemed to be moving closer to George Canning, who, before serving in Pitt's ministry, had been a protégé of Sheridan. Sheridan's career ended in 1812 when he failed to win back his seat in Stafford.

In thirty-two years in Parliament Sheridan enjoyed three brief spells in government: as Under-Secretary for Foreign Affairs in the short-lived Rockingham administration of 1782; as Joint Secretary to the Treasury in the Fox-North coalition in 1783 and finally, in January 1806, as Treasurer of the Navy in the Ministry of All the Talents. This was a post vacated by the much younger George Canning which Sheridan had been promised almost twenty years previously at the time of the first Regency Crisis.[6] This was the rather feeble reward for having been 'Thirty years a Whig Politician and six and twenty years in Parliament, and having expended full £20,000 of my own money to maintain my seat there and in all the course of political life struggling thro' great di[f]ficulties and risking the existence of the only Property I had'.[7] That Sheridan did not have more opportunities to serve in government is due to his party loyalty and the antagonism of George III to the Rockingham/Foxite Whigs. But that Sheridan did not rise higher within the party when the opportunity afforded is due in large measure to the conservative aristocratic ethos of the leaders of that party, including Fox. Why and how Sheridan became a Foxite Whig is, therefore, a central question.

The evidence concerning Sheridan's earliest political thinking indicates little common ground with the Rockingham Whigs. A letter published in the *Public Advertiser* on 16 October 1769, chiefly intended to criticize the style of a correspondent who signed himself 'Novus', contained an oblique defence of Lord Bute, who was regarded by the Newcastle/Rockingham Whigs as the tool of George III and the means of their downfall in 1762.[8] A draft for an essay entitled *Essay on Absentees*, probably written about 1778, criticized the behaviour of Irish landlords, such as the Marquis of Rockingham and other Whig landowners, for the problems which their absenteeism caused in Ireland.[9] Jottings made probably in 1776 for a reply to Johnson's *Taxation No Tyranny* had, however, shown sympathy for the Whig point of view on the issue of America, in that Sheridan sought to show that taxation of the American colonists could not be justified by theories of virtual representation.[10]

Sheridan was drawn first into metropolitan Whig social life, and then into Whig politics, for two principal reasons. First, his marriage to the beautiful singer, Elizabeth Linley, who was much sought after for private recitals in the homes of the nobility, obtained for Sheridan an entry to Devonshire House society, at the heart of the Whig élite. Subsequently, in 1780, Georgiana, Duchess of Devonshire, a member of the Spencer family, was to exert the Spencer interest in Stafford to help secure Sheridan's election to the House of Commons.[11]

The second factor was Sheridan's developing friendship with Charles James Fox. Thomas Moore relates that Fox was immediately impressed by Sheridan's wit on first meeting him, probably in 1776 or 1777.[12] At that time Fox himself was only just moving towards political co-operation with the Rockingham Whigs under the influence of Edmund Burke.[13] As a former member of North's government, and the son of Henry Fox, who loomed almost as large as Bute in the Whig demonology, Fox was hardly an orthodox Whig. Fox presided over Sheridan's election to the Literary Club on 11 March 1777 and after the success of *The School for Scandal* later that year was known to regard Sheridan as 'the first Genius of these times'.[14] Apart from mutual admiration there was their shared family connections with the deposed Stuart dynasty to draw them together. Fox, whose first two names were more than usually significant, could trace his ancestry back through his mother and the Dukes of Richmond to Charles II. In contrast with Sheridan, Fox could lay claim to high aristocratic pedigree, but the uncle of Sheridan's grandfather had been secretary to James II in exile and his grandfather's cousin had been knighted during the 1745 Jacobite rebellion by the Young Pretender.[15]

From a letter written on 4 January 1773, it is clear that Sheridan had been contemplating a career in politics. Rejecting a life of private enjoyment he asked, 'Was it meant that we should shrink from the active Principles of Virtue, and consequent[ly] of true Happiness . . .?'[16] It was not surprising that Sheridan's ambition was kindled by the admiration of members of the political élite. Sheridan now saw a political life as the means to social elevation and personal satisfaction. As he put it in another letter, written on 24 February 1773,

> The Track of a Comet is as regular to the eye of God as the orbit of a planet . . . as God very often pleases to let down great Folks from the elevated stations which they might claim as their Birthright, there can be no reason for us to suppose that He does not mean that others should ascend etc.[17]

Speaking in the House of Commons in June 1804 he uttered similar sentiments: 'there is nothing of honour, emolument or wealth which is not within the reach of a man of merit . . . I would call on the humblest peasant to defend his son's title to the great seal of England.'[18]

Such views were too advanced for the Whig party to which Sheridan became attached through his connection with Fox. But Sheridan's talents were useful assets to the forces fighting Lord North's alleged incompetence and the supposed growth of executive power which threatened to unbalance the constitution. In particular, Sheridan was able to provide a link between the Whig leaders in Parliament and the sources of extra-parliamentary discontent. He contributed to a periodical, *The Englishman*, addressed to the 'freeholders of England', urging them to turn against the alleged corruption of the North ministry. Along with other Whigs, Sheridan was present at the founding meeting of the Westminster Committee of Association, established to join the pressure for parliamentary reform being exerted by Christopher Wyvill's county association movement; two months later he was present at the inaugural meeting of the Society for Constitutional Information. Under Sheridan's chairmanship a sub-committee of the Westminster Association, established to enquire into the 'state of the Representation', produced a report which considered that the representative system was even more unfair at representing property (assessed through regional land tax contributions) than electors. It was perhaps because of the influence of Sheridan and Fox that the Westminster Committee was diverted from more radical solutions than those being advocated by Wyvill's country gentlemen, but as popular pressure for reform began to decline, so Sheridan's attendances at committee meetings became fewer.[19] When Sheridan entered the House of Commons in

September 1780 he was already an established Foxite. A promising political future seemed to beckon as North's ministry tottered.

In Parliament Sheridan consolidated his position as a loyal Foxite. He was at least as vehement as Fox in his condemnation of Shelburne's behaviour during the Rockingham administration and did not hesitate to follow Fox into opposition when Shelburne succeeded Rockingham as First Lord of the Treasury. There is some doubt as to what he really thought about the wisdom of the Fox-North coalition and of introducing the East India Bill at that time,[20] but Sheridan later played a prominent part in attacking Pitt's own Bill, introduced in 1784, and in the impeachment proceedings against Warren Hastings, in each case with the intention of vindicating Fox's coalition government and its actions.[21] In 1788 Sheridan wrote *A Comparative Statement of the Two Bills for the Better Government of the British Possessions in India*, which contained a systematic attack on the principles underlying Pitt's style of government. He was central to the Foxites' attempts to create a favourable impression of themselves in the newspapers and he took over the difficult, but vital, brief of opposition spokesman on financial and taxation affairs, in which Fox had no interest at all.[22] He was a zealous proponent of the view that the manner in which Pitt and the King were able to overwhelm the Fox-North coalition in 1783–4 was proof of a constitutional crisis, in which the House of Commons was losing power and influence as a result of the contrivances of a wily, ambitious king and unscrupulous ministers. Although he supported parliamentary reform when the question was brought forward in Parliament, Sheridan did not offend the conservative aristocratic Whigs by unnecessarily pressing the issue. When he was asked to bring forward the question of reform of the notoriously corrupt Scottish burghs by a committee of delegates from the burghs in 1787, he brought forward his motion very late in the session. Even after 1789, when there was more political capital to be gained from supporting such a measure, as popular interest in reform revived under the impact of the French Revolution, Sheridan was cautious in his approach, prompting the historian John Cannon to comment that his campaign on behalf of the burghs had 'the impetuosity of a slow bicycle race'.[23] Parliamentary reform was never a fundamental principle of Foxite belief. Sheridan, more than most politicians of his generation, was aware of the value of courting extra-parliamentary opinion, but even he was reported to have said in November 1794 'in the hearing of Lord Fitzwilliam' at Brooks's that it was 'the present intention of the Friends of the People to abandon all thoughts of Parliamentary

Reform unless called for by two-thirds of the People'.[24] If this is true, Sheridan was obviously trying to conciliate those aristocrats whose fear of reform in the context of the French Revolution was driving them into alliance with Pitt.

In spite of Sheridan's manifest loyalty and usefulness, tension was generated within the party by Sheridan's equally manifest ambition. He believed his talents entitled him in due course to a position of leadership. This did not fit the Whig view that for liberty to survive in the balanced constitution established at the Glorious Revolution, the leading parts in government must be undertaken by men of wealth, property and education, who could be relied upon to be independent and were thus immune to the blandishments of ambitious kings.[25] Such men could only be aristocrats and they took on governmental office as an obligation and not primarily as an object of ambition.

Particularly worrying to the other Foxites was Sheridan's closeness to the Prince of Wales. In 1786 Sheridan had been involved in trying to sort out the Prince's finances – a grave embarrassment to the Foxites who had so clearly attempted to secure the Prince's favour. It was Sheridan who managed to save the situation in 1787, after Fox had denied there was any truth in the rumour of a marriage between the Prince and Mrs Fitzherbert. This exploit enhanced Sheridan's position at Carlton House and irritated Fox. Fox was further irritated by Sheridan's assumption of a leadership role in November 1788 when the Regency Crisis developed while Fox was abroad. The Duchess of Devonshire recorded two quarrels between Fox and Sheridan at this time – on 20 December and 2 January.[26] Fox was not the only one to be alarmed at Sheridan's assumption of a position of eminence. Charles Grey believed Sheridan had deliberately humiliated him in front of the Prince.[27] Later in 1789 another quarrel between Grey and Sheridan nearly produced a duel.[28] The Duke of Portland was reported to be offended by the close consultation between the Prince and Sheridan in November 1788[29] and at the end of January 1789 Portland declared his determination 'not to act with Mr Sheridan in council'.[30]

More significantly for the events to come, Sheridan's relations with Burke were deteriorating. Burke was deeply irritated by the manner in which both Sheridan and Fox began to lose interest in the impeachment of Warren Hastings once it became clear that it would not undermine Pitt. To Burke, the Hastings trial was a moral issue, not a question of party politics. Sheridan's advance presented a direct challenge to Burke's own influence over Fox; the fact that Burke's advice during the Regency Crisis was ignored seemed to demonstrate the effects of Sheridan's rise. Fox's enthusiastic support for the removal of the legal penalties on the Dissenters seemed to show that Fox was being pushed in the direction of more radical and dangerous ideas and this was ascribed to Sheridan's influence. This impression was confirmed by the enthusiastic reception that Fox and Sheridan gave to the French Revolution.

Burke's resentment exploded on 9 February 1790 in the debate on the Army Estimates, when Burke and Fox clashed openly on the subject of the French Revolution. Sheridan then vehemently disagreed with Burke.[31] Although Sheridan seems 'to have expressed some contrition for his conduct on the very evening the conversation passed',[32] there was no wish for reconciliation on Burke's part. From this point on, there was an open struggle for the nature of the Whig party's beliefs. Sheridan was depicted by Burke and his son – and others alarmed at his apparent influence over Fox – as a dangerous demagogic manipulator. In Burke's opinion 'They who cry up the French Revolution, cry down the [Whig] Party', which was 'an aristocratic Party . . . a Party, in its composition and in its principles connected with the solid permanent long possessed property of the Country.'[33] Sheridan and others in the party were said to be 'running into Democracy'.[34]

In reality, Sheridan, and others like Charles Grey, whose social origins were more elevated, sought a moderate parliamentary reform for conservative reasons. Moderate reform was the best means of restoring the constitutional balance framed in the Revolution Settlement of 1689 and of conciliating the extra-parliamentary reformers to the substance of that settlement. Nor were the aristocratic Whig leaders to whom Burke was appealing taken in by Burke's claim that Fox and Sheridan had become the leaders of the 'New French Whigs' who cared not at all for the traditional Whig approach. There was a degree of resentment at the way in which Burke seemed to polarize the situation, pushing Fox into a more determined defence of the French Revolution and benefiting Pitt's government by dividing the opposition. But Sheridan's humble origins and rapid rise to political prominence, together with his connections with the popular societies, made him ideal for fostering the aristocrats' fears. The satirical prints delighted in portraying Sheridan as a revolutionary regicide.[35] Burke's claim that Sheridan intended to put himself at the head of a spirit of innovation and to gain by the resulting confusion had plausibility. This propaganda, articulated in the context of the issues raised by the French Revolution, derived from antecedent tensions and rivalries based on resentment of Sheridan as a parvenu who did not know the proper limits to set to his own political ambition.

Sheridan's radicalism in the 1790s consisted of support for a measure of parliamentary reform to reverse the growth in executive power when there was sufficient popular support for such a measure; resistance to Pitt's innovatory, repressive legislation of the 1790s; and rejection of the war against France as unnecessary and insidious, designed to extend executive power in Britain and restore despotism in France. With all this Fox could agree. Where they differed might have been in Sheridan's stated belief that Britain's constitution helped to create 'a people among whom all that is advantageous in private acquisition, all that is honourable in public ambition [is] equally open to the efforts, the industry and the abilities of all – among whom no sullen line of demarkation (*sic*) separates and cuts off the several orders from each other'.[36] Fox, on the other hand, told Lord Holland, just before the Whig split in 1794, 'You know I am one who think both property and rank of great importance in this country in a party view'.[37] By 1799, regarding the political situation in Britain with despair, he wrote that he could not 'help feeling every day more and more, that in this country at least, an aristocratic party is absolutely necessary to the preservation of liberty'.[38] Although Fox carried little or no ideological baggage, he recognized that the only way to power after Pitt's resignation in 1801, and then after his death in 1806, was through broadening the party to bring in those aristocratic elements whose prejudices were not compatible with Sheridan's ambition. Sheridan was to reap little reward for continuing the parliamentary fight against Pitt during the Foxite secession.

Lord Holland told James Mackintosh that Sheridan's failure to reach the highest levels of party leadership was due to his 'peculiarities' rather than to Whig snobbery. He claimed that if distinctions based on birth mattered 'They were in fact less in the real and practical estimation of the Party called Whigs than of that of the Society in which they lived'.[39] For a party that claimed to stand for the public interest, aristocratic exclusivity was hard to admit openly. Lady Bessborough stated that she 'should approve of a great deal in his [Sheridan's] language and conduct . . . but then a great deal is quite disgusting and it is impossible to trust him for a moment'.[40] Before the French Revolution Sheridan had been portrayed as Bardolph or compared with Joseph Surface.[41] But behind-the-scenes intrigue, whether at Carlton

House or in Grub Street, was one way in which Sheridan had made himself useful to the Whigs. And there was an argument, conceded even by Lady Holland, that Sheridan was driven to intrigue to overcome the prejudice he encountered.[42] In the early nineteenth century, when the Whigs maintained their unity through the long years of opposition by developing a Foxite cult,[43] there was a need to denigrate Sheridan because detailed examination of his career could expose serious shortcomings in Fox's. In 1818 Lord Byron told Thomas Moore, who was preparing his biography: 'The Whigs abuse him; however, he never left them, and such blunderers deserve neither credit nor compassion . . . Don't let yourself be led away by clamour, but compare him with the coalitioner Fox, and the pensioner Burke, as a man of principle, and with ten hundred thousand in personal views and with more in talent for he beat them all *out* and *out*.'[44] How justified was Whig exclusion of Sheridan on the basis of 'peculiarity'?

Sheridan's refusal to join the secession from Parliament in 1797, his advocacy of a united patriotic resistance to the danger of a French invasion and his willingness to support the Volunteer movement set up to counteract this threat – all this irritated his colleagues.[45] The apparently loyalist and aggressively anti-Napoleonist sentiments given voice in *Pizarro* bewildered them; Fox described it as the 'worst thing possible'.[46] More significantly, Fox was greatly exasperated by Sheridan's attempt to bolster the Addington government against the possibility of Pitt's return to office and consequently his rejection of the idea of an understanding with the Grenvilles in opposition to Addington. Sheridan was not alone in opposing an arrangement of political co-operation with the Grenvilles, however informal,[47] but in opposing such a link Sheridan exposed the Foxites and the Grenvilles to the same sort of condemnation that had been so damaging to the Fox-North coalition – that an unprincipled alliance was trying to restrict the king's choice of ministers. Sheridan and other anti-Grenville Foxites believed such an alliance would damage their reputation. But a sub-text to this argument was a battle for influence over Fox and the Prince of Wales. Grey was a keen supporter of co-operation with the Grenvilles, even if it meant co-operation with Pitt.[48] Fox was not in the best of health and such was his diffidence about politics that he could retire at any time. Sheridan was known to be keen to take over the prestigious constituency of Westminster in this event. Battle had been joined for the succession to Fox as leader and Sheridan had the audacity to regard himself as a realistic contender. But in the quarrel over parliamentary tactics between 1801 and

1804 Sheridan lost the battle for Fox's ear and confidence to Grey and consequently lost any hope of asserting his right to a leading position in any ministry the Foxites and their new allies might form.

Sheridan's behaviour during this quarrel provided some evidence to those who wished to prove that he lacked integrity and could not be trusted. In December, 1802, he was accused of inserting in the newspapers 'puffs' of himself alongside 'the most violent abuse' of Fox.[49] Fox claimed that he remained sympathetic to Sheridan in spite of the provocations afforded by his behaviour both in and out of Parliament, and indeed he expressed willingness for Sheridan to succeed him in Westminster. Referring to Sheridan's alleged interference in the newspapers, he told Denis O'Bryen 'that what I most feel in it is the advantages it gives to those who hate him . . . to justify suspicions which in my conscience I believe to be wholly unfounded'.[50] Yet Fox himself described Sheridan as 'mad with vanity and folly'[51] just two days before the latter made a speech calling upon Members of Parliament to show unanimity and 'not to waste that time and those talents in party spirit and intrigue, which might be so much more worthily employed in performing the sublime and animated duties of patriotism'.[52] On hearing this, Fox considered that Sheridan had 'outdone his usual outdoings. Folly beyond all the past'.[53]

Sheridan's relations with Fox reached their lowest point in early 1804, just before Pitt returned to power. Unwisely he allowed Thomas Creevey to overhear him 'damning Fox in the midst of his enemies'.[54] Creevey believed that Sheridan was 'basely playing an under game as Fox's friend in the event of defeat to him and his Dr'.[55] Although Sheridan admitted to his wife that he saw 'Fox every day – and Addington almost every evening',[56] he had never made any secret of his goodwill towards Addington's government, once it had become clear that Addington was no mere Pittite stooge. Sheridan's conduct did possess integrity, however galling it was to his colleagues. Opposition to Pitt provided a connecting thread of consistency through his conduct. Although he had called for a spirit of patriotic unity to resist French aggression in 1798, he had at the same time stated his 'irreconcilable' enmity to Pitt's government as well as his 'unaltered and unalterable' attachment to Fox and his political principles.[57] The rationale of his support for Addington was that he had made peace with the French and destroying him would only produce Pitt's return to power. Pitt was damnable in Sheridan's eyes. He practised a debased, cynical and unprincipled form of politics for the purposes of personal advancement. He had fatally weakened the cause of reform in British politics by allowing the king to defy the majority of the House of Commons in 1783, and the combined effect of the revolutionary war and the accompanying repressive legislation had been to undermine British liberties and the balanced constitution itself. Sheridan's support for Addington was only the converse of hostility to Pitt. Sheridan was scrupulous in refusing any position for himself or his son in Addington's ministry unless the Foxites came in as a body – unlike George Tierney who accepted the post of Treasurer of the Navy, but nevertheless, because of his friendship with Grey, later went on to become a leader of the Whigs in the House of Commons. Once the return of Pitt to government was assured, Sheridan could with consistency resume co-operation with Fox, even in concert with the formerly Pittite Grenvilles. Sheridan might, with justification, claim that he had remained loyal to Foxite principles, even if that had involved friction with Fox himself. He did, however, continue to differ from Fox in believing that Napoleon was motivated by a desire for territorial conquest and not for peace. He also believed it was unwise to agitate the issue of Catholic emancipation for the purpose of embarrassing Pitt while George III remained on the throne, because the only result would be to raise Catholic hopes, simply to have them dashed against the king's intransigence, with possibly disastrous consequences in Ireland. In both these judgements he was arguably more astute than Fox and Grey. When the Foxites finally took office in 1806, with the Grenvilles and the followers of Sidmouth, the Whig leaders could easily claim that Sheridan was too much of a maverick to claim the senior position in the ministry which his long service to the party and his abilities deserved. Consequently Sheridan felt no qualms about opposing his own government's plans for the country's defences in July 1806.[58]

Having crushed Sheridan's aspirations for high office, the Whig leaders, Grey and Grenville, made sure that Sheridan did not inherit Fox's seat in Westminster after his death in September 1806. Although Sheridan successfully insisted on his candidature in the general election held shortly after the by-election, the Whig party leaders did not over-exert themselves in Sheridan's interest, although he was elected. He was not so fortunate in the general election of May 1807, after the collapse of the Talents Ministry. Westminster's independent electors could no longer trust the Whigs or their representatives to support the cause of reform and Sheridan was only able to return to Parliament as Member of Parliament for a pocket borough in the gift of the Prince.[59]

Thereafter, the Whigs and Sheridan drifted further apart. Significantly, when Grey moved to the House of Lords on the death of his father in November 1807, Grenville placed an absolute veto on any aspirations Sheridan, Whitbread and Windham might have had to take over Grey's role as leader of the Whigs in the House of Commons.[60] All three were non-aristocrats. In July 1808, Grey could tell Lady Holland 'As to Sheridan's conduct in a party view that is past praying for; and in truth it is of no consequence.'[61] By 1810 Sheridan had acquired an amused detachment from the squabbles over leadership among the Whigs in the Commons. He told Lady Bessborough that the struggle for pre-eminence 'threaten'd to subdivide the subdivisions of Op[position] till they became like Atoms known to exist, but too numerous to count – and too small to be felt'.[62] After Canning's resignation from the Portland ministry in 1809, Sheridan tried to establish closer relations with him. Lady Holland described Canning as one who 'abhors titles and the aristocracy of hereditary nobility'.[63] In 1810 Sheridan claimed that he would defend Canning 'thro' thick and thin'.[64] Alliance with Canning was a means of maintaining liberal principles while at the same time challenging the exclusive, aristocratic ethos represented by Grey and Grenville.

Any remaining connection Sheridan might have had with the party led by Grey and Grenville was shattered by the events of 1810–12. With the onset of the King's terminal illness in November 1810, proceedings were set in train for the establishment of a regency. Grenville and Grey were thoroughly angered when their proposed draft for the Prince's reply to the terms of the regency offered by Perceval was altered by Sheridan. Haughtily, Grey told his wife that he had remonstrated 'on the impropriety of having the advice which Ld. Grenville and I were called upon to give subjected in this manner to the examination of an inferior council'.[65] Sheridan was accused of undermining the Prince's official advisers in the manner of Bute or Shelburne, but even Lord Holland had to admit that there was nothing official in the position of Grey and Grenville.[66] Inevitably, Sheridan was blamed for the failure of the Whigs to gain office when the limited regency came to an end and George III's incapacity seemed permanent. Holland was aware, however, that Sheridan had hoped for the non-cabinet post of Chief Secretary to Ireland in a ministry headed by Grey and Grenville. This was 'peremptorily rejected by Lord Grenville . . . Lord Grenville and Lord Grey showed upon that and every other occasion a repugnance to consult or to court him'.[67] Grey said that sending Sheridan to Ireland would have been like sending a man with a lighted torch into a magazine of gunpowder, but if it were merely a question of 'giving him a place, however high, with large emoluments, nobody would be more ready to consent to it than I should be'.[68] This was precisely the stipulation that Fitzwilliam had made in 1792 when he had said that Sheridan 'might have a lucrative place, but never could be admitted to one of trust and confidence'.[69] Finally the Whig leaders claimed that they had been deliberately misled by Sheridan into thinking that they would not be able to have control of appointments within the Prince's Household if they came into office after the assassination of Perceval in May 1812. Acting under this impression the Whig leaders refused to form a government. Sheridan was therefore given the blame for the re-establishment of a ministry unsympathetic to Catholic emancipation, under the leadership of Lord Liverpool. Thus Sheridan's reputation for double-dealing and untrustworthiness was assured.[70] But Sheridan had written to the Prince to tell him that 'a proscription of Lord Grey in the formation of a new administration would be a proceeding equally injurious to the estimation of your personal dignity and the maintenance of the Public Interests'.[71] Sheridan seems to have worked towards a coalition of groups united in their policy on the war, on the Catholic question and on Ireland; what he called 'that extended and efficient administration which the country was desirous of having'.[72] Sheridan did not want to see the continuation of an anti-Catholic administration and he refused to consider playing any part in such an administration.

In the summer of 1812 Sheridan declared his determination to work with Canning in politics from then on.[73] Anxious to prove his independence from the Prince of Wales and his ministers, he offered himself once again for his old constituency of Stafford at the general election held in October. He came bottom of the poll. The *Staffordshire Advertiser* claimed that there had been 'groundless reports' spread to injure his cause by 'vulgar and illiterate people'.[74] Sheridan claimed he had been denied money he was owed by the Drury Lane Theatre trustees under Samuel Whitbread's chairmanship.[75] Possibilities of a return to the House of Commons as representative for Wootton Bassett and subsequently Westminster came to nothing. Sheridan's political career, including his influence with the Prince, was at an end.

Writing to William Eden on 16 January 1789, the Archbishop of Canterbury, noticing the rivalries among the Foxite Whigs, drily observed that 'it is thought that things are not yet ripe enough for the manager of Drury Lane to be manager of the House of Commons'.[76] The anonymous writer of a political pamphlet published in 1794 perceptively pointed out that Sheridan had 'quit a path [in the theatre] which must have led to honest fame and competence, to prostitute his talents to a faction, who, though they pretend to reject the pretensions of illustrious extraction, still are secretly so much swayed by ancient prejudice, that they will never acknowledge the son of an actor as their leader, however superior may be his capacity'.[77] Making sure that his message was quite clear, the author added that it was Sheridan's fate 'to live for ever the drudge of a party who distrust him while they employ him; who despise his obscure birth, while they avail themselves of his talents'.[78]

The party into which Sheridan was drawn by his friendship with Charles Fox was an aristocratic party. For those who constituted the Rockingham Whig party, known after 1782 as the Foxite Whig party, the preservation of political liberty was essentially a matter of balancing out powers within the state and particularly of preventing the development of an over-mighty executive, especially monarchical, power. The Rockinghams, descendants of the 'Old Corps' Whigs who had monopolized governmental office in the previous two reigns, had adopted and adapted the arguments of the opposition to their predecessors. In the Rockingham view, however, aristocrats were cast as the guardians of constitutional liberty because not only did they possess a physical stake in the country, through the ownership of land, but they possessed the independent means to guarantee their capacity to act independently, and thus to withstand the tendency inherent in a monarchy to degenerate into despotism. Fox's objection to Pitt and Addington was that they lacked the personal fortune to be anything other than royal puppets, whereas Grenville, by contrast, had the wealth and intelligence which gave him the freedom to challenge the Crown, if the need arose. Unlike Pitt, the Grenvilles were seen as capable of becoming good party men.

Sheridan could happily agree, especially after the events of 1783–4, that the overwhelmingly important question in British politics was the danger of a growth in executive power at the expense of Parliament and the country's liberties. He could support the Whigs out of conviction, not just because of personal connections. In Shelburne's machinations in 1782 Sheridan could sense the motions of an ambitious king; the installation of Pitt in power in 1783 evinced a contempt for Parliament; Pitt's reforms of the government in India and of the trading relationship with Ireland betrayed a system hostile to constitutional rights. The repressive legislation of the 1790s convinced Sheridan that there was a deep-laid plot to introduce despotism into the country.[79] Even as late as February 1810 Sheridan could state his belief that the source of the downfall of the nations of Europe, under the Napoleonic flail, was 'the want of that salutary controul (*sic*) upon their governments, that animating source of public spirit and national exertion', provided by a free press.[80] All this could be accepted by the most aristocratic of Whigs. What could not be accepted was Sheridan's blithe assertion that 'it was the most amiable and valuable fruit of our happy constitution, that every path of honourable ambition was open to talents and industry, without distinction of ranks'.[81] Sheridan's views on liberty went beyond the traditional Whig view to something more akin to the nineteenth-century Liberal belief in equality of opportunity. Equally unsettling to his more traditional colleagues was his recognition that politics could not be confined to the Palace of Westminster. Sheridan was assiduous and adept at cultivating a wide range of political contacts outside Parliament, particularly among the popular societies and within the journalistic field.

Professor John Cannon has shown that between 1782 and 1820 sixty-five individuals held Cabinet office of whom forty-three were peers and of the remaining twenty-two fourteen were sons of peers. By his reckoning only six were genuinely non-aristocratic.[82] Of these, only William Windham could put forward any claim to having been a Rockinghamite/Foxite Whig. Significantly, two of the others on the list, Addington and George Canning, were linked politically with Sheridan. It is true that in 1806–7 the Whigs were prepared to admit Addington – a man whose origins and abilities they had previously scorned – to the Cabinet table, but on this occasion it suited their own political ambition to do so; Addington had already been raised to the peerage as Lord Sidmouth and he was from outside the party, which somehow made it more acceptable. Sheridan and Whitbread, both non-aristocratic Foxites, were excluded. Sheridan was forced to accept that cultivating the Prince of Wales and acquiring influence in the extra-parliamentary world would not be enough to overcome Whig social prejudices. By 1812 Sheridan was of the opinion that only a new party could cater for the man of talent with liberal convictions. Pittite 'Tories' were unwilling to force reform on unwilling, reactionary monarchs, although men of humble extraction could prosper well enough in their ranks if they possessed enough talent and were prepared to sacrifice any reforming proclivities. Whigs had the right ideas about civil, religious and political liberties, but remained wedded to traditional ideas of rank and deference.

In one of his last speeches in Parliament, Sheridan declared that he would never 'endure that this great country must be suffered to go drooping to perdition, because there are none but those two parties competent to direct its energies'.[83] But, failing to be elected in 1812, he never had the opportunity to see whether forging a political alliance with that other scion of the theatrical world, George Canning, would produce anything of substance in a party view. After his death in 1816 he was buried in Poets' Corner. Even in death the Whigs insisted on keeping him in his proper place.

Notes

1 *Memoirs, Journal and Correspondence of Thomas Moore*, ed. Lord J. Russell (London, 1853–6), iii, 233.

2 W. Hinde, *George Canning* (London, 1973), p. 21 (quoting from Leeds City Archives, Harewood MSS. 2: George Canning to his mother, 13 June 1791.)

3 *The Parliamentary History of England from the Earliest Period to the Year 1803*, ed. W. Cobbett (London, 1806–20), xxii, 415 (cited hereafter as *PH*).

4 *PH*, xxv, 766.

5 *Betsy Sheridan's Journal: Letters from Sheridan's Sister 1784–86; 1788–90*, ed. W. LeFanu (London, 1960), p. 58 (15–20 June 1785).

6 British Library Add. MSS. 41579 fo. 4; The Journal of Lady Elizabeth Foster.

7 *The Letters of Richard Brinsley Sheridan*, ed. C. Price (Oxford, 1966), ii, 260: To the Duke of Bedford, 12 February 1806.

8 Ibid. i, 6–11. Sheridan's father had been granted a pension by the Bute government and Henry Fox, the father of Charles James, led for the government in the House of Commons when Bute was First Lord of the Treasury.

9 T. Moore, *Memoirs of the Life of Richard Brinsley Sheridan* (single volume edition, London, 1825), pp. 205–10.

10 Ibid., pp. 110–12.

11 Price, *Letters*, i, 135: to the Duchess of Devonshire, 19 September 1780.

12 Moore, *Life of Sheridan*, p. 211.

13 L. G. Mitchell, *Charles James Fox* (Oxford, 1992), pp. 25–45. In view of Sheridan's later difficulties with the Whigs' aristocratic ethos, and the fact that Sheridan's primary political attachment was to Fox, not the Rockinghamite leadership, it is significant that Mitchell states (p. 25) that 'In 1782, Fox was not a Whig in the sense that he had foreclosed on all other options . . . The lack of firm principle, which had marked his early years, still gave him total flexibility.'

14 *The Dramatic Works of Richard Brinsley Sheridan*, ed. C. Price (Oxford, 1973), i, 331, quoting from Folger Shakespeare Library, Washington DC, Folger MS. Wb. 478 opp. p. 254.

15 I am grateful to Professor Ian Christie for drawing my attention to the Jacobite connections in Sheridan's family; W. Sichel, *Sheridan* (London, 1909), i, 209–18.

16 Price, *Letters*, i, 72: to Thomas Grenville, 4 January 1773. Thomas Grenville was the elder brother of William Wyndham Grenville, 1st Baron Grenville, who led the Whig party jointly with Grey after Fox's death. Thomas Grenville had been a pupil in Sheridan's father's school of oratory at Bath.

17 Price, *Letters*, i, 77: to Thomas Grenville.

18 *The Parliamentary Debates from the year 1803 to the present time*, ed. T. C. Hansard (London, 1812–20), ii, 728–38. (Hereafter *PD*).

19 BL Add. MSS. 38593–5: Minutes of the Westminster Committee of Association.

20 *Memorials and Correspondence of Charles James Fox*, ed. Lord J. Russell (London, 1853–7), ii, 21–5: Lord John Townshend to Lord Holland, 15 June and 23 June 1830; *PH*, XXIV, 490; J. Watkins, *Memoirs of the Public and Private Life of the Rt Hon. Richard Brinsley Sheridan, with a particular account of his family and connections* (London, 1817), i, 240–50; Moore, *Journal*, ii, 316; *PH*, xxvi, 187.

21 *PH*, xxiv, 1199; xxvi, 274–302.

22 L. T. Werkmeister, *The London Daily Press 1772–92* (Nebraska, 1963), pp. 10–12, 69–70. A. Aspinall, *Politics and the Press c. 1780–1850* (London, 1949), pp. 271–2; Scottish Record Office, Blair Adam MSS: W. Woodfall to W. Adam, 24 February 1784.

23 J. A. Cannon, *Parliamentary Reform 1640–1832* (Cambridge, 1972), p. 113.

24 *Political Memoranda of the 5th Duke of Leeds*, ed. O. Browning (Camden Society, 1884), pp. 209–10.

25 See E. A. Smith, *Lord Grey 1764–1845* (Oxford, 1990), p. 11.

26 Sichel, *Sheridan*, ii, 418, 422–3.

27 Chatsworth House, Derbyshire, MSS. Journal of Lady Elizabeth Foster, 2 December 1788.

28 *Ibid.*, 5 June 1789.

29 Duke of Buckingham and Chandos, *Memoirs of the Courts and Cabinets of George III, from original family documents* (London, 1853), i, 451.

30 *The Journal and Correspondence of William, Lord Auckland*, ed. Bishop of Bath and Wells (London, 1861–2), ii, 279.

31 *PH*, xviii, 344–72.

32 *The Life and Letters of Sir Gilbert Elliot, 1st Earl of Minto, 1750–1806*, ed. Countess of Minto (London, 1874), i, 351.

33 *The Correspondence of Edmund Burke*, general ed. T. Copeland (Cambridge, 1958–70), vii, 52–63: Burke to W. Weddell, 31 January 1792.

34 Ibid., 409: R. Burke to Fitzwilliam, 16 August 1793.
35 M. D. George, *English Political Caricature: A Study of Opinion and Propaganda, 1793–1832* (Oxford, 1959), pp. 213–21.
36 *PH*, xxxi, 1072.
37 Russell, *Memorials and Correspondence*, iii, 67.
38 Ibid., 149.
39 L. G. Mitchell, *Holland House* (London, 1980), p. 67.
40 *The Private Correspondence of Lord Granville Leveson Gower, 1781–1821*, ed. Castalia Countess Grenville (London, 1916), i, 427: Lady B to GLG, 17 August 1803.
41 M. D. George, *Catalogue of Political and Personal Satires preserved . . . in the British Museum* (London, 1978), vi, nos. 6974; 7380; 7528; *Morning Post*, 14 August 1788.
42 *The Journal of Elizabeth, Lady Holland (1791–1811)*, ed. Earl of Ilchester (London, 1908), i, 221–2.
43 Mitchell, *Fox*, p. 262; Mitchell, *Holland House*, chapters 2 and 3.
44 *Byron: A Self-Portrait. Letters and Diaries 1798 to 1824*, ed. P. Quennell (Oxford, 1990), p. 432.
45 *PH*, xxxvi 1698; *Morning Chronicle*, 9 February 1804.
46 *Recollections of the Table-Talk of Samuel Rogers*, ed. A. Dyce (3rd edition, London, 1856), p. 97.
47 Moore, *Sheridan*, pp. 607–8. Beinecke Library, Yale University, Im. Sh. 53+w825a.
48 Smith, *Grey*, pp. 89–91.
49 BL Add. MSS. 47566 fos. 134–5: Fox to D. O'Bryen, 24 December 1802.
50 Ibid.
51 Russell, *Memorials and Correspondence*, iii, 412.
52 *PH*, xxxvi, 1698.
53 Russell, *Memorials and Correspondence*, iv, 11.
54 *The Creevey Papers: A Selection from the Correspondence and Diaries of the late Thomas Creevey M.P. 1768–1838*, ed. Sir H. Maxwell (London, 1903), i, 21: Creevey to Currie, 21 January 1804.
55 Ibid., i, 25: Creevey to Currie, 2 April 1804. Addington was disparagingly referred to as 'the Doctor' because his father had been a mere physician.
56 Price, *Letters*, ii, 215–6: to his wife 27 February 1804.
57 *PH*, xxxiii, 1427.
58 *PD*, vii, 1115.
59 See C. A. Clayton, *The Political Career of Richard Brinsley Sheridan* (unpublished D. Phil. thesis, Oxford University, 1992), chapter VI.
60 J. J. Sack, *The Grenvillites, 1801–1829. Party Politics and Factionalism in the Age of Pitt and Liverpool* (London, 1979), p. 135.

61 Durham University Library, Grey MSS: Grey to Lady Holland, 2 July 1808.
62 Granville, *Private Correspondence*, ii, 353: Lady B to GLG, 1810.
63 *Lady Holland's Journal*, i, 217.
64 Granville, *Private Correspondence*, ii, 353.
65 Grey MSS: Grey to Lady Grey, 12 January 1811.
66 Lord Holland, *Further Memoirs of the Whig Party*, ed. Lord Stavordale (London, 1905), p. 84.
67 Ibid., p. 73.
68 Grey MSS: Grey to Lady Grey, 29 January 1811.
69 *The Diaries and Correspondence of James Harris, 1st Earl of Malmesbury*, ed. by his grandson (London, 1844), ii, 465.
70 See Sir J. Barrington, *Personal Sketches of his Own Times* (London, 1827), i, 298–9.
71 Price, *Letters*, iii, 158: To the Prince of Wales, 1 June 1812.
72 *PD*, xxiii, 623.
73 Granville, *Private Correspondence*, ii, 444: G. Canning to GLG, 18 August 1812.
74 *Staffordshire Advertiser*, 17 October 1812.
75 Price, *Letters*, iii, 163: to Samuel Whitbread, 1 November 1812.
76 *Auckland Correspondence*, ii, 267.
77 *The Whig Club or a Sketch of the Manners of the Age* (London, 1794), p. 19.
78 Ibid., p. 24.
79 *PH*, xxxii, 665.
80 *PD*, xv, 341.
81 *PD*, xvi, 33. Speech of 23 March 1810.
82 J. Cannon, *Aristocratic Century, The Peerage of Eighteenth-Century England* (Cambridge, 1984), p. 117.
83 *PD*, xxiii, 612.

9

The ruin of a public man: the rise and fall of Richard Brinsley Sheridan as political reformer

MARC BAER

In order to appreciate Sheridan's career as a political reformer, this chapter examines high politics and extra-parliamentary radicalism in mid and late Georgian England, as well as certain visual evidence which bridges the worlds of patrician and popular politics. Each of these inquiries reveals a distinct representation of Sheridan. To England's élite, Sheridan became something of a loose cannon; radicals came to see him as corrupt oligarchy personified; and visual sources created the image of a theatrical, place-hunting drunk. Sheridan in fact presented too many facets to an age in which large segments of the politically active population thought dichotomously – loyalism versus radicalism, Pitt versus Fox, Britain versus France. At the same time a new politics was emerging in the early nineteenth century, most strikingly in London. Sheridan, however, was too closely identified with the old century, a victim of success in achieving his political status. One key to each of the representations and therefore the failure of Sheridan as reformer was his inability to separate theatre from politics. In 1782 Sheridan resolved 'to give myself up thoroughly and diligently to a Business and a Pursuit which whether I am right or not is more to my fancy and Feelings'.[1] Innate theatricality helped establish Sheridan's reputation as an orator in and out of the House of Commons, and as well in the role he performed as the poor but incorruptible politician.[2] The real man was seen as altogether different, as neither virtuous nor benign but venal. Failure thus was the price paid for crossing boundaries – between theatre and politics, between House of Commons and election crowd, between oligarchy and democracy, between past and present. I begin by asking how, in the late eighteenth century, Sheridan invented himself politically. I then consider visual sources, demonstrating how Sheridan's image was contested by caricaturists and others. The chapter concludes with one of the most famous elections in British history.

Sheridan's political career before 1806 developed from three turning points. First, not being born into whiggery, Sheridan fashioned political space from friendships with Charles James Fox and the Prince of Wales. From 1780 Sheridan was represented visually with Fox, and shortly thereafter with the Prince. The Foxites gambled that their association with the Prince, the 'reversionary interest', would ensure their political futures, but instead the relationship only earned them the enmity of George III. The King told Lord North in 1783 that he could neither 'forget or forgive' the Foxites' role in alienating his son from him,[3] which doomed men like Sheridan to a lifetime of opposition. Sheridan moved from dabbling in political journalism to a role in the 1780s–90s as press manager for the Rockingham (later Foxite) Whigs. He was elected Member of Parliament for Stafford in 1780, a seat he held until 1806. The same election saw Pitt returned to parliament for the first time, and Fox chosen for the borough of Westminster. These three young men, whose careers were so intertwined during the next three decades, were remarkably similar: unconcerned with religion or paying bills; abusers of drink; reformers by instinct who could trim sails when they had to.

From the regency crisis in 1788–9 to the death of Fox in 1806, Sheridan and his mentor crossed swords over Fox's role as party leader and Sheridan's desire to be both independent and esteemed.[4] That their virtues and vices were so similar kept them closer than otherwise might have been the case.[5] Sheridan's conduct during the regency crisis helped produce splits among the Foxites, men such as Charles Grey and Thomas Creevey coming to distrust Sheridan's motives.[6] The closer Sheridan drew to the Prince, who at times functioned as a Whig leader, the greater the friction between Sheridan and Fox.[7] By the end of the 1780s, Sheridan had developed the skills and reputation for intrigue which were to shape the rest of his political career.

His fragile position within whiggery was both strengthened and weakened by the second turning point, Sheridan launching himself as a parliamentary reformer who also had credentials with 'the people', a role he cultivated into the early nineteenth century.[8] He was involved with the Westminster Committee, the most radical and forceful association in the movement of that name. Sheridan's first public political presence was alongside Fox at Westminster Hall in February 1780, when he presented the Committee's reform resolutions, and for his trouble there followed the first satirical attack on him. Fox asked Sheridan to chair a subcommittee of

8 James Gillray, *The Hopes of the Party*, 19 July 1791.

the Westminster Committee, whose report issued that May called for reforms anticipating Chartism by fifty years.[9] Shortly thereafter Sheridan became a charter member of the Society for Constitutional Information, an organization of establishment reformers which met in Westminster until its demise in 1794.[10] These experiences in the 1780s taught Sheridan and other reform-minded Whigs the limits of politics out of doors, and that intrigue with the Prince was a more direct means to power – an end they had failed to achieve by the time of the demise of the association movement.

The third turning point was Sheridan's reaction to the French Revolution and subsequent wars with France. The ascendancy of Pitt blunted reformism, making reformers more reactive and dependent upon the 'reversionary interest'. Reform became politically problematized in the 1790s, both within the élite and between parliamentary and extra-parliamentary reformers. Nevertheless, publicly and in parliament Sheridan helped maintain the viability of reform. Moving in intersecting circles of Whigs and radicals, he participated in the banquet celebrating the first anniversary of the fall of the Bastille, as well as the November 1795 Palace Yard meeting protesting against the Seditious Meetings and Treasonable Practices Acts. Sheridan helped found the Friends of the People in April 1792 with Charles Grey and other impatient Whigs, men dissatisfied with lack of movement in parliament on the reform issue. In January 1795 Sheridan offered a motion to repeal suspension of habeas corpus. At the end of the decade he worked with Sir Francis Burdett on the inquiry into the Cold Bath Fields prison.[11] That they were understood to be allies of a kind was reflected in Sheridan appearing as a partner of Burdett in a number of prints.[12] Sheridan's politics thus tended to fragment his party: conservative Whigs like Earl Fitzwilliam moved toward Pitt, while at the same time Sheridan competed with Grey and George Tierney for recognition, leading Fox to conclude 'Sheridan will never do anything quite wrong in politics, but whether he will ever go on very steadily and straightforward I doubt'.[13] By early 1804 Sheridan was giving limited support to Henry Addington,[14] who had replaced Pitt as prime minister, which did nothing to encourage Foxites about his steadiness. For his radical politics, however, Sheridan was accused of being an anti-patriot by opponents such as Charles Abbot, who concluded Sheridan was 'acting himself, hand and heart, with the most desperate Jacobins'[15] (see Plate 8). Allowing for hyperbole, such a characterization reflects a widespread perception of Sheridan's ambiguous behaviour in and out of the House of Commons in the 1790s regarding war and peace, pressing reform or temporizing so as to defeat Pitt, joining potential governments or remaining in opposition.

In his progress in high politics, then, Sheridan became as much a liability as an asset for his colleagues. With the failure of reform from above, the Foxite opposition became more hesitant. At this moment, however, a reform movement was emerging among segments of the artisanal and middling classes in London. Fox and Sheridan appeared more ambivalent about reform in the late 1790s because of pressure from organizations such as the London Corresponding Society.[16] Thus Sheridan moved slowly in the management of a bill to reform the Scottish burghs, which cause he championed in the House of Commons. This ambiguity frustrated the plebeian reformers, some of whom were to re-emerge in the radical Westminster of 1807.

With other reform-minded Whigs, Sheridan was involved in Westminster elections in the 1780s–90s in the cause of Fox and his allies.[17] Fox informed his Westminster agent in 1802 that he desired Sheridan 'should have my Seat, and that I would do any thing I could to forward such an object', but was dissuaded from so acting by other Whigs.[18] After his own return for Stafford in 1802, Sheridan had his solicitor leak a letter to the press: 'indeed had Mr Sheridan stood for Westminster on Mr Fox's retirement as was at one time reported young [Tom] Sheridan would have been infallibly returned for Stafford with the same unanimity as his Father.'[19] Such indiscretions led colleagues like Lord Holland to think the worst about Sheridan's ambitions regarding Fox's seat; Holland recalled Sheridan wanting to succeed Fox as Member of Parliament for Westminster back in the 1790s.[20] While that is an overstatement, Holland reflected the distrust of Sheridan held by many Whigs.

Westminster had a ratepayer franchise, with the poll in 1806 surpassing 10,000, making it a democratic constituency in an oligarchic age. But not until the very end of the eighteenth century did the lower orders become politically proactive.[21] It was particularly this borough which saw the birth early in the nineteenth century of an extra-parliamentary radical movement, the product of the failure in the 1790s of parliamentary reform. Sheridan became one focus of radical frustration with Whig rhetoric and actions. Thus it is important to consider what interested caricaturists about Sheridan's character and politics, for in turn their work would shape the public perception of him.

Sheridan was one of most widely caricatured individuals in the late Georgian era, identifiable in hundreds of prints, which speaks to his success in establishing his presence as a public man. The 1780s saw certain damaging images established, in particular greed for office and power, as well as impecuniousness. *The Funeral Procession of Mrs Regency* portrays Fox and Sheridan as mourners supporting a grief-stricken Prince; 'Impertinent Tradesmen' complain about 'Congreve Dick, who probed our Pockets to the Quick'.[22] These images would become hardened as time went on, as would that of Sheridan as trouble-maker for the Foxites. A print of 1799 displays a seesaw balanced on the back of John Bull, with Sheridan in the centre, Pitt higher and Fox lower. Sheridan says to Fox, 'You know I am Jack of both sides', Fox responding, 'You always work to keep him up and me down.'[23]

Satires, whether verbal or visual, signify a set of characteristics within the matrix of a political culture. The symbols associated with Sheridan were powerful, interlocking, and negative. Virtually every print from 1788 onward displays a blotched face and bloated body; others show Sheridan in

9 James Gillray, detail, *Sans-Culottes, feeding Europe with the Bread of Liberty*, 12 January 1793.

a dishevelled, drunken stupor, at times as Silenus or Bacchus.[24] In nearly twenty prints beginning in 1786 Sheridan's money problems were worked visually into images of beggars, or ragged creatures (cf. Plate 9). *The Cries of London* mixes metaphors: Sheridan appears as a poor hawker, holding a playbill, 'the Clamourous Creditors or Execution upon Execution with the Farce of Tumble Down Dick'.[25]

The repeated association of Sheridan with republicanism marks him as moving against the tide of loyalism. Sheridan appeared often as the Prince's lackey, therefore as an opponent of George III; a print of 1788 shows a drunken Prince and Sheridan bursting into the King's bedroom.[26] Sheridan was portrayed on several occasions as a regicide; in Plate 8, Fox raises an axe while Sheridan (who wishes 'I had hold of the Hatchet') grips George III. Sheridan was frequently accused of being pro-French, that is, anti-British, in over twenty prints 1792–1808 (see Plate 9), with the greatest concentration in 1794, the year the opposition fragmented.

Even a friend such as the Duchess of Devonshire could remark that Sheridan 'cannot resist playing a sly game',[27] hence the frequent accusations of insincerity. Sheridan appears in prints as favouring 'no popery', picking the pocket of the Prince, and as a sans-culotte who wears the bonnet rouge while holding a flag inscribed 'God Save the King No Jacobins'.[28] Political allies saw Sheridan's insincerity as connected to theatricality. Sir Gilbert Elliot remarked in 1788, on Sheridan's speech at the Hastings impeachment, 'his coming on so much in the character of a favourite actor, called on by the public, for the gratification of their taste and pleasure, to give them a specimen and display of eloquence and oratory, must put the real business so much aside', and the Hastings speech produced mixed results visually.[29] Approximately one in every ten prints of Sheridan associates him with some element of the theatre. Theatre explained who Sheridan was: as Bardolph, face bloated with drink, or performing as the lackey of the Duke of Norfolk.[30] Sheridan was portrayed as a clown, zany, mountebank, and as Punch.[31] One of most powerful of these images was Sheridan as Harlequin, that is, a buffoon, inaugurated by James Gillray in 1802.[32] Some forty prints identified Sheridan as Harlequin (cf. Plate 13). While this may have reflected public opinion, more likely it created it. A handbill from the November 1806 election combined many of these symbols in attacking Sheridan as the 'Son of an obscure *Irish Player* . . . this *Harlequin Son* of a *Mountebank Father* was indulged by some few of the depraved Nobility of the age with admission into their society, as a kind of *hired Jester*, whose grossness of conversation was calculated to stimulate their already too luxuriant debauchery'[33] (cf. Plate 12). Such statements reveal the tension between love of theatre and resentment when its luminaries were perceived as upstarts.

Sheridan was often portrayed in visual satires as desperate for place in any government. One print depicts him obsequiously referring to his enemy the king, 'oh! how I long to kiss that dear Hand'.[34] But this fails to match the vicious power of a Gillray print, wherein thirty-two voracious piglets representing the Fox-Grenville coalition scramble for office; Gillray places Sheridan prominently in the centre, but so positioned that others reach their goal before him.[35] Though not in the cabinet, Sheridan was seen as representing the spirit of the government; on one occasion he appears alongside Fox, exclaiming, 'surely there is enough to satisfy us all'.[36]

A final theme evident in nearly fifty prints was Sheridan as Fox's deputy, in which Sheridan appears as an object of conversation, a companion or fellow conspirator, beside or behind the party leader, as in Plates 8–10. Thus he is Fox's accomplice with a crowbar labelled 'Begum Sophistry' while wearing a mask (of deceit), attacking the door to a building labelled 'Treasury' defended by Pitt.[37] These prints were powerful precisely because they worked so many veins. That Sheridan was frequently cast as supporting Fox meant he never gained but always lost in reputation. Thus when Sheridan took up an anti-French stance in the late 1790s ahead of Fox, he was shown as insincere rather than independent; an exasperated Fox expressed concern about the 'incurable itch' that Sheridan had for 'distinguishing his conduct from that of those with whom he wishes to be supposed united'.[38]

Caricaturists found it difficult to reconceptualize Sheridan and thus the continuities were very powerful. Artists did not work in a vacuum, but drew upon earlier themes and symbols; likewise viewers read across prints and through symbols. Prints worked because of the multiplicity of symbols, for example Plate 9, *Sans-Culottes, Feeding Europe with the Bread of Liberty*, wherein a ragged Fox and Sheridan, wearing bonnets rouges, force-feed John Bull small loaves of bread labelled 'Liberty', while each picks John's pockets; Sheridan is shown with a blotched face.

One example of how visual symbols interacted with political polemic to define the representation of Sheridan was the work of William Cobbett. Fox had appeared as Proteus in an early print,[39] and Cobbett drew upon some of those same negative characteristics in casting Sheridan as a changeling. Cobbett's attack began in August 1803, in letters addressed to Sheridan in his *Political Register*; the following January these reappeared in a book, *The Political Proteus*, analyzing Sheridan's speeches. The letters responded to attacks by Sheridan in the House of Commons on Cobbett, his *Register*, and his patron William Windham.[40] Cobbett then criticized Sheridan's patriotism by assailing *Pizarro*, Sheridan's role in the Hastings impeachment as revealing his lack of 'political constancy', and his 'endless maze of inconsistencies'.[41] Sheridan was accused by Cobbett of bringing theatrical speech into the House (a complaint Pitt made in the Commons in 1783), and of using his ownership of Drury Lane to manipulate press and public alike.[42] Many of these themes appear in two Gillray prints which were published earlier that year.[43] The constellation of topics by Cobbett and the caricaturists – misapplied theatre, insolvency, revolutionary politics, bloated or otherwise physically deformed appearances, double-dealing – later reappear, deepening the disapproving representation of Sheridan.[44] A Pittite pamphlet-writer also reproached Sheridan as a changeling, asking which of Fox's principles Sheridan was continuing, 'democratical or aristocratic'.[45] Critics did not have to agree politically to damage Sheridan visually or lexically.

Having discussed political character and political caricature, we come now to the events of 1806–7. These require close reading, because they reveal both how oligarchy worked and where it was falling apart, how Sheridan used a system he knew well and how it destroyed him.

William Pitt's death led to the formation of the Ministry of All the Talents in January 1806, a coalition of Whig factions led by Fox and Lord Grenville. Sheridan did not get a cabinet seat, but was appointed Treasurer of the Navy, with £4,000 per annum and an official residence in Somerset Place in the heart of Westminster. Although he resented the slight,[46] Sheridan continued to be pictured in the front ranks of his party, as in Plate 10. Fox was seriously ill for much of 1806, and evidence suggests Sheridan was organizing the succession.[47] When Fox died on 13 September Sheridan, assuming his party's leaders knew his intentions, immediately announced for the vacant Westminster seat.[48]

Sheridan soon discovered, however, 'scandalous tricks play'd', that his governmental colleagues had in fact already arranged to have Fox succeeded by Lord Percy, the Duke of Northumberland's 21-year old son.[49] Planning for this had begun that summer and continued as Fox lay dying, and is best understood as currying favour with the Duke. The Marquis of Buckingham told his brother Lord Grenville in early August that their cousin the Duke had approached him about his son. Grenville then communicated with Northumberland in late August that he would support Percy.[50] (There was no love lost between Sheridan and Grenville, for Sheridan had tried to wreck the emerging Foxite-Grenville coalition three years earlier.[51]) Grenville's second in command, Charles Grey (now Lord Howick), wrote to the Duke of Northumberland to offer his support as well. The government then leaked information to the press, that if Sheridan stood he might lose his Treasurership of the Navy. All this took place while Sheridan operated on information that his leaders would make no move until Sheridan stated his intentions about Westminster.[52]

10 Charles Williams, *Blowing-Up-the New Opposition*, March 1806.

Why did his governmental colleagues play Sheridan for a fool? Certainly it was not a case of honest mistakes – Grey failing to consult Grenville until it was too late, Northumberland and Grenville both thinking they were obliging the other.[53] Mrs Creevey suggested an answer in a letter of 15 September: 'None of the present party wish . . . to quarrel with [Sheridan], yet perhaps they may all think . . . that with his present ambitious hostility he might make the being member for Westminster a most troublesome engine for mischief.' Lord Holland remarked similarly a week later: he feared what Sheridan might do now, 'but considering his *connexions* [with the Prince], talents and appearance of steadiness to the mob and public I fear there is too much disposition to set him at defiance and too great a desire to get rid of him altogether than is either prudent or perhaps right.'[54]

All the while the relationship between the Whigs and the Westminster radicals increased in acrimony. Francis Place recalled Percy as 'a very young man, without pretension to talents of any kind'.[55] More important was Cobbett, who sensed in the summer of 1806 that if Fox died the political situation would become quite fluid.[56] In this he reflected a print which showed an ailing Fox visited by his colleagues, including Sheridan who has in his pocket a 'Scheme for a New Administra[tion]'.[57] On 9 August 1806 Cobbett began a year-long series of letters in his *Political Register* addressed to the Westminster electorate. 'In the City of Westminster,' Cobbett argued, '. . . there is less excuse for base conduct, than there is in almost any other body of electors . . . In your hands is now placed the fate of the people of England, as far as regards their political liberties.'[58] Cobbett maintained an assault on Sheridan in the pages of the *Political Register* for months.[59] Burdett and Samuel Whitbread were approached by radicals to stand, but pledged themselves to Percy. Frustrated, the Westminster radicals continued the search for a candidate.[60]

Sheridan knew he could not win in Westminster without 'the Protection of the Government', and with pressure from the Prince he stepped aside for Percy at an election meeting on 18 September.[61] In standing down Sheridan claimed he did so of his own free will, using as an excuse loyalty to Stafford. But simultaneously Sheridan penned the following as a motion at the meeting: 'That the long and faithful services of Mr S. in Parliament, his uniform support of all the Principles and measures . . . his almost unrivall'd Talents and his devoted attachment to his late departed Friend do eminently qualify him – to succeed Mr Fox as Member for Westminster.' He added: 'At the same time this meeting cannot but acquiesce in the motives which induce him to withdraw himself on the present occasion in the sanguine hope that upon a future opportunity they may be enabled to manifest the high sense the[y] entertain of his merits.'[62]

Percy was returned unopposed on 7 October, at a cost to his father of about £2,500. Much of the money went on a fête after the election, which degraded Westminster in the eyes of the radicals. Francis Place thought, 'Almost every man I knew was much offended with the whole of the proceedings and with all who were concerned in them.' Cobbett in turn was outraged by the contrived chairing of Percy, blaming Sheridan and the 'intrigues and frauds of the Whig Club'. Cobbett helped radicalize the borough further by shaming Westminster electors, accusing them of being 'menial servants of a few great families', and the failure to find an alternative

11 Isaac Cruikshank [*Frontispiece to the Imposter Unmasked*], [1806].

to Percy in 1806 made men like Place realize that permanent political organization was the only way to prepare for the future.[63]

A month later parliament was dissolved, forcing new elections. Once again, Sheridan declared his intention to contest Westminster, assuming he would stand alongside Percy.[64] Sheridan, however, had infuriated the Duke of Northumberland by working behind the scenes to undermine his son's position in Westminster while publicly supporting him, Cobbett publicizing the Duke's displeasure with Sheridan.[65] In addition Northumberland was irritated with the Talents government for dissolving parliament seventeen days after Percy's election, and by the failure to contain Sheridan's activities; 'Two elections for Westminster in one month and Mr Sheridan for a colleague was too much for a person even of less delicate feelings than a Percy to bear.'[66] Art reflected life, so that in Plate 11 Cruikshank has a dog with the head of Percy urinating on Sheridan's boot, while in Plate 12 Gillray puts the Duke on the side of Sheridan's radical opponent.

With Percy gone, the government indicated they would support a Sheridan candidature.[67] The Whig leaders first recruited an admiral, Sir Samuel Hood, for the second seat, and subsequently arranged a coalition between Hood and Sheridan.[68] Although Hood had been selected by Grenville because he was non-partisan, the Westminster radicals considered him a Tory. The Hood-Sheridan coalition thus had the appearance of renewing the arrangements in place since 1790 of government and opposition splitting the representation of Westminster, thereby avoiding a contested election.[69] James Paull, a radical who claimed to be a political disciple of Burdett, and formerly an ally of Sheridan in the House of Commons, entered the contest on 27 October with radical support; Sheridan conveyed to friends that 'Paul[l] will give him a great deal of trouble'.[70]

On his own at first Sheridan performed poorly, according to Lord Holland's subsequent account because he 'thought, in his inordinate vanity, that he might defy the Court, the Aristocracy, and the Reformers'. Although Sheridan acknowledged problems, Holland's account is neither trustworthy nor sufficiently complex. The Duke of Bedford, for example, did not hesitate to use his influence in Westminster in support of Sheridan and Hood, but he also blamed the internecine conflict between Sheridan and Northumberland for dividing the Whigs, thus encouraging the entry of

12 James Gillray, *View of the Hustings in Covent Garden*, 15 December 1806.

Paull into the contest.[71] Sheridan's larger problem concerned perception. Like the caricaturists, politicians on the right saw Sheridan as no different from the radicals, while radicals like Place saw Whigs such as Sheridan as 'trading politicians, Tories out of place, who cared little for the people further than they could be made to promote their own interests'.[72] This outlook was reflected in a print which had the Talents ministry under assault by both radicals and the followers of Pitt.[73]

From the outset Sheridan understood he was to have 'some rough work on the Hustings'.[74] Burdett charged Sheridan with hypocrisy regarding reform, the opening salvo of a continuous attack on Sheridan's passing himself off as a reformer while in opposition but doing nothing in office, a theme articulated as well by Cobbett and in election songs.[75] The first line of one of these, 'Lo! Corruption stalks forward in Liberty's guise', reflected a theme prominent in satirical prints[76] (see Plate 9).

For much of the fifteen-day election Paull topped the poll, Sheridan remaining mired in third place. Radicals relentlessly directed barbs at Sheridan about his failure to pay creditors, as in Plates 11 and 12. In response to a statement of Sheridan on the public debt, a man in an election crowd exclaimed '*Hear! Hear! Hear! Sheridan; Richard Brinsley Sheridan*, DETESTS BREAKING FAITH WITH CREDITORS!', which perhaps he had noticed in a print.[77] Through the medium of anonymous handbills, the radicals hammered Sheridan for living in luxury at the expense of Westminster tradesmen, the typical approach being to contrast the 'Honest Men of the *middling* Class' with a spendthrift placeman (cf. Plate 12). Dangerously for Sheridan's political future, it was precisely among these 'middle classes of society' that the Westminster radicals were at work.[78]

Sheridan blamed his late start in organizing the borough on bad advice and an address of 5 November claimed 'a systematical arrangement of canvass is established', which is perhaps when the bribery began which was alleged by various sources. As well there is evidence aristocrats intimidated tradesmen, of the use of force by hired toughs, and of Treasury influence directly and indirectly through the press.[79] The spectre of a Paull victory helped raise money from as far away as Scotland, but the Whigs remained anxious that Sheridan would be unable to defeat Paull.[80] On the seventh day of the poll, 10 November, Hood passed Paull, and Sheridan, although still third, made his greatest gain to date; these developments may have resulted from the averred corrupt practices.

Sheridan's strategy in 1806 was to claim Fox's mantle, which necessitated winning Westminster on his own. But in fact he ruined his long-term position by alienating the Westminster radicals in the course of the election. Paull assailed Sheridan on the very ground Sheridan claimed, namely independence. The response was to attack Paull's humble background – he was the son of a tailor – an approach which could only hurt Sheridan. A well-organized procession, which began at the Shakespeare Tavern, the Sheridan campaign's headquarters, incorporated symbols of tailors – including a goose and cabbages – which functioned as ritualized abuse. In turn the affair reappeared in political caricatures.[81] The goose and cabbages were part of a long tradition in popular culture and caricature, hence their deep resonance with the people of Westminster. A pamphlet decried the possibility of a 'rabble Representative', while a newspaper pointed to Paull as 'a man of the most obscure birth, without education, a petty speculator in Eastern traffic and a contemptible speaker, whose folly and ignorance were the subject of ridicule in the last House of Commons'. Accusations of Paull's being pro-French and a democrat were all the more ironic given Sheridan's past positions.[82] This pattern hurt Sheridan in the eyes of many common folk in Westminster, so that opinion may have been less pro-Paull than anti-Sheridan. In particular it played into the hands of Cobbett, who reacted strongly to the attack on his side's manliness and their treatment 'as low and insignificant men'.[83] There is some feel of Sheridan no longer maintaining 'steadiness to the mob' in Plate 11.

Sheridan passed Paull on the eleventh day and finished in second place. There was an extensive chairing, which Sheridan probably organized himself, less genuine and more theatrical than such events had been in Westminster.[84] Nevertheless, there were in Sheridan's triumph a number of warning signals. First, this was the third straight contested Westminster election in which the radical candidate increased his percentage of the poll. Second, the oligarchs were not well organized, and conflict continued between Sheridan and Hood supporters.[85] Third was the voting behaviour of the Westminster electorate. Hood finished with 5478 votes, Sheridan with 4758 and Paull with 4481. While 68.7 per cent of Paull's voters were plumpers (votes for a single candidate alone when electors were permitted to vote for two candidates), 79.9 per cent of Sheridan's were split votes, mainly with Hood – which meant that Sheridan was dependent upon his coalition partner for his second place finish. As well, he relied upon others for money. Cobbett claimed the election cost the Sheridan side £13,000. While this is probably an exaggeration, Sheridan was too heavily dependent for his own good upon Whig subscribers during and after the election.[86]

Whig discourse about 'the people' had come to be perceived as contemptible by radicals who were developing a notion of 'the people' which looked remarkably like themselves. Fox had lost hope in the possibility of reform, observing in 1805 that 'it will be next to impossible in our times to revive any zeal in favour of it'.[87] Burdett denounced the Foxites, 'those who so long maintained the principles of Freedom with those who had uniformly shewed themselves its most implacable enemies'.[88] Sheridan in particular had developed a reputation for insincerity when it came to reform.[89] Thus when oligarchs expressed anxiety about managing elections in Westminster, or as one put it, that 'there is a most factious spirit rising in the country (I cannot give a stronger proof than the numbers Mr Paull polled in Westminster)', they understood that in Westminster the plebeians were out in front of the patricians.[90] In terms of this transition, Sheridan was on the wrong side.

The importance of the November 1806 election therefore was that it drove a permanent wedge between Whigs and radicals. The Middlesex election in which Burdett was defeated by two ministerial-backed Whigs was linked to Westminster; the anti-Sheridan *History of the Westminster and Middlesex Elections in the Month of November 1806* was already in press by late November.[91] Place believed that Paull's strong showing had a 'considerable effect in convincing many of the electors that they were of more consequence in an election than they had conceived'.[92] The radicals had been defeated by superior organization and political showmanship, and the influence of ground landlords directly on electors and indirectly through vestries. Since the radicals could not compete with influence, they focussed on the other two factors in 1807. Sheridan might have had six years to prove his worth; instead the parliament lasted only six months. Three elections in a span of eight months allowed continuity of purpose and organization on the radical side,[93] but tended to fragment the Whigs.

The Westminster radicals, unable to forgive Sheridan for what they perceived as apostasy, had no alternative but retribution. Caricatures after the election kept up the assault, focussing particularly on how Sheridan had ruined his creditors financially, and on his supposed political hypocrisy (see Plates 11 and 12). A six-part 'progress' told the story of an imaginary Member of Parliament whose behaviour recalls the complaints against Sheridan.[94] Immediately after the 1806 election Paull brought a petition against Sheridan's return. The petition was taken up in February 1807 but subsequently dismissed by the House of Commons as 'false and scandalous', in part because Sheridan could appeal to his parliamentary colleagues against Paull's witnesses, 'so low, so vulgar, so contradictory in their accounts'.[95] George Canning believed Sheridan guilty, but he would not attend the debate on 2 March because, had it carried it 'must absolutely ruin him'.[96] This incident added another chapter to the manichean struggle of democracy versus oligarchy, and again Cobbett appealed through the *Political Register* to Westminster electors against the Whigs.[97]

When in April 1807 George III jettisoned the Talents ministry and dissolved parliament, Place and other Westminster radicals appealed to Paull and Burdett to stand with their support. Most radicals were eventually so irritated by Paull's behaviour they aligned with Burdett, who agreed to stand but refused to offer any support to the campaign.[98] Cobbett made clear the importance of this election: if Westminster electors returned Burdett, 'you will have done more for the country, in the space of fourteen days, than has been done for it, during the last hundred years'.[99]

While the Westminster radicals prepared for the contest, there was disarray among the Whigs. The new Portland government did not signal its intentions about how many candidates it would start, Lord Percy's name was bandied about once again, and Paull remained unpredictable. It transpired that Lord Cochrane entered as a reformer, while the local brewer John Elliot eventually stood with support from the Portland government.[100] Sheridan feared Burdett would siphon off his own supporters: 'If B. stands most of my Troups will support him'.[101] Though Cochrane was ignored by the radicals, his candidature was a serious threat as well for Sheridan, for in contrast to Hood he was a naval officer who championed reform of the navy as well as the political system.

Paull attacked Sheridan for alcoholism, being a toady of the Prince, irreligion, and 'by the most profligate extravagancies reduc[ing] honest tradesmen to penury and despair'.[102] Burdett's supporters were still smarting from the abuse of the last campaign; according to Place 'the ridicule which was cast upon us almost disabled them from acting', which may explain how the radicals were able to raise by subscription nearly all the £1300 they spent.[103] But hard work produced only desultory results during the first two days. The radicals, copying Sheridan's side in the previous election, then organized a procession: 'The number did not exceed 250 but it decided the election', and votes as well as money flowed their way.[104] As a sign matters were not going well Tom Sheridan met with Burdett's committee, asking for a coalition. This overture was turned down, as were two more.[105]

By 17 May Sheridan knew he could not win, although he continued to keep up a good face.[106] The numbers when polling ended had Burdett first with 5134, Cochrane second with 3708, and Sheridan third with 2646. Writing in 1826, Place claimed that so as not to shame Sheridan the radicals allowed his supporters to poll fraudulent votes.[107] No poll book from 1807 survives, but looking at the distribution of votes Place's comment seems dubious. Sheridan received 592 plumpers – a *decline* of 363 since 1806; with roughly the same percentage of plumpers in his total (22.4 per cent in 1807 versus 20.1 per cent in 1806), his total fell by more than 2,000 votes, which meant he slipped from second to third place. Some 1527 voters, 57.8 per cent of Sheridan's total vote, split Burdett-Sheridan.[108] So whereas one radical newspaper read the 1807 Westminster campaign as a spectacular triumph in the battle of oligarchy versus democracy – 'the whole influence of aristocracy ranged against the well-organized endeavors of a free people'[109] – evolution rather than revolution seems the better metaphor. Sheridan lost the election of 1807 in November 1806; the Whigs had been losing ground to radical candidates in Westminster since 1790.

Gillray completed Sheridan's humiliation with a print of a scene before the hustings where the five candidates are trying to get to top of a pole/poll (Plate 13); a corpulent Sheridan dressed as Harlequin struggles at the bottom. To Sheridan the defeat in 1807 was 'the most unfortunate occurrence of my life. It was a real misfortune which I can never get over. It was my total ruin as a public man'.[110] He continued to play an active role in politics, for example in the regency crisis of 1810. But Sheridan was forced to come into parliament as the Prince's nominee for Ilchester, and he was left after 1807 with a debt 'which has press'd upon me grievously'.[111] His financial ruin was completed in 1809 when Drury Lane was destroyed by fire.

Sheridan continued to cause trouble for fellow Whigs from his standing with the Prince, and at least in parliament he remained a reformer.[112] But he was slipping, and the prints charted his decline, ending with an almost humanoid Sheridan picking a man's pocket and lamenting his exclusion from the Regent's 'Tory' government; his former colleagues made Sheridan the scapegoat for this fiasco. By now Sheridan was moving from foreground to background in many prints, signifying his political marginalization.[113]

The Talents government had fought the November 1806 election in Westminster as if it were an eighteenth-century contest, intimidating

13 James Gillray, *Election-Candidates*, 20 May 1807.

tradesmen, urging aristocrats to use all their influence, and utilizing traditional agents.[114] Remarks by Lord John Townshend and George IV about how the patrician interest could have brought Sheridan in for Westminster 1812 reveal unwillingness to comprehend the new wind sweeping the borough.[115] Nor did Sheridan appreciate the changes in the political world. At the 1814 Westminster by-election he was once more a candidate, along with Henry Brougham and several others. Sheridan may have scouted the seat late in 1813 when it was possible Cochrane would go to the Lords, and he was active at the outset of the campaign in 1814: 'I have the Whig *support* made known to me thro' the Duke of Norfolk . . . After what has pass'd between me and Lord Sidmouth I cannot doubt the support of Government.' But 'desparing of supplies' and with his former colleagues backing Brougham, Sheridan was forced to withdraw.[116] One of the last prints of Sheridan reveals an almost indiscernible Harlequin quoting Cardinal Wolsey: 'If I had serv'd my God with half the Zeal I serv'd my Prince, He would not have deserted me in my nakedness.'[117]

Operating within Georgian political culture, Sheridan acted reasonably given his background and how he perceived the system worked for men like him and for the Foxite opposition generally. Before his 1807 defeat the Foxites needed Sheridan's gifts in parliament and his friendship with the Prince, fearing if they discarded him he would destroy them with his still-formidable powers of rhetoric[118] (cf. Plate 10). Looking at him through Westminster, however, suggests an alternative reading of his career. After the November 1806 election Cobbett stated that without Paull's challenge the nation would have accepted Sheridan's claim to have inherited Fox's mantle, but 'we exhibited him in his true colours; and, in those colours he will be seen unto the end of his days'.[119] The visual evidence discussed here would suggest Cobbett was closer to the truth than Sheridan would have wished; thus Plate 11, while in Plate 12 Gillray, himself a political reactionary, has Paull's supporters focussed on their candidate while Sheridan's partisans – and an anguished Sheridan himself – look fearfully towards the crowd.

If one demand of the Westminster radicals was for respect of the middle classes on the part of patricians, another was efficiency in government. As Treasurer of the Navy in the Talents ministry, Sheridan also failed. An individual in an election crowd in November 1806 exclaimed, 'Oh, damn your checks Sherry, they're worth nothing', a reflection on the debts arising from the splendid parties given in the official residence of the Treasurer of the

Navy while there was a war on and he failed to pay tradesmen[120] (cf. Plate 11); all this prophesied the end of the age of sinecures. As a survivor in an oligarchical political culture, Sheridan was forced to operate during the transition to a proto-democratic political culture in precisely the place, radical Westminster, where the transition was being invented. It was thought at the time that what happened in 1807 was a harbinger; in the words of Cobbett, 'This election is the beginning of a new era in the history of parliamentary representation.'[121] And so it was.

Notes

1 *The Letters of Richard Brinsley Sheridan*, ed. C. Price (Oxford, 1966), i, 141; cf. F. G. Stephens and M. D. George, eds., *Catalogue of Prints and Drawings in the British Museum* (hereafter *BMC*) (London, 1870–1954), 6248.

2 Cf. P. Fitzgerald, *Lives of the Sheridans* (London, 1886), i, 267; G. Pellew, *Life and Correspondence of Henry Addington, First Viscount Sidmouth* (London, 1847), ii, 105.

3 Quoted in E. A. Smith, *Whig Principles and Party Politics* (Manchester, 1975), p. 101.

4 M. Sadler, *The Political Career of Richard Brinsley Sheridan* (Oxford, 1912), pp. 37–8; J. C. Hobhouse, Baron Broughton, *Recollections of a Long Life* (London, 1909–11), iii, 22–3; *Correspondence of George, Prince of Wales*, ed. A. Aspinall (London, 1963–71), iii, 349–54.

5 C. J. Fox, *Memorials and Correspondence of C. J. Fox*, ed. Lord J. Russell (London, 1853–7), iii, 206, 388, 420–1, 436–7; iv, 11, 429–30.

6 *Prince of Wales*, i, 364–6; see also iv, 519–20 n.5 and 531 n.1; T. Creevey, *The Creevey Papers*, ed. H. Maxwell (London, 1903), i, 21–2, 25–6; *Fox Correspondence*, ii, 23–4; Broughton, *Recollections*, iii, 128.

7 Duke of Buckingham and Chandos, *Memoirs of the Court and Cabinets of George III* (London, 1853–5), i, 151; W. Sichel, *Sheridan* (London, 1909), ii, 414.

8 *Letters*, ii, 262–3.

9 Westminster Committee, Minutes, BL Add. MSS 38593, fos. 9–19, 38–44; *London Courant*, 15 July 1780.

10 F. D. Cartwright, *The Life and Correspondence of Major John Cartwright* (London, 1926), i, 120.

11 *The Correspondence of Edmund Burke*, gen. ed. T. W. Copeland (Cambridge 1958–70), vi, 126, vii, 57–8; *Fox Correspondence*, iii, 126; J. Farington, *The Farington Diary*, ed. J. Greig (London, 1923–8), i, 108 ff.; *Letters*, ii, 134–5.

12 *BMC* 9416, 9511, 10417, 10540, 10605, 10622; cf. M. W. Patterson, *Sir Francis Burdett and His Times* (London, 1931), i, 151; *Letters*, ii, 242 and n. 4.

13 Quoted in R. G. Thorne, ed., *The House of Commons, 1790–1820* (London, 1986), p. 148; cf. *Letters*, ii, 142 n. 2; Elizabeth, Lady Holland, *Journal of Elizabeth Lady Holland, 1791–1811*, ed. Earl of Ilchester (London, 1908), i, 220–4.

14 *Letters*, ii, 211–13, 216.

15 C. Abbot, Baron Colchester, *The Diary and Correspondence of Charles Abbot, Lord Colchester*, ed. Charles, Lord Colchester (London, 1861), i, 23; cf. Historical Manuscripts Commission, *Manuscripts of J. B. Fortescue Preserved at Dropmore* (London, 1915), vii, 180.

16 *Prince of Wales*, iii, 341–2.

17 *Letters*, i, 135–6, ii, 38–9; Sichel, *Sheridan*, i, 454–5, ii, 87–93; J. Watkins, *Memoirs of Sheridan* (London, 1817), p. 65; E. Sheridan, *Betsy Sheridan's Journal*, ed. W. LeFanu (London, 1960), p. 111; *The Times*, 14 June 1796; *BMC* 7342.

18 Fox MSS, BL Add. MSS 47566, f. 118, and see also f. 67; *Fox Correspondence*, iii, 366.

19 *Letters*, ii, 185–6 and n. 4; *The Times*, 26 June 1802; *Courier*, 30 June 1802.

20 Henry, Lord Holland, *Memoirs of the Whig Party During My Time*, ed. Henry, Lord Holland (London, 1852), i, 90 and ii, 63, and see Creevey, *Creevey Papers*, i, 195; but cf. T. Moore, *Memoirs of the Life of the Right Honourable Richard Brinsley Sheridan*, 3rd edn. (London, 1825), ii, 338–9 and Sichel, *Sheridan*, ii, 280.

21 Place Papers, BL Add. MSS 27838, fos. 18–20.

22 Artist unknown, published 29 April 1789, Henry E. Huntington Library, Pr. Box 206/1; cf. the pamphlet *The Death, Dissection, Will and Funeral Procession of Mrs Regency* (London, 1789), and *The Funeral Procession of Miss Regency*, engraved by James Gillray, 29 April 1789, *BMC* 7526.

23 *See Saw- -or, a New Mode of Digestion for John Bull*, published by W. Holland, Prints and Photographs Division, Library of Congress (hereafter LC), British Political Cartoon Prints, Social Satires, and Illustrated Broadsides (hereafter PC) 3, 1 October 1799; cf. *The Rival Managers*, published by W. Holland, LC PC 3, June 1799.

24 *Bubbles of Opposition*, engraved by James Gillray, 19 July 1788, *BMC* 7342; see also *BMC* 7894, 11079, 10972, 11860, 11864, 11888, and 11312.

25 *The Cries of London*, artist unknown, LC PC 3, May 1797; cf. *BMC* 10714–16, 10726, 10728.

26 *Filial Piety!*, engraved by Thomas Rowlandson, 25 Nov. 1788, *BMC* 7378; cf. M. D. George, *English Political Caricature* (Oxford, 1959), i, 198.

27 Sichel, *Sheridan*, ii, 400.

28 *Guy-Vaux, or the 5th of November*, artist unknown, [c. 1800], LC PC 3, and cf. *BMC* 7387, 9972 and 10572.

29 G. Elliot, *Life and Letters of Sir Gilbert Elliot*, ed. Countess of Minto (London,

1874), i, 208; cf. Creevey, *Creevey Papers*, i, 16, and two 1788 prints by William Dent: George, *Catalogue*, vi, 499 and *BMC* 7331; see also *BMC* 7273.

30 *BMC* 7380, 10969.

31 *BMC* 6384, 7273, 7633, 8690, 10459; cf. Sichel, *Sheridan*, i, 92–101.

32 *BMC* 9916.

33 A Calm Observer, *To the Independent Electors of Westminster*, in *History of the Westminster Election in the Month of November 1806* (London, 1807), pp. 129–31.

34 *BMC* 10526.

35 *BMC* 10540; see also *Letters*, ii, 259–63.

36 *BMC* 10562.

37 *House-Breaking before Sun-Set*, LC PC 3, 6 Jan. 1789.

38 *Fox Correspondence*, iii, 272; cf. *Journal of Lady Holland*, i, 220.

39 *Proteus Ye 2d in Sev'ral among his MANY publick CHARACTERS*, LC PC 3, 12 Jan. 1784.

40 W. Cobbett, *The Political Proteus: A View of the Public Character and Conduct of R. B. Sheridan* (London, 1804), p. 30.

41 Cobbett, *Political Proteus*, pp. 68 ff., 119–20, 129–30; cf. *BMC* 9396–9, 9402, 9406–7, 9417.

42 Cobbett, *Political Proteus*, pp. 201–2, 207–9, 219 ff.; *Debrett's History, Debates and Proceedings of Both houses of Parliament* (London, 1792), ix, 274; Fitzgerald, *Lives of Sheridans*, i, 269. On providing disinformation to the press see *BMC* 7510.

43 *BMC* 9972, 10088; cf. *Cobbett's Weekly Political Register*, 10 Sept. 1803; George, *Catalogue*, vi, 190.

44 For example, *BMC* 10459.

45 *Fox's Title Disputed* (London, 1806), p. 46.

46 *Prince of Wales*, v, 343–4 and n. 1.

47 *Journal of Lady Holland*, p. 172.

48 *Letters*, ii, 277.

49 *Letters*, ii, 275–8; cf. J. Gore, *Creevey's Life and Times* (New York, 1934), p. 32; *An Eulogium on the Right Honourable C. J. Fox Delivered by the Honourable Mr. Sheridan* . . . (Nottingham, 1806), p. 7.

50 *Dropmore Papers*, viii, 260, 333, and see also 330, 350.

51 BL Add. MSS 34079, f. 81; see also Moore, *Sheridan*, ii, 336–7.

52 BL Add. MSS 31158, f. 199, and cf. W. A. Lindsay, *A History of the House of Percy* (London, 1902), ii, 458; *Political Register*, 27 Sept. 1806.

53 Thus Holland, *Memoirs of Whig Party*, ii, 62, and Moore, *Sheridan*, ii, 339.

54 Gore, *Creevey's Life and Times*, p. 31; cf. *Dropmore Papers*, viii, 336; *Prince of Wales*, v, 439 n. 2.

55 Francis Place Papers, BL Add. MSS 27850, f. 12.

56 *Political Register*, 7 Feb. 1807.

57 *BMC* 10589.

58 *Political Register*, 20 Sept. 1806.

59 See *Letters*, ii, 277 n. 1; *History of Westminster Election*, p. 308.

60 Burdett Papers, Bodleian Library, MSS English History B. 200, f. 143; Whitbread MSS, Bedford Record Office, w/1/1985; *Morning Chronicle*, 24 Sept. 1806; *London Chronicle*, 25 Sept. and 4 Oct. 1806; *Westminster Journal*, 27 Sept. and 4 Oct. 1806; *Political Register*, 4 Oct. 1806.

61 *Letters*, ii, 278 and n. 1, 281; *Lord Granville Leveson Gower . . . Private Correspondence, 1781 to 1821*, ed. Castalia, Countess Granville (London, 1917), ii, 212; *Prince of Wales*, v, 430–1, 438, 444; *Dropmore Papers*, viii, 338–9; *Westminster Journal*, 20 Sept. 1806.

62 *Letters*, ii, 278 n. 1; cf. *ibid.* 279–81 and Place Papers, BL Add. MSS 27850, fos. 12–15, 22.

63 Place Papers, BL Add. MSS 27850, fos. 6, 19–22, 37–41; *Political Register*, 11 Oct. and 15 Nov. 1806.

64 *Letters*, ii, 286, 288; Watkins, *Sheridan*, p. 348.

65 *Prince of Wales*, v, 501–2; *Dropmore Papers*, viii, 400; *Address to Richard Brinsley Sheridan on the Public and Private Proceedings During the Late Election at Westminster*, 2nd edn (London, 1807), p. 3; *Gower Correspondence*, ii, 219; *Political Register*, 27 Sept., 11 Oct. and 22 Nov. 1806; *History of Westminster Election*, pp. 237–46; *Morning Chronicle*, 19 Nov. 1806.

66 *Letters*, ii, 288 n. 2; *Prince of Wales*, v, 449–50, 484, 501–2; vi, 18 and n. 1, 67 n. 3, 95–7; *Dropmore Papers*, viii, 414; *History of Westminster Election*, pp. 203, 244–6.

67 *Letters*, ii, 286, 288.

68 *Prince of Wales*, vi, 19; *Letters*, ii, 290; *Morning Chronicle*, 6 Nov. 1806.

69 *Dropmore Papers*, viii, 400; *History of Westminster Election*, pp. 2–5; cf. Place Papers, BL Add. MSS 27849, f. 52.

70 *Political Register*, 1 Nov. 1806; *Gower Correspondence*, ii, 225; cf. V. Foster, *The Two Duchesses* (London, 1898), p. 299.

71 Holland, *Memoirs of Whig Party*, ii, 64; *The Times*, 8 Nov. 1806; *History of Westminster Election*, pp. 298, 306; *Dropmore Papers*, viii, 414; *Prince of Wales*, vi, 67 n. 2, 69–70 n. 1.

72 *Dropmore Papers*, viii, 421; *Prince of Wales*, vi, 204 n. 3; cf. Place Papers, BL Add. MSS 27850 f. 6, 27838, f. 18, and 27842, f. 42; Sir F. Burdett, *A Letter to the Freeholders of Middlesex* (London, 1806); *Political Register*, 2 Aug. 1806.

73 *BMC* 10697.

74 *Letters*, ii, 291.

75 *Political Register*, 8 Nov. 1806; *History of Westminster Election*, p. 82, and see also pp. 111, 130, 175.

76 *History of Westminster Election*, pp. 26, 36, 101.

77 *Political Register*, 29 Nov. 1806; cf. *BMC* 10606.

78 *History of Westminster Election*, pp. 81–2, 96–7, 101, 111–13, 129, 132, 155, 175, 304; *Address to Sheridan*, pp. 3, 15; *Prince of Wales*, vi, 218, 259; *Exposition of the Circumstances Which Gave Rise to the Election of Sir Francis Burdett* . . . (London, 1807), pp. 5–6.

79 *History of Westminster Election*, pp. 52, 207, 211–12, 301; *The Times*, 8 and 22 Nov. 1806, 20 Apr. 1807; *Political Register*, 20 Sept. and *Westminster Journal*, 8 Nov. 1806; *Prince of Wales*, vi, 218; Holland, *Memoirs of the Whig Party*, ii, 64; *Dropmore Papers*, viii, 417; *Address to Sheridan*, pp. 3–4, 16; HMC, *Manuscripts of the Earl of Lonsdale* (London, 1893), p. 224.

80 *Prince of Wales*, vi, 67 n. 3, 70; *Letters*, ii, 300; *Dropmore Papers*, viii, 424–30, 439; *Gower Correspondence*, ii, 227; H. Leveson-Gower, *Hary-O: the Letters of Lady Harriet Cavendish, 1796–1809*, eds. G. Leveson-Gower and I. Palmer (London, 1940), p. 157.

81 *London Chronicle*, 8 Nov. 1806; *BMC* 10608; cf. Plate 12.

82 *History of Westminster Election*, pp. 70–1, 81, 141; *Morning Chronicle*, 8 Nov. 1806; cf. *London Chronicle*, 8 and 18 Nov. 1806.

83 *Political Register*, 22 Nov. 1806; *Address to Sheridan*, pp. 5, 14–17, 42; *History of Westminster Election*, pp. 302–3.

84 See Gower, *Hary-O*, pp. 165–7; D. Stuart, *Dearest Bess* (London, 1955), p. 154; *Address to Sheridan*, pp. 41–2; *History of Westminster Election*, pp. 265–7, 305; *Courier*, 20 Nov. 1806; *Political Register*, 29 Nov. 1806.

85 *Dropmore Papers*, viii, 427–30; *Letters*, ii, 294–5; see also *The Times*, 7 Nov. 1806 and *History of Westminster Election*, p. 93.

86 *Political Register*, 28 Feb. 1807; *Prince of Wales*, vi, 69–70, 75–6; cf. *Dropmore Papers*, viii, 430.

87 Wyvill Papers, North Yorkshire Record Office 7/2/183, f. 3.

88 Patterson, *Burdett*, ii, 483.

89 *Journal of Thomas Moore*, ed. W. S. Dowden (Cranbury, NJ, 1983–91), i, 95; G. Rose, *Diaries and Correspondence of the Right Hon. George Rose*, ed. L. V. Harcourt (London, 1860), ii, 169–70.

90 Quoted in J. A. Hone, *For the Cause of Truth: Radicalism in London, 1796–1821* (Oxford, 1982), p. 156; cf. *Dropmore Papers*, viii, 358; *Political Register*, 22 Nov. 1806; *Exposition of the Circumstances*, pp. 3–5.

91 *Political Register*, 1 and 22 Nov. and 20 Dec. 1806; *History of Westminster Election*, pp. 83–4, 87, 92. *View of the Hustings in Covent Garden*, Plate 12, was the frontispiece in later editions.

92 Place Papers, BL Add. MSS 27850, fos. 23–7.

93 Cf. Place Papers, BL Add. MSS 27850, f. 66.

94 *The Progress of a Corrupt Senator*, drawn by George Woodward, engraved by George? and Robert? Cruikshank [Dec. 1806–Jan. 1807], Huntington Library, Pr. Box 212.9/86.

95 Parliamentary Paper 1807, vii, *Minutes of Evidence Taken at the Bar of the House Upon Taking Into Consideration the Petition of James Paull*; *History of Westminster Election*, pp. 308–9; *Courier*, 27 Nov. 1806; *Hansard's Parliamentary Debates*, ix, 158; Foster, *Two Duchesses*, pp. 307–8; cf. *BMC* 10708, and *The Westminster Buggabo*, LC PC 3, 9 March 1807.

96 *Prince of Wales*, vi, 139–40 n. 1; see also H. B. Lytton, *The Life of Henry John Temple, Viscount Palmerston* (London, 1870), i, 54.

97 *Political Register*, 7 Feb. 1807, and see also 28 Feb. and 14 Mar. 1807; cf. Place Papers, BL Add. MSS 27838, f. 18v; Cobbett Papers, BL Add. MSS 22906, f. 254.

98 J. H. Tooke, *A Letter to the Editor of The Times* (London, 1807) and *A Warning to the Electors of Westminster* (London, 1807); Place Papers, BL Add. MSS 27850, fos. 43–7 and 27838 fos. 11–12; Cobbett Papers, BL Add. MSS 22906, f. 280; *Exposition of the Circumstances*, pp. 7–10.

99 *Political Register*, 16 May 1807.

100 *The Times*, 29 Apr., 8–14 May 1807; Place Papers, BL Add. MSS 27850, fos. 42, 79; Buckingham, *Courts and Cabinets*, iv, 175.

101 *Letters*, iii, 7–8; cf. Foster, *Two Duchesses*, p. 310.

102 Place Papers, BL Add. MSS 27850, f. 71.

103 Place Papers, BL Add. MSS 27850, fos. 75, 78 and 27838, f. 342; *Exposition of the Circumstances*, pp. 27–8.

104 Place Papers, BL Add. MSS 27838; fos. 18–19; *Exposition of the Circumstances*, pp. 10–11, 15.

105 Place Papers, BL Add. MSS 27838, f. 20.

106 *Letters*, iii, 9–10.

107 Place Papers, BL Add. MSS 27850, fos. 80–1.

108 *Exposition of the Circumstances*, p. 18.

109 *Independent Whig*, 24 May 1807.

110 Quoted in *Prince of Wales*, vi, 68 n.3; cf. *The Ghost of a Rotten Borough*, artist unknown, 17 May 1807, Huntington Library, Coll. Caricatures 226132, and *Independent Whig*, 24 Nov. 1807.

111 *Letters*, iii, 194; see also *Prince of Wales*, vi, 68 n. 3.

112 *Dropmore Papers*, ix, 329, 334; *Journal of Lady Holland*, ii, 283; *BMC* 11531, 11547; George, *Catalogue*, vii, 926.

113 *BMC* 11323, 11705, 11709, 11730, 11855, 11860, 11864, and 11888–90; *A Sale of Fox Hounds*, LC PC 3, 17 March 1812; cf. Moore, *Sheridan*, ii, 426.

114 *Dropmore Papers*, viii, 417, 427, 433.

115 Whitbread MSS W1/1926; J. W. Croker, *The Croker Papers*, ed. L. J. Jennings (London, 1884), i, 305–6.

116 *Letters*, iii, 190–2, 194–5; Place Papers, BL Add. MSS 27850, fos. 276–8, and 27840, fos. 236–7.

117 *BMC* 12181.
118 *Fox Correspondence*, iii, 460; Whitbread MSS w1/889, 892; cf. Holland, *Memoirs of the Whig Party*, ii, 62; *Gower Correspondence*, ii, 307.
119 Quoted in *History of Westminster Election*, p. 306.
120 *Sheridaniana* (London, 1826), pp. 192, 199; Watkins, *Sheridan*, pp. 338–9; *BMC* 10703; cf. Lytton, *Palmerston*, i, 54.
121 *Political Register*, 30 May 1807; cf. H. Hunt, *Memoirs* (London, 1820–2), ii, 252; *Independent Whig*, 24 May 1807.

10

On producing Sheridan

A conversation with PETER WOOD

You staged two Sheridan plays at the National Theatre, The Rivals *in 1983 and* The School for Scandal *in 1990.*

Yes. I'm glad I did them in chronological order because I think there's a great difference in kind between the two plays, and the director at his peril regards them as the same animal. They aren't. There's no question that *The School for Scandal* is an artificial comedy about an artificial society in an artificial city whereas *The Rivals* is essentially a human comedy based on superb characterization, actually taking place in what was then the country, the city of Bath. I have to say to begin with that I find *The School for Scandal* very chilly indeed whereas *The Rivals* is a particular pleasure and joy. Only this morning when I was reading the first big scene with Jack and Sir Anthony I fell out of bed laughing. I think this play has such power. Somehow it seems to me that once Sheridan has been accepted into grand London society, he loses something. It's no longer needful to him to write plays. His life as a playwright lasted the short period of four years. You can feel the match burning out in *The School for Scandal*. I think in any case it's extremely dangerous to embark on a Sheridan comedy nowadays. I'm glad I produced my favourite *The Rivals* when I did, before the dark time of deconstructive thinking and revisionism and AIDS and militant feminism and political correctness engulfed our culture, before English culture turned in the direction of Germany because it was economically advantageous to do so, before we felt the effects of their cultural guillotine which followed the war in 1945 and left the Germans bereft of a belief in their own artistic heritage. What I deeply resent is this, that we do not have the mainstream tradition in our theatre that exists for instance both in Japan and China, and it really upsets me to think that we cannot, without being criticized for it, do a pro-

14 The generations collide: Sir Anthony Absolute (Michael Hordern) and Jack Absolute (Patrick Ryecart) in a scene from Peter Wood's 1983 production of *The Rivals*.

duction of *The School for Scandal* or of *The Rivals* in the costume of the period, with the manners of the period, with costumes being worn as far as possible with the grace of the period, and with the aim of to some extent finding some means of communication with a vanished tradition of rhetoric and oratory which was so essential to the plays. Just think about the shape of the scene between Jack and Sir Anthony, which is a miracle in the way in which it comes to a rhetorical conclusion. Don't you long when watching the televised Parliament to see *Sheridan* stand up and really say something, even perhaps wake up those bland grey-suited mediocrities!

Yet take care – the patience of a saint may be overcome at last! – but mark! I give you six hours and a half to consider of this: if you then agree, without any condition, to do every thing on earth that I choose, why – confound you! I may in time forgive you – If not, z—ds! don't enter the same hemisphere with me! don't dare to breathe the same air, or use the same light with me; but get an atmosphere and a sun of your own! (*The Rivals* II.i.383–9)

It's not just good, it's magnificent. And it's not only large, but the scene is superbly constructed in musical terms to reach a performance pitch which will allow what is said to be said. That is what is dazzling about it. But of course you have to have the bellows to perform it, and unfortunately lungs have got smaller. There is no longer any tradition of articulate speech. Nobody can deliver it. They all say 'sorta' and 'kinda'. In fact it's rude, people tell you in berating interviews, for someone to speak in perfectly formed sentences, as if somehow that's improper, unsuitable, not in keeping with the times. That's the root of the trouble.

The French director's cry over the years, 'Allez jusq'au bout' (Stay with it), is highly relevant to Sheridan because he writes in a way that requires you to go to the end and go there you must. Unfortunately now, because of television dialogues, because of the question and answer techniques, you can't. Actors today don't seem to have the bottle. It's a very great issue this, that shallow breathing has become the fashion. And not only that – language today has lost its energy and vitality. They've both gone.

Now let's consider the social difficulties of performing the plays and let us think to begin with simply about how we could find anybody who would 'play the music'. Because this is the hard part. Verdi's *Il Trovatore* is rarely performed because you can't engage four matched singers at one time. Much the same thing is true of the scenes in *The Rivals*. It's not the same in *The School for Scandal*. What's interesting about that play is that it is not written affectionately in respect of character. Right at the first line of *The Rivals* you get this wonderful feeling – it's like the beginning of *Hamlet*:

(Wood adopts a broad Somerset accent) What! – Thomas! – Sure 'tis he? – What! – Thomas – Thomas! (*The Rivals* I.i.1)

It's beautiful that – it really is. With it *The Rivals* springs into extravagant life.

It would be good if you could tell us what exactly you mean by the 'chilly' nature of The School for Scandal.

Nobody's fond of anybody. It's as simple as that. *The School for Scandal* is an intimidating play. There's a very famous anecdote about it which you may know. The actors were so intimidated that at one early performance Lady Sneerwell began with 'The snakes are all inserted, Mr. Paragraph?', to which the reply came, 'Yes, your majesty' – whereupon Snake bowed and left the stage. It's probably apocryphal but the point is that it does indicate the chary way in which the actor approaches *The School for Scandal*, because in fact at no point does it beat with the rhythm of life – and in this respect it's quite unlike *The Rivals*.

It's worth saying here that *The Rivals* is graced by four great egos, obviously Malaprop, obviously Sir Anthony, so utterly unabashable, but more importantly Faulkland and of course Lydia. Those two are so hell-bent on their own romantic problems that they destroy absolutely everything in their path. They will not be diverted from their thinking. 'So! – there will be no elopement after all!' is the end of the matter for Lydia (IV.ii.108), and Faulkland can reduce Julia to tears, he can say that he has killed a man, he can behave in an abominably cruel fashion, simply because it is the romantic ego which is driving him forward. And it is very interesting that the romantic ego should manifest itself there in that form just ahead of the Byronic notions which are still in the future, still thirty years away.

That's what makes the play such a joy for the players, that you have these four great egos present. The characters in *The School for Scandal* have none of this egotistical energy. Candour, for example, has nothing of that force, Lady Sneerwell is the pathetic victim of her lustful passion, and both the Teazles are victims too in their own way. The great ego, on the other hand, has a zestful driving force. The ego is the rider. And that is a very powerful difference between the two plays and what makes *The School for Scandal* so chilling.

Is there some parallel between the loss of humanity passing from The Rivals *to* The School for Scandal *and the loss of humanity you detect now?*

Yes, unquestionably. Eric Hobsbawm says, 'The destruction of the past is one of the most characteristic and eerie phenomena of the late twentieth century. Most young men and women at the century's end grow up in a sort of permanent present lacking any organic relation to the public past of the times they live in.'[1] All those mechanistic, robotic forms of producing words do the most appalling things to the naturalness of received speech.

There's far less idiosyncratic delivery. You can say that with the death of Ralph Richardson idiosyncratic delivery virtually left the stage. He has been memorably described by Ken Tynan as having 'a mode of speech that democratically regards all syllables as equal'. Gone for ever?

I think that the traditions of music have a great deal to do with it as well. I feel that the repetitive forms as represented by Glass and Reich for instance – the whole minimalist approach to music – have their influence upon speech. It's typical that the revolt against this should be occurring through music. All of a sudden the popularity of Gregorian Chant and Górecki suggests that the public in a parched land is trying to find its way back to tradition.

Are you suggesting that it might be possible to perform Sheridan successfully again some day?

Yes, I would like to think somebody somewhere might have the breath to deliver it as it wants to be delivered.

When you were doing The Rivals *was there anything in your mind of the difficulties you feel there are now?*

Do you know, they hardly existed then. It's not that long ago either, only 1983. Feminism was young, heroine was not a dirty word. In fact we had four heroines and one of them was Bath, a sort of Serenissima on the Avon. But do you know that if anyone now attempted the sort of arrant pulchritude of that design, it would be written off as sentimental.

I remember the excellent ensemble work in your production of The Rivals, *with Geraldine McEwan and Michael Hordern playing into each other's hands beautifully.*

But the difference between *The Rivals* and *The School for Scandal* is that Sir Anthony in *The Rivals* in the scene with Jack after eating a breakfast egg can invert the shell and smash it with his egg spoon as if it were Jack's skull. You can't use business of that kind in *The School for Scandal.* That play doesn't allow for the ordinary activities of life. For instance, the billiard game between Lucius and Bob, that kind of director's motor, could not be inserted in *The School for Scandal.* The only thing I could find for the

15 John Neville as Sir Peter Teazle engulfed by newsprint in Peter Wood's 1990 production of *The School for Scandal*.

scandal-mongers to do in *The School for Scandal* was all to sit there embroidering the most enormous tapestry – which wasn't good. The idea was that they were all stitchers, stitching everything up.

You couldn't any longer put on my production of *The Rivals* on the London stage. You could still do it in Chichester but not any more in London. And this is very odd. In less than ten years the critics could say of my production of *The School for Scandal*, 'This is *The School for Scandal* as it used to be.' By contrast the 1983 notices for *The Rivals* were chummy and charming, 'the best *Rivals* we have ever seen'.

The interesting thing is that when people attempt to do period pieces like these in some other way, they just aren't funny. They look silly in modern dress, like the Glyndebourne production of *Don Giovanni* (1994) in Armani suits.

Do you think it would be true to say that dress in the late eighteenth century itself was a kind of rhetoric?

Of course, and not just dress but the use of gloves too and 'the nice conduct of a clouded cane'. It's not for nothing that even early on in the performance tradition Hazlitt says what he does about Moses' being the only person who looks right and who behaves correctly. Mrs Candour, he complains, has the coarseness of a barmaid and Crabtree seems to have mistaken one of his stable-boys for his nephew, Sir Benjamin.[2]

In the Garrick Club, I think I'm right in saying, there hangs a very elegant portrait by Zoffany of Robert Baddeley as the original Moses.

Yes, he was one of the group who played in this play that was scarcely changed over a period of about twenty years. Think, twenty years later they were still playing it.

What does interest me in the oriental theatre or the Jewish theatre even today – or Nestroy in the Burgtheater in Vienna – is that performances can still be put on with complete success in their own original style, as if somehow that was still allowed. Find me a Shakespearean production in the major classical theatre where anybody is wearing an Elizabethan costume. There isn't such a thing. It's as if we've done exactly what the Germans have done – cut ourselves off from a centuries-old theatrical tradition.

Do you think that there is a danger of fossilization if the major emphasis is on preserving the continuity of tradition?

Of course this can happen if the performers allow fossilization to occur. But I don't think that is to do with the style and manner of the presentation. In a consciously traditional production every actor can still respond to the pressures the play presents him with and find his own originality in response to them. I don't think there is any need for it all to end in a varicose condition. Surely parts as good as those that Sheridan provides will call forth the players. If *The Rivals* were done more, it would breed Anthony Absolutes.

Within the tradition, you find again the humanity that first expressed itself?

Absolutely. When it comes down to it, if you put on a play in modern dress, what does this mean, what does it say? Are we demanding that all the social *mores* associated with modern dress must be observed in the performance?

If so, today's Lady Teazle couldn't be persuaded to step behind the screen. Or are we saying that, while wearing modern dress, we are still caught up in the antique mode of performance?

Do you think that, if our own culture were more humane, it would be possible to put on performances of Sheridan's plays without loss of human energy?

Certainly. Today if you'd got a group of West Country speaking people to stage *The Rivals*, you'd get something like a contemporary version of the humanity which I feel the desiccated and facsimile-speech around us has lost. In my Cambridge days we put on *Julius Caesar* in an attempted reconstruction of Elizabethan pronounciation and it was the living Somerset that saved the day! Everything is fax nowadays. Even the chat's faxed! It could be argued that our major subsidised theatres don't keep in performance a properly extensive repertory of plays from the other centuries.

Do you think that the health of the theatre has to do with how confidently it can reach back into its own past?

The difficulties associated with this have to do with the training of the performer. The drama schools prepare their students for the lucrative world of television with its attendant advertisements and voice-overs.

To what extent is good acting a matter of skill rather than of fundamental human understanding? Would it be true to say that The School for Scandal *and* The Rivals *fall on either side of this divide?*

The marvel of the screen scene – and this is what makes *The School for Scandal* so chilling – is that it is built intricately, like tiny parts of a watch, to fit perfectly together, but this in a way is what is the matter with it. You are made aware of the dazzling technical skill of the design. The great foursome in *The Rivals* doesn't work nearly as well mechanically, but the quartet of Jack, Lydia, Sir Anthony and Mrs Malaprop defines each of them with such precise individuality. In some sense Jack so clearly represents the human standpoint. He is one of us. I assure you that, had *The School for Scandal* preceded *The Rivals*, in terms of more mature technique alone the *Rivals* four-hander would have been managed as deftly and elegantly as the screen scene. Sheridan would have held humanity and technique in a perfect equilibrium.

The secret of the screen scene, of course, is that the interloper Charles is like Jack, he's one of us, and, after all the superb dramatic complications, it is he who actually seizes and throws down the screen. It's Charles that makes the situation explode. We accept it all because it seems so natural, but in fact it's a supreme instance of situational invention. It brings situation comedy to life. We'd had comedy of mistaken identity, we'd had people hiding in cupboards before then, but we'd never had situations as piquant or as brilliant or as involved, and that is Sheridan's legacy.

The real difference between the screen scene and the four-hander in *The Rivals* is that there is no tension in the earlier play. There can't be because there's no foreseeable threat. One just assumes that when Lydia's love is given the seal of approval, she will say, 'How wonderful!' In fact she's quite put out. Sheridan surprises us by giving her the contrary reaction. On the other hand, in the screen scene there's a very real threat. A marriage is in peril. Lady Teazle may be discovered and it's that tension which makes the screen scene so much stronger.

With Oscar Wilde, of course, situation comedy works every bit as brilliantly. Sheridan, you know, is the bone that Wilde is chewing on. Wilde could not have set up Jack's mourning entry in the second act of *The Importance of Being Earnest* without Sheridan.

Do you feel that Sheridan and Wilde are very much in the same dramatic tradition?

The whole body of our comic drama is Irish, not English at all. The English theatre is very unwilling to acknowledge the fact that the history of its comedy owes everything to seven great Irish dramatists, Congreve, Farquhar, Sheridan, Boucicault, Wilde, Shaw and Beckett.

What happened between Wilde and Sheridan?

The rise of the novel caused plausibility to enter the field. Plausibility is the backbone of the novel as it is of the cinema. The moment plausibility enters, artificiality hides behind the screen.

Can we put together the plausible and the implausible in the play that Sheridan wrote just before he entered politics, The Critic *(1779)? The reason why I like the end of* The Critic *is that it takes something very theatrical at a pitch of energy and something patriotic and fuses them together.*

The one thing people of a younger generation have missed – and no description of mine will ever help – is the performance of *The Critic* with Olivier as Puff and Richardson as Burleigh at the Albery, then the New Theatre. The ending was superb, magnificent – and it was played as patriotic farce. There were a whole lot of cut-outs at stage level – we call them ground-rows – which represented the waves, and Puff was in the middle of them, directing the armada and the charges of artillery and everything else. He was standing astride one of these ground-rows when suddenly he went up in the air and he looked as if he was riding a horse and disappeared into the sky. Pure magic!

And you have the Shakespearean sense that theatrical triumph and farce are so close together?

Absolutely true, and da Ponte and Mozart have exactly the same quality. The modern theatre seems very reluctant to laugh. Where's it going to end? What are we going to do? Where's the laughter? Why can't anybody laugh any more? Is it politically incorrect to laugh?

Eighteenth-century audiences undoubtedly laughed. They fought for their seats and they were very vocal when they got to them. How much of the difference between what happens now in the theatre and what happened in Sheridan's day is attributable to different audience reaction?

Today's audience supposes itself to be watching ART. Sheridan's audience was looking at the funnies. The story goes that Sheridan would nearly always stroll along outside Drury Lane when *The School for Scandal* was playing to hear the laugh that occurred when the screen fell. We are so far distant from the manners of the time that we cannot feel anxious that the Teazles' marriage is in jeopardy, and laughter unfortunately depends upon tension. So today we laugh politely but our laughter would not be heard outside on the pavement. Today the director's responsibility with a classic comedy is to help the play to be funny. In Sheridan's time no director could stop the play being funny.

It is always said that there was constant uproar in the eighteenth-century auditorium. If there was, how could the audience have understood the plays' exposition? Think of the key differences between the two brothers that are made clear at the start of *The School for Scandal*, and the Beverley plot as laid out in the first scene of *The Rivals*. How could you know that Jack was Beverley if you hadn't taken in that scene?

Do you see any hope for the kind of change of attitude which would make it possible to stage Sheridan's comedies again as you would like to?

You mean, to present the plays in terms that do not smack of cleverness and *auteur* direction? One thinks immediately of the work done in the musical field by the performers on the one hand and also very importantly the instrument-makers on the other. They have striven with extraordinary diligence and extraordinary belief in what they're doing to produce what they hope, what they would have wished to be the authentic sound of the music, whether it is the authentic sound of the piano and the violins in a Beethoven piano concerto or whether it is the authentic sound of the *Matthew Passion* by Bach. Well, all right, the theatre always lags a long way behind the other arts, it drags its feet, and revolutions have almost come and gone before they are absorbed by the theatre. But it would be good to think that perhaps one day the instrument-makers, that is to say the people who train people to use their voices and to use that superb and supple instrument, the English language, the finest language in the world for dramatic speech or indeed for rhetoric, – that perhaps the instrument-makers can breed up a race of executants, of instrumentalists, who can use their brains and their larynx to make those splendid rolling sounds of Sheridan ring in our ears and cause us to have some real envy for the way in which people spoke in Sheridan's time.

Notes

1 *The Independent on Sunday*, 9 October 1994, p. 4.

2 The references are to a review article by William Hazlitt in the *Examiner* (15 October 1815) of a production of *The School for Scandal* at Covent Garden (quoted in *Sheridan: Comedies*, Casebook ed. P. Davison (Macmillan, 1986), pp. 136–7).

Select bibliography

Abbot, C., Baron Colchester, *The Diary and Correspondence of Charles Abbot, Lord Colchester*, ed. Charles Lord Colchester. 3 volumes (London, 1861)

Address to Richard Brinsley Sheridan on the Public and Private Proceedings During the Late Election at Westminster, 2nd edn (London, 1807)

Alston, W. P., *Philosophy of Language* (Englewood, 1964)

Aristotle, *On Rhetoric*, trans. G. A. Kennedy (New York and Oxford, 1991)

Aspinall, A., ed., *Correspondence of George, Prince of Wales*. 8 volumes (London, 1963–71)

Politics and the Press c. 1780–1850 (London, 1949)

Auburn, M. S., *Sheridan's Comedies: Their Contexts and Achievements* (Lincoln, NB, 1977)

Auckland, Lord, *The Journal and Correspondence of William, Lord Auckland*, ed. Bishop of Bath and Wells (London, 1861–2)

Barrington, J., *Personal Sketches of his Own Times*. 3 volumes (London, 1827–32)

Benzie, W., *The Dublin Orator: Thomas Sheridan's Influence on Eighteenth-Century Rhetoric and Belles Lettres* (Leeds, 1972)

Bickerstaff, I., *The Hypocrite* (London, 1769)

The Plain Dealer (London, 1766)

Billig, M., *Arguing and Thinking: A Rhetorical Approach to Social Psychology* (Cambridge, 1987)

Ideology and Opinions: Studies in Rhetorical Psychology (London, 1991)

Bond, E. A., ed., *Speeches of the Managers and Counsel in the Trial of Warren Hastings*. 4 volumes (London, 1859–61)

Braunmuller, A. R. and J. C. Bulman, eds., *Comedy from Shakespeare to Sheridan* (Newark, Delaware, 1986)

Brunsdon, P. J., 'The Association of the Friends of the People', unpublished MA thesis, University of Manchester (1961)

Buckingham and Chandos, Duke of, *Memoirs of the Court and Cabinets of George III*. 4 volumes (London, 1853–5)

Burdett, Sir F., *A Letter to the Freeholders of Middlesex* (London, 1806)

Burke, E., *The Correspondence of Edmund Burke*, gen. ed. T. W. Copeland. 10 volumes (Cambridge, 1958–78)

Butler, C., *Reminiscences*. 2 volumes (London, 1824–7)

Byron, Lord, *Byron: A Self-Portrait, Letters and Diaries 1798 to 1824*, ed. P. Quennell (Oxford, 1990)

Canning, G., *The Letter-Journal of George Canning*, ed. P. Jupp (London, 1991)

Cannon, J. A., *Parliamentary Reform 1640–1832* (Cambridge, 1972)

Aristocratic Century, The Peerage of Eighteenth-Century England (Cambridge, 1984)

Cartwright, F. D., *The Life and Correspondence of Major John Cartwright* (London, 1926)

Cibber, C., *The Non-Juror* (Dublin, 1759)

Clayton, C. A., *The Political Career of Richard Brinsley Sheridan* (unpublished D.Phil. thesis, Oxford University, 1992)

Cobbett, W., *The Political Proteus. A View of the Public Character and Conduct of R. B. Sheridan, Esq.* (London, 1804)

Cohen, M., *Sensible Words: Linguistic Practice in England, 1640–1785* (Baltimore, 1979)

Colley, L., *Britons: Forging the Nation 1707–1837* (New Haven and London, 1992)

Creevey, T., *The Creevey Papers*, ed. Sir H. Maxwell. 2 volumes (London, 1903)

Croker, J. W., *The Croker Papers*, ed. L. J. Jennings. 3 volumes (London, 1884)

Cumberland, R., *The Battle of Hastings* (London, 1778) (in the Bodleian Library, Oxford)

Darlington, W. A., *Sheridan* (London, 1933)

Davies, T., *Memoirs of the Life of David Garrick*. 2 volumes (London, 1808)

Davison, P., ed. *Sheridan's Comedies* (Macmillan Casebook, 1986)

Deuchar, S., *Painting, Politics & Porter* (Whitbread, 1984)

Durant, J. D., *Richard Brinsley Sheridan* (Twayne, 1975)

Ehrman, J., *The Younger Pitt: The Years of Acclaim* (London, 1969)

Elliot, G., *Life and Letters of Sir Gilbert Elliot*, ed. Countess of Minto. 3 volumes (London, 1874)

Exposition of the Circumstances Which Gave Rise to the Election of Sir Francis Burdett . . . (London, 1807)

Farington, J., *The Farington Diary*, ed. J. Greig. 8 volumes (London, 1923–8)

Fitzgerald, P., *Lives of the Sheridans*. 2 volumes (London, 1886)

Foster, V., *The Two Duchesses* (London, 1898)

Fox, C. J., *Memorials and Correspondence of C. J. Fox*, ed. Lord J. Russell. 4 volumes (London, 1853–7)

Garrick, D., *The Letters of David Garrick*, ed. D. M. Little and G. M. Kahrl. 3 volumes (Cambridge, Mass., 1963)

The Plays of David Garrick, ed. H. W. Pedicord and F. L. Bergmann. 7 volumes (Carbondale, 1982)

George, M. D., *English Political Caricature: A Study of Opinion and Propaganda, 1793–1832* (Oxford, 1959)

Catalogue of Political and Personal Satires preserved in the British Museum (London, 1978)

Goodwin, A., *The Friends of Liberty: The English Democratic Movement in the Age of the French Revolution* (London, 1979)

Gore, J., *Creevey's Life and Times* (New York, 1934)

Lord Granville Leveson Gower . . . Private Correspondence, ed. Castalia, Countess Granville. 2 volumes (London, 1916)

Griffith, E., *The School for Rakes* (Dublin, 1769)

Harris, J., *The Diaries and Correspondence of James Harris, 1st Earl of Malmesbury*, ed. by his grandson. 8 volumes (London, 1844)

Highfill, Jr, P. H., K. A. Burnim and E. A. Langhans, *A Biographical Dictionary of Actors, Actresses, Musicians, Dancers, Managers & Other Stage Personnel in London, 1660–1800*. 16 volumes (Carbondale, IL, 1973–93)

History of the Westminster Election in the Month of November 1806 (London, 1807)

Hinde, W., *George Canning* (London, 1973)

History of the Westminster Election. Second edition (London, 1785)

Hobhouse, J. C., Baron Broughton, *Recollection of a Long Life*. 6 volumes (London, 1909–11)

Hogan, C. B., *The London Stage, 1660–1800, Part Five, 1776–1800*. 3 volumes (Carbondale, IL, 1968)

Holland, Elizabeth, Lady, *Journal of Elizabeth Lady Holland, 1791–1811*, ed. Earl of Ilchester. 2 volumes (London, 1908)

Holland, Henry, Lord, 3rd Baron, *Memoirs of the Whig Party During My Time*, ed. Henry, Lord Holland. 2 volumes (London, 1852)

Further Memoirs of the Whig Party, ed. Lord Stavordale (London, 1905)

Hone, J. A., *For the Cause of Truth: Radicalism in London, 1796–1821* (Oxford, 1982)

Howell, W. S., *Eighteenth-Century British Logic and Rhetoric* (Princeton, 1971)

Hume, R. D., ed., *The London Theatre World, 1660–1800* (Carbondale, IL, 1980)

Hunt, H., *Memoirs*. 3 volumes (London, 1820–2)

Kearful, F. J., *Molière Among the English 1660–1737* in *Molière and the Commonwealth of Letters*, ed. R. Johnson, Jr, E. S. Neumann, G. T. Trail (Mississipi, 1975)

Kelly, H., *The School for Wives* (Belfast, 1774)

Leeds, Duke of, *Political Memoranda of the 5th Duke of Leeds*, ed. O. Browning (Camden Society, 1884)

Leith, D. and G. Myerson, *The Power of Address: Explorations in Rhetoric* (London, 1989)

Leveson-Gower, H., *Hary-O: The Letters of Lady Harriet Cavendish*, eds. G. Leveson-Gower and I. Palmer (London, 1940)

Lindsay, W. A., *A History of the House of Percy* (London, 1902)

Little, D. M. and G. M. Kahrl, eds., *The Letters of David Garrick*. 3 volumes (Cambridge, MA, 1963)

Locke, J., *An Essay Concerning Human Understanding* (Chicago, 1952)

Loftis, J., *Sheridan and the Drama of Georgian England* (Oxford, 1976)

Lytton, H. B., *The Life of Henry John Temple, Viscount Palmerston* (London, 1870)

Medbourne, M., *Tartuffe* (London, 1670)

Mitchell, L. G., *Charles James Fox and the Disintegration of the Whig Party 1782–1794* (Oxford, 1971)

Holland House (London, 1980)

Charles James Fox (Oxford, 1992)

Moore, T., *Memoirs of the Life of the Right Honourable Richard Brinsley Sheridan*. Second edition. 2 volumes (London, 1825)

Memoirs, Journal, and Correspondence of Thomas Moore, ed. Lord J. Russell. 8 volumes (London, 1853–6)

Morwood, J., *The Life and Works of Richard Brinsley Sheridan* (Edinburgh, 1985)

Murphy, A., *Know Your Own Mind* (London, 1777)

The School for Guardians (Dublin, 1767)

The Life of David Garrick (Dublin, 1801)

Patterson, M. W., *Sir Francis Burdett and His Times*. 2 volumes (London, 1931)

Pellew, G., *Life and Correspondence of Henry Addington, First Viscount Sidmouth* (London, 1847)

Price, C., ed., *The Letters of Richard Brinsley Sheridan*. 3 volumes (Oxford, 1966)

ed., *The Dramatic Works of Richard Brinsley Sheridan*. 2 volumes (Oxford, 1973)

Rae, W. F., *Sheridan, a Biography*. 2 volumes (London, 1896)

Reid, C., 'Patriotism and rhetorical contest in the 1790s: the context of Sheridan's *Pizarro*' in *Comedy: Essays in Honour of Peter Dixon*, ed. Elizabeth Maslen (London, 1993)

Reid, L., *Charles James Fox: A Man for the People* (London, 1969)

Reinert, O., *Drama* (Boston, 1964)

Rhodes, R. C., *Harlequin Sheridan* (Oxford, 1933)

Rogers, S., *Recollections of the Table-Talk of Samuel Rogers*, ed. A. Dyce (London, 1856)

Rose, G., *Diaries and Correspondence of the Right Hon. George Rose*, ed. L. V. Harcourt (London, 1860)

Sack, J. J., *The Grenvillites, 1801–1829, Party Politics and Factionalism in the age of Pitt and Liverpool* (London, 1979)

Sadler, M., *The Political Career of Richard Brinsley Sheridan* (Oxford, 1912)

Sheldon, E. K., *Thomas Sheridan of Smock-Alley* (Princeton, 1967)

Sheridan, E., *Betsy Sheridan's Journal*, ed. W. LeFanu (London, 1960)

Sheridan, F., *The Dupe* (London, 1764)
A Journey to Bath, ed. W. F. Rae (London, 1902)
Sheridan, R. B., *An Eulogium on the Right Honourable C. J. Fox Delivered by the Honourable Mr Sheridan* . . . (Nottingham, 1806)
The Speeches of the Right Honourable Richard Brinsley Sheridan. 3 volumes (London, 1842; rpt New York, 1969)
The Letters of Richard Brinsley Sheridan, ed. C. Price. 3 volumes (Oxford, 1966)
The Dramatic Works of Richard Brinsley Sheridan, ed. C. Price. 2 volumes (Oxford, 1973)
Plays, ed. C. Price (Oxford, 1975)
The Critic, ed. D. Crane (New Mermaids, London, 1989)
Sheridaniana (London, 1826)
Sichel, W., *Sheridan* (London, 1909)
Skinner, Q., 'Sheridan and Whitbread at Drury Lane, 1809–1815', *Theatre Notebook*, xvii (1962/3), 40–6, 74–9
Smith, E. A., *Whig Principles and Party Politics* (Manchester, 1975)
Lord Grey 1764–1845 (Oxford, 1990)
Sprat, T., *History of the Royal Society*, ed. J. Cope and H. W. Jones (St Louis, 1958)
Stephens, F. G. and M. D. George, *Catalogue of Prints and Drawings in the British Museum* (London, 1870–1954)
Stone, Jr, G. W., *The London Stage, 1660–1800, Part Four, 1747–76*. 3 volumes. (Carbondale, IL, 1962)
Stone, Jr, G. W. and G. M. Kahrl, *David Garrick: A Critical Biography* (Carbondale, IL, 1979)
Stuart, D., *Dearest Bess* (London, 1955)
Tasch, P. A., *The Dramatic Cobbler* (Lewisburg, 1971)
Thorne, R. G., ed., *The House of Commons, 1790–1820* (London, 1986)
Tooke, J. H., *A Letter to the Editor of The Times* (London, 1807)
A Warning to the Electors of Westminster (London, 1807)
Van Laun, H., 'Les Plagiaires de Molière en Angleterre', *Le Molièriste*, xxvi (May 1881), pp. 52–62
Villiers, G., Duke of Buckingham, *The Rehearsal*, ed. D. E. L. Crane (Durham, 1976)
Watkins, J., *Memoirs of the Public and Private Private Life of the Rt Hon. Richard Brinsley Sheridan* (London, 1817)
Werkmeister, L. T., *The London Daily Press 1772–92* (Nebraska, 1963)
The Whig Club or a Sketch of the Manners of the Age (London, 1794)
Wiesenthal, C. S., 'Representation and Experimentation in the Major Comedies of Richard Brinsley Sheridan', *Eighteenth-Century Studies*, xxv (3) (Spring 1992)
Wilcox, J., *The Relation of Molière to Restoration Comedy* (Columbia, 1938)
Worth, K., *Sheridan and Goldsmith* (Macmillan, 1992)

Wraxall, N., *The Historical and Posthumous Memoirs of Sir Nathaniel Wraxall*, ed. H. B. Wheatley. 5 volumes (London, 1884)
Wycherley, W., *The Plain Dealer*, ed. J. L. Smith (London, 1979)
Wyrick, D. B., *Jonathan Swift and the Vested Word* (Chapel Hill, 1988)

Alphabetical list of plays mentioned

Page references to these plays will be found under the author's name in the index

A Bold Stroke for a Wife – Centlivre
A Christmas Tale – Garrick
A Journey to Bath – Frances Sheridan
Alexander the Great – Ozell
All's Well That Ends Well – Shakespeare
Amphytrion – Dryden
Artaxerxes – Thomas Arne
As You Like It – Shakespeare
A Trip to Scarborough – Sheridan
Blue Beard – Colman
Captain O'Blunder – Sheridan
Cato – Addison
Celedon and Florimel – Dryden and Cibber
Coriolanus – Shakespeare
Eugénie – Beaumarchais
Every Man in his Humour – Jonson
False Delicacy – Kelly
Hamlet – Shakespeare
Harlequin's Invasion – Garrick
Henry VIII – Shakespeare
Irene – Johnson
Isabella – Garrick
Jane Shore – Rowe
Julius Caesar – Shakespeare
King Lear – Shakespeare
Know Your Own Mind – Murphy
Le Bourgeois Gentilhomme – Molière

Le Misanthrope – Molière
Le Tartuffe – Molière
Le Testament – Fontenelle
Love à-la-Mode – Macklin
Love for Love – Congreve
Love in a Village – Bickerstaff
Love Makes a Man – Cibber
Love's Last Shift – Cibber
Macbeth – Shakespeare
Matilda – Francklin
Measure for Measure – Shakespeare
Midas – O'Hare
Miss in Her Teens – Garrick
Monsieur de Porceaugnac – Molière
Much Ado About Nothing – Shakespeare
Othello – Shakespeare
Pizarro – Sheridan
Richard Coeur de Lion – Elizabeth Sheridan and Burgoyne
Richard II – Shakespeare
Richard III – Shakespeare
Romeo and Juliet – Shakespeare
Rule a Wife and Have a Wife – Beaumont and Fletcher
St Patrick's Day – Sheridan
Selima and Azor – Collier
Semiramis – Ayscough
She Stoops to Conquer – Goldsmith
She Wou'd and She Wou'd Not – Cibber
Sir Thomas Overbury – Savage
Tamerlane – Rowe
Tartuffe – Medbourne
The Alchemist – Jonson
The Agreeable Surprise – O'Keeffe
The Barber of Seville – Beaumarchais
The Battle of Hastings – Cumberland
The Beaux' Stratagem – Farquhar
The Beggar's Opera – Gay
The Busy Body – Centlivre
The Camp – Sheridan

Alphabetical list of plays mentioned

The Careless Husband – Cibber
The Clandestine Marriage – Colman and Garrick
The Confederacy – Vanbrugh
The Conscious Lovers – Steele
The Constant Couple – Farquhar
The Country Wife – Wycherley
The Critic – Sheridan
The Distress'd Mother – Phillips
The Double Dealer – Congreve
The Duel – O'Brien
The Duenna – Sheridan
The Dupe – Frances Sheridan
The Fair Penitent – Rowe
The Fathers – Fielding
The Forty Thieves – Ward and Colman
The Funeral – Steele
The Gamester – Moore
The Generous Imposter – O'Beirne
The Glorious First of June – Sheridan
The Haunted House – Cobb
The Hypocrite – Bickerstaff
The Hypocrite – Shadwell
The Importance of Being Earnest – Wilde
The Irish Widow – Garrick
The Jealous Wife – Colman
The Liar – Foote
The London Merchant – Lillo
The Man of Mode – Etherege
The Merchant of Venice – Shakespeare
The Merry Wives of Windsor – Shakespeare
The Miser – Fielding
The Mourning Bride – Congreve
The Non-Juror – Cibber
The Old Bachelor – Congreve
The Padlock – Bickerstaff
The Plain Dealer – Wycherley
The Prophecy – King
The Provok'd Husband – Vanbrugh

The Provok'd Wife – Vanbrugh
The Recruiting Officer – Farquhar
The Refusal – Cibber
The Rehearsal – Buckingham
The Relapse – Vanbrugh
The Rivals – Sheridan
The Roman Actor – Massinger
The School for Guardians – Murphy
The School for Lovers – Whitehead
The School for Rakes – Griffith
The School for Scandal – Sheridan
The School for Wives – Kelly
The Siege of St Quintin – Hook
The Spanish Friar – Dryden
The Statesman – Dent
The Stranger – Kotzebue (trans. Thompson)
The Suspicious Husband – Hoadly
The Tempest – Shakespeare
The Twin Rivals – Farquhar
The Way of the World – Congreve
The Way to Keep Him – Murphy
The West Indian – Cumberland
The Winter's Tale – Shakespeare
The Wonder – Centlivre
Twelfth Night – Shakespeare
Venice Preserv'd – Otway

Index